EDUCATIONAL EVALUATION METHODOLOGY

Educational Evaluation Methodology: THE STATE OF THE ART

EDITED BY RONALD A. BERK

The Johns Hopkins University Press • Baltimore and London

The Johns Hopkins University Press, Baltimore, Maryland 21218
The Johns Hopkins Press Ltd., London

Library of Congress Cataloging in Publication Data

Main entry under title:
Educational evaluation methodology.
    "A product of the second annual Johns Hopkins University
National Symposium on Educational Research (NSER),
held in Washington, D.C., in November 1979."
    1. Educational surveys—United States—Congresses.
2. Educational research—United States—Congresses.
I. Berk, Ronald A.

LB2823.E44   379.1'54   80-8859
ISBN 0-8018-2518-0   AACR2

To My Parents

CONTENTS

PREFACE

THIS BOOK provides an assessment of the state of the art of educational evaluation methodology. It is a product of the second annual Johns Hopkins University National Symposium on Educational Research (NSER), held in Washington, D.C., in November 1979.

THE SYMPOSIUM

The idea for a symposium was first suggested to me by Gilbert B. Schiffman. The state-of-the-art concept applied to the symposium was stimulated by the divisional state-of-the-art addresses presented at the 1978 American Educational Research Association Conference. The need for a "research symposium" with a practical orientation became obvious as I observed that much of the research generated year after year did not seem to be reflected in classroom and school district practices. Consequently, despite the sophisticated research dissemination methods available, a gap between research findings and their implementation in practice was evident. The symposium was seen as one possible vehicle to bridge the gap.

Purposes. The symposium was conceived as a mechanism for assembling research scholars on a topic of national concern to educational researchers and practitioners. The scholars selected to participate in the second symposium have contributed substantially to the advancement and understanding of program evaluation methodology through their publications and their direction of major evaluation projects. Their task was to synthesize the research on the topic that has been amassed over the past twenty years and translate the results into guidelines that evaluators can use and issues that researchers can investigate.

The presentations provided a state-of-the-art assessment of the methodological underpinnings of educational program evaluation in terms of what has been done, what should be done, and what still needs to be done. The symposium dealt only with the quantitative approach to program evaluation for two reasons: (1) a significant number of the problems encountered in conducting an evaluation relates to assessing program effects and (2) there is growing recognition by decision makers that affective arguments and qualitative information alone are insufficient; quantitative evidence of program effectiveness is essential for sound decision making.

Advisory board. The annual theme and invited speakers for the symposium are chosen according to the recommendations of the NSER Advisory Board. I gratefully acknowledge the useful contributions of the 1979 board members: Joan Bollenbacher, Robert L. Brennan, Lois E. Burrill, Carmen J. Finley, Lorraine R. Gay, Ronald K. Hambleton, David J. Kleinke, James M. McPartland, William B. Michael, and Lorrie A. Shepard. Robert L. Brennan's suggestions for structuring the 1979 NSER were particularly valuable.

Audience. The symposium was designed to attract researchers from universities, private corporations and R & D laboratories, and practitioners at the federal, state, and local levels of research and evaluation. The response to the 1979 symposium was enthusiastic. More than 270 distinguished educators from thirty-four states, Canada, Mexico, and Bermuda attended the symposium.

ACKNOWLEDGMENTS

The symposium and this book represent the culmination of a tremendous amount of work by several individuals. I am delighted to mention the contributions of a few who deserve special credit. First, I extend my deepest appreciation to the eleven authors and to Carol Kehr Tittle (University of North Carolina), Herbert I. Weisberg (The Huron Institute), David R. Rogosa (The University of Chicago), and Michael H. Kean (School District of Philadelphia), who served as discussants at the symposium, for sharing their expertise and exhibiting rare patience and cooperation. The administrative and financial support given by Dean Roman J. Verhaalen, Elaine C. Davis, and Keith E. Glancy of the Evening College of The Johns Hopkins University made it all possible. Lynn E. Wilkinson and Sharon D. Custis coordinated the symposium with ingeniousness and alacrity. Henry Tom, social sciences editor of The Johns Hopkins University Press, furnished invaluable assistance in the early stages and many helpful suggestions throughout the publication process. Finally, I thank Ilse M. Harrop for her assistance with the symposium.

EDUCATIONAL EVALUATION METHODOLOGY

INTRODUCTION RONALD A. BERK

A RECENT national study of Title I program evaluations found that *evaluation* is typically perceived as synonymous with *achievement testing* at both the state and local levels (Forgione, Kaplan, & Orland, 1979; Goettel et al., 1977). It is often viewed as a necessary evil, conducted to please someone else, with little apparent relevance to local programmatic concerns. Another investigation indicated that local districts do not use program evaluation results either as a basis for judging program effectiveness or as a guide for program decision making (David, 1978, p. 37). Criticisms of the design and utilization of local educational evaluations have been documented extensively for over a decade (see, for example, Guba, 1969; Stufflebeam et al., 1971; Worthen & Sanders, 1973). Clearly, if one attempted to identify an Achilles' heel in the field of education, it is most likely that evaluation practices would receive a large number of nominations.

The overall quality of local evaluation efforts leads one to believe that either a sophisticated methodology does not exist or, if it does, practitioners are not applying it for one reason or another. As the succeeding pages will demonstrate, a vast body of evaluation methodology literature is available. Perhaps the form in which the information is conveyed or the manner in which it is disseminated may be stifling the use of sound methodology in practice. A brief historical overview of evaluation practices and methodological developments should provide some insight into this problem.

HISTORICAL OVERVIEW

The first program evaluation in the United States was Joseph Mayer Rice's comparative study of the spelling performance of over thirty thousand students in a large city school system in 1897. Evidence of what was labeled "evaluation activity" was quite sparse until the 1950s. The only noteworthy

1

evaluation activities in the intervening years consisted of Ralph Tyler's evaluation of the Eight-Year Study and the development of school and college accreditation procedures during the 1930s. Both of these activities were actually measurement activities. This association between measurement techniques or testing and the term *evaluation* was to characterize evaluation practices for the next fifty years.

1950s. During the 1950s, there were numerous large-scale evaluations of social action programs in public housing, delinquency prevention, psychotherapeutic treatments, and the like undertaken at the national and international levels. Educational program evaluations were rare.

1960s. Program evaluations grew dramatically in all fields in the 1960s. Exemplary of the large-scale educational evaluation projects were Project TALENT (Flanagan et al., 1964), the Westinghouse–Ohio University evaluation of Head Start (Cicirelli, 1969; Cicirelli, Cooper, & Granger, 1969), the National Assessment Program beginning in 1964, and the Coleman report on school desegregation (Coleman et al., 1966). Unfortunately some of those evaluations were criticized severely for their statistical analyses (see, for example, Bowles & Levin, 1968; Cain & Watts, 1970; Campbell & Erlebacher, 1970; Mosteller & Moynihan, 1972). These criticisms prompted several reevaluations of the original data, especially in the case of Head Start (Barnow, 1973; Smith & Bissell, 1970).

Many of the evaluation studies in these post-Sputnik years accompanied major innovations in the school curriculum. Perhaps the greatest single boost to educational evaluation during this period was the U.S. Congress's passage of the Elementary and Secondary Education Act in 1965 (ESEA). This act required for the first time that state and local education agencies evaluate the effectiveness of their Title I and Title III programs. The pervasive impact of this mandate was to be felt in the years that followed.

1970s. Both the quantity of program evaluations and the size of their budgets increased during the seventies. Due in large part to direct federal support, the budgets for several large-scale projects averaged about $100,000. Several ongoing evaluations of compensatory education programs had 10- to 20-million-dollar budgets. The evaluations of "Sesame Street" were illustrative of these commitments (cf. Ball & Bogatz, 1970; Bogatz & Ball, 1971; Cook et al., 1975; Diaz-Guerrero et al., 1976; Lesser, 1974).

Attached to these federal funds were more stringent evaluation requirements, stated in the Education Amendments of 1974, the 1976 Amendments to the Vocational Education Act, and the 1978 Amendments to the Bilingual Education Act. The 1974 legislation related to Title I programs was by far the most explicit to date. It designated the evaluation models a school district could use to evaluate its Title I programs as well as the scale for reporting the achievement test gains (Normal Curve Equivalent). The models were de-

veloped by the RMC Research Corporation under contract with the U.S.
Office of Education (Horst, Tallmadge, & Wood, 1975; Tallmadge & Horst,
1976).

In addition to the expanding role of the federal government in educational
program evaluation in the 1970s, there was a burgeoning of evaluation
methodology literature—textbooks, casebooks, and journals. More than fifty
volumes were published on the evaluation of social action programs and
educational programs. These volumes fell into two main categories: (1) those
that extricated methodological procedures and strategies for conducting
evaluations, and (2) those that examined and critiqued the application of the
procedures to specific programs. The two-part *Handbook of Evaluation Research* compiled by Guttentag and Struening, published by Sage in 1975, best
exemplifies both of these orientations. The Sage Publication series *Evaluation
Studies Review Annual* that began in 1976 followed in a similar vein.

The actual methodologies that emerged seemed to draw upon extant
methodologies in measurement, research, and statistics from a variety of
disciplines including education, psychology, sociology, and the administrative sciences. Program evaluation methodology constituted a synthesis and
extension of a variety of scientific methods in order to answer policy questions
regarding the status of particular programs.

While evaluations were implemented and the various models and methodological procedures were tested at the local, state, and national levels, it wasn't
until 1975 that a journal devoted to evaluation research, *Studies in Educational Evaluation,* was founded. This was followed by *Evaluation Quarterly*
in 1977 (retitled *Evaluation Review* in 1980), *Evaluation and Program Planning* and *Evaluation and the Health Professions* in 1978, and *Educational
Evaluation and Policy Analysis* in 1979. The first and last journals were the
only ones that dealt exclusively with the issues and problems in educational
evaluation. Furthermore, despite the fact that national standards for educational and psychological testing have been available for fifteen years, it has
been only within the past four years that any serious commitment was evi-
denced toward establishing national guidelines and standards for educational
evaluation (see Stufflebeam, chapter 7).

These developments indicate that educational evaluation practices have not
kept pace with methodological advances. The foregoing chronology of evaluation practices and methodology suggests that the most significant events
were concentrated within the past twenty years. There are four considerations that lend credence to the notion that educational program evaluation
is in its infancy: (1) the recency of the evaluation methodology literature, (2)
the stringent requirements imposed on federally supported program evaluations in the mid to late seventies, (3) the creation of the first educational
evaluation journal in 1975, and (4) the lack of national standards for conduct-

ing program evaluations. In addition, evaluation practices at the state and local levels connote that probably Worthen and Sanders's observations in 1973 (pp. 7–8) still hold true today: "Despite the newly developed evaluation strategies, . . . the methodology of evaluation [remains] fuzzy in the minds of most evaluators. . . . Perhaps the major reason [is] that the useful information on evaluation plans and techniques [is] badly fragmented and [appears] in a variety of sources, some of which [are] fugitive materials."

DEFINITION OF EVALUATION

One of the first definitions of evaluation was proposed by Ralph Tyler (1942) within the context of the Eight-Year Study at Ohio State University. Evaluation was defined as the process of determining whether the objectives of a program have been achieved—congruence between performance and objectives. Since then, the definitions that have appeared in the evaluation literature have been numerous and diverse (e.g., Alkin, 1972; Cooley & Lohnes, 1976; Cronbach, 1963, 1977; Fink & Kosecoff, 1980; Freeman, 1977; Guba, 1966; Popham, 1975; Posavac & Carey, 1980; Provus, 1967, 1971; Scriven, 1967; Stake, 1967; Stufflebeam et al., 1971; Walberg, 1974; Wolf, 1979). A critical survey of these definitions revealed that there was a single common thread running through all of them: *evaluation is the process of providing information for decision making.* This concept of evaluation as a political decision-making tool is expressed most clearly in the definition by Stufflebeam et al.: "the process of delineating, obtaining, and providing useful information for judging decision alternatives" (1971, p. 36). This comprehensive and extremely popular definition was an outgrowth of the work of the Phi Delta Kappa National Study Committe on Educational Evaluation from 1968 to 1970.

Outside of the field of education there has been a particularly heavy emphasis on the application and utilization of scientific research methods in the definition of evaluation related to public service and social action programs (e.g., Rutman, 1977; Suchman, 1967). This component suggests a rigor and precision in evaluation methodology that is not only appropriate but also highly desirable in educational program evaluations.

The definition of evaluation advanced in this volume constitutes an amalgam of both the information-for-decision-making and research-methods characteristics:

Evaluation is the process of applying "scientific procedures" to collect "reliable and valid information" to make "decisions" about an "educational program."

Four major elements are stressed. First, the application of "scientific procedures" reflects the methodological orientation of this book. The strategies described herein represent the confluence of developments in measurement theory, research design, applied statistics, and computer technology from several social and behavioral science disciplines. Second, the collection of "reliable and valid information" qualifies the type of information and implies the use of formal data-gathering instruments (tests, scales, and/or questionnaires) that have established psychometric properties. Third, the making of "decisions" based upon decision theory and the principles of educational administration designates the specific use of the information. Fourth, the preceding three elements are restricted to "educational programs." This focuses all evaluation activities on the assessment of program effects* in educational systems and the statistical and policy significance of those effects. The subsequent decisions about the continuance, termination, and/or modification of an educational program are guided primarily by the evidence of program effectiveness.

This definition reflects the traditional *quantitative paradigm* of evaluation as opposed to the qualitative paradigm. The prominent features of both approaches have been succinctly described by Reichardt and Cook (1979): "the quantitative paradigm is said to have a positivistic, hypothetico-deductive, particularistic, objective, outcome-oriented, and natural science world view. In contrast, the qualitative paradigm is said to subscribe to a phenomenological, inductive, holistic, subjective, process-oriented, and social anthropological world view" (pp. 9-10). Staunch proponents of the former stress the use of randomized and quasi-experimental designs à la Campbell and Stanley (1966), Cook and Campbell (1979), and Riecken et al. (1974); advocates of the latter urge the use of ethnographic techniques, case studies, and participant observation (see Filstead, 1979; Guttentag, 1973; Rist, 1977; Stake, 1978; Weiss & Rein, 1970; Wilson, 1977).

PURPOSES OF THE BOOK

This book attempts to determine the state of the art of educational program evaluation methodology. Given the previous definition, this methodology is restricted to the quantitative paradigm. The contribution of the book to the evaluation literature will depend largely on how well it accomplishes the following purposes: (1) to clarify the terminology and jargon related to the methodology; (2) to synthesize the research that has accumulated over the past twenty years; (3) to translate the research results into forms meaningful and useful to evaluators and researchers; and (4) to bring into sharp focus the major issues in educational evaluation that have been resolved and those that need resolution. In particular, by supplying evaluators with concrete direc-

---

*This emphasis on program effects has also been referred to as impact or product evaluation.

tions for planning and implementing an evaluation and reporting its findings, it is hoped that ultimately the overall quality of program evaluations will be improved.

Probably any volume that claims to present a state-of-the-art assessment of any research domain is doomed to the flaw of some omission. The topics chosen for review in this volume have been judged essential for the proper design, execution, analysis, and interpretation of a program evaluation. Admittedly, other important topics germane to quantitative evaluation methodology such as educational objectives, sampling, cost-effectiveness analysis, and the decision-making process were omitted or only partially treated. A consideration of ethical and legal issues and the entire domain of qualitative evaluation methodology were also bypassed. Those omissions were due primarily to the time constraints of the symposium from which the chapters originated. The failure to present the qualitative paradigm should not be misconstrued to mean that it is perceived to be an inferior approach to evaluation. Even Campbell (1974) and Cronbach (1975) have attested to the merits of the qualitative techniques. In fact, it has been indicated that there is a strong degree of complementarity between the quantitative and qualitative approaches. Perhaps the utilization of multiple methods will provide the most exhaustive evaluation of a particular program and also reduce the biases inherent in the disparate methods. Evaluators interested in qualitative techniques should consult Filstead (1970), Guba (1978), and Patton (1980).

ORGANIZATION OF THE BOOK

The book is divided into seven chapters. Each chapter is preceded by introductory remarks that provide a linkage among the chapters and a summary of chapter highlights. The topics covered are arranged sequentially and correspond to some of the key steps in conducting an evaluation. A deliberate effort has been made to address the most pressing practical problems and thorny technical issues that an evaluator must confront.

For ease of use by evaluators and researchers, each of the first six chapters that deals with a step in the evaluation process is organized into five main parts: (1) "Introduction," which defines the topic and explains its significance in educational evaluation; (2) "Review," which provides a critical survey of all major strategies, methods, and conceptualizations directly related to the topic; (3) "Suggestions for Future Research," which list the specific types and areas of research that still need attention; (4) "Guidelines for Evaluators," which discuss the implications of the recommended strategy(s) for evaluations conducted at the district, state, and national levels; and (5) "References," which provide a complete and easily accessible list pertinent to the specific topic.

INTENDED USES OF THE BOOK

Consistent with its structure, contents, and orientation, this volume should be used as a handbook for practicing evaluators, as a textbook for graduate students learning educational evaluation, and as a reference book for researchers studying evaluation methodology issues and problem areas. It can also serve as a resource for workshops for teachers on program and curriculum evaluation. The treatment of the topics throughout the book presumes the reader has had at least basic coursework in measurement and research methods. Some of the material in chapters 3, 4, and 5 also requires a working knowledge of analysis of variance and multiple regression.

REFERENCES

Alkin, R. C. Evaluation theory development. In C. H. Weiss (ed.), *Evaluating action programs: Readings in social action and evaluation*. Boston: Allyn & Bacon, 1972. P. 107.

Ball, S., & Bogatz, G. A. *The first year of "Sesame Street": An evaluation* (PR-70-15). Princeton, N.J.: Educational Testing Service, October 1970.

Barnow, B. S. *Evaluating Project Head Start* (Discussion paper 189-73). Madison: Institute for Research on Poverty, University of Wisconsin, 1973.

Bogatz, G. A., & Ball, S. *The second year of "Sesame Street": A continuing evaluation* (PR-71-21). Princeton, N.J.: Educational Testing Service, November 1971.

Bowles, S., & Levin, H. M. The determinants of scholastic achievement—An appraisal of some recent evidence. *Journal of Human Resources*, 1968, *3*, 3-24.

Cain, G. G., & Watts, H. W. Problems in making policy inferences from the Coleman Report. *American Sociological Review*, 1970, *35*, 228-242.

Campbell, D. T. Qualitative knowing in action research. Kurt Lewin Award address, Society for the Psychological Study of Social Issues, at the annual meeting of the American Psychological Association, New Orleans, September 1974.

Campbell, D. T., & Erlebacher, A. How regression artifacts in quasi-experimental evaluations can mistakenly make compensatory education look harmful. In J. Helmuth (ed.), *The disadvantaged child*, Vol. 3, *Compensatory education: A national debate*. New York: Brunner/Mazel, 1970. Pp. 185-210.

Campbell, D. T., & Stanley, J. C. *Experimental and quasi-experimental designs for research*. Chicago: Rand McNally, 1966.

Cicirelli, V. G. Project Head Start, a national evaluation: Brief of the study. In D. G. Hays (ed.), *The Britannica review of American education*. Chicago: Encyclopaedia Britannica, 1969. Pp. 235-243.

Cicirelli, V. G., Cooper, W. H., & Granger, R. L. *The impact of Head Start: An evaluation of the effects of Head Start on children's cognitive and affective development*. Athens: Westinghouse Learning Corporation and Ohio University, 1969. (Distributed by Clearinghouse for Federal Scientific and Technical Information, U.S. Department of Commerce, National Bureau of Standards, Institute for Applied Technology, PB 184328.)

Coleman, J. S., Campbell, E. Q., Hobson, C. J., McPartland, J. M., Mood, A. M., Weinfield, F. D., & York, R. L. *Equality of educational opportunity.* Washington, D.C.: U.S. Government Printing Office, 1966.

Cook, T. D., Appleton, H., Conner, R. F., Shaffer, A., Tamkin, G., & Weber, S. J. *"Sesame Street" revisited.* New York: Russell Sage Foundation, 1975.

Cook, T. D., & Campbell, D. T. *Quasi-experimentation: Design and analysis issues for field settings.* Chicago: Rand McNally, 1979.

Cooley, W. W., & Lohnes, P. R. *Evaluation research in education.* New York: Irvington, 1976.

Cronbach, L. J. Course improvement through evaluation. *Teachers College Record,* 1963, *64,* 672–783.

Cronbach, L. J. Beyond the two disciplines of scientific psychology. *American Psychologist,* 1975, *30,* 116–127.

Cronbach, L. J. Remarks to the new society. *Evaluation Research Society Newsletter,* 1977, *1,* No. 1.

David, J. L. *Local uses of Title I evaluations.* (Report EPRC 21). Menlo Park, Calif.: Stanford Research Institute, July 1978.

Diaz-Guerrero, R., Reyes-Lagunes, I., Witzke, D. B., & Holtman, W. H. Sesame Street around the world/Plaza Sesamo in Mexico: An evaluation. *Journal of Communication,* 1976, *26,* 145–154.

Filstead, W. J. (ed.). *Qualitative methodology: Firsthand involvement with the social world.* Chicago: Markham, 1970.

Filstead, W. J. Qualitative methods: A needed perspective in evaluation research. In T. D. Cook and C. S. Reichardt (eds.), *Qualitative and quantitative methods in evaluation research.* Beverly Hills: Sage, 1979. Pp. 33–48.

Fink, A., & Kosecoff, J. *An evaluation primer.* Beverly Hills: Sage, 1980.

Flanagan, J. C., Davis, F. B., Dailey, J. T., Shaycoft, M. F., Orr, D. B., Goldberg, I., & Neyman, Jr., C. A. *Project TALENT, The identification, development, and utilization of human talents: The American high school student.* Pittsburgh: University of Pittsburgh Press, 1964.

Forgione, Jr., P. D., Kaplan, B. A., & Orland, M. E. Evaluation of compensatory education programs: Problems, promising strategies and recent trends. Paper presented at the annual meeting of the American Educational Research Association, San Francisco, April 1979.

Freeman, H. E. The present status of evaluation research. In M. Guttentag (ed.), *Evaluation studies review annual* (Vol. 2). Beverly Hills: Sage, 1977. Pp. 17–51.

Goettel, R. J., Kaplan, B. A., Orland, M. E., Forgione, Jr., P. D., & Huff, S. M. *A study of the administration of the Elementary and Secondary Education Act (ESEA), Title I in eight states: Volume 5, a synthesis report* (TR77-5645). Syracuse: Syracuse Research Corporation, October 1977.

Guba, E. G. *A study of Title III activities: Report on evaluation.* Bloomington: National Institute for the Study of Educational Change, Indiana University, October 1966.

Guba, E. G. The failure of educational evaluation. *Educational Technology,* 1969, *9,* 29–38.

Guba, E. G. *Toward a methodology of naturalistic inquiry in educational evaluation* (CSE Monograph Series in Evaluation, No. 8). Los Angeles: Center for the Study of Evaluation, University of California, 1978.

Guttentag, M. Subjectivity and its use in evaluation research. *Evaluation,* 1973, *1,* 60–65.

Horst, D. P., Tallmadge, C. K., & Wood, C. T. *A practical guide to measuring project impact on student achievement.* Washington, D.C.: U.S. Government Printing Office, 1975.

Lesser, G. S. *Children and television.* New York: Random House, 1974.

Mosteller, F., & Moynihan, D. P. (eds.). *On equality of educational opportunity.* New York: Vintage, 1972.

Patton, M. Q. *Qualitative evaluation methods.* Beverly Hills: Sage, 1980.

Popham, W. J. *Educational evaluation.* Englewood Cliffs, N.J.: Prentice-Hall, 1975.

Posavac, E. J., & Carey, R. G. *Program evaluation: Methods and case studies.* Englewood Cliffs, N.J.: Prentice-Hall, 1980.

Provus, M. M. *Big city Title I evaluation conference.* Pittsburgh: Pittsburgh Public Schools, 1967.

Provus, M. M. *Discrepancy evaluation.* Berkeley: McCutchan, 1971.

Reichardt, C. S., & Cook, T. D. Beyond qualitative versus quantitative methods. In T. D. Cook and C. S. Reichardt (eds.), *Qualitative and quantitative methods in evaluation research.* Beverly Hills: Sage, 1979. Pp. 7–32.

Riecken, H. W., Boruch, R. F., Campbell, D. T., Caplan, N., Glennan, T. K., Pratt, J. W., Rees, A., & Williams, W. *Social experimentation: A method for planning and evaluating social intervention.* New York: Academic Press, 1974.

Rist, R. C. On the relations among educational research paradigms: From disdain to detente. *Anthropology and Educational Quarterly,* 1977, *8,* 42–49.

Rutman, L. (ed.). *Evaluation research methods: A basic guide.* Beverly Hills: Sage, 1977.

Scriven, M. The methodology of evaluation. In R. W. Tyler, R. M. Gagné, and M. Scriven (eds.), *Perspectives of curriculum evaluation* (AERA Monograph Series on Curriculum Evaluation, No. 1). Chicago: Rand McNally, 1967. Pp. 39–83.

Smith, M. S., & Bissell, J. S. Report Analysis: The impact of Head Start. *Harvard Educational Review,* 1970, *40,* 51–104.

Stake, R. E. The countenance of educational evaluation. *Teachers College Record,* 1967, *68,* 523–540.

Stake, R. E. Should educational evaluation be more objective or more subjective? More subjective! Invited debate at the annual meeting of the American Educational Research Association, Toronto, March 1978.

Stufflebeam, D. I., Foley, W. J., Gephart, W. J., Guba, E. G., Hammond, R. L., Merriman, H. O., & Provus, M. M. *Educational evaluation and decision making.* Itasca, Ill.: F. E. Peacock, 1971.

Suchman, E. A. *Evaluative research.* New York: Russell Sage Foundation, 1967.

Tallmadge, G. K., & Horst, D. P. *A procedural guide for validating achievement gains in educational projects.* Mountain View, Calif.: RMC Research Corporation, 1976.

Tyler, R. W. General statement on evaluation. *Journal of Educational Research,* 1942, *35,* 492–501.

Walberg, H. J. (ed.). *Evaluating educational performance*. Berkeley: McCutchan, 1974.

Weiss, R. S., & Rein, M. The evaluation of broad-aim programs: Experimental design, its difficulties, and an alternative. *Administrative Science Quarterly*, 1970, *15*, 97–109.

Wilson, S. The use of ethnographic techniques in educational research. *Review of Educational Research*, 1977, *47*, 245–265.

Wolf, R. M. *Evaluation in education*. New York: Praeger, 1979.

Worthen, B. R., & Sanders, J. R. *Educational evaluation: Theory and practice*. Worthington, Ohio: Charles A. Jones, 1973.

1 DESIGNING EVALUATIONS FOR DIFFERENT PROGRAM ENVIRONMENTS ANTHONY S. BRYK AND RICHARD J. LIGHT

P*lanning an evaluation study of an educational program has become an increasingly complex task in recent years. There are usually a multiplicity of factors that influence a program's operation and its eventual success or failure. The possibility of understanding the program effect or impact rests with the structure of the evaluation design. The selection of a design that is appropriate for the characteristics of the program and the type of information that it must yield for decision making should be based on a scrupulous examination of available alternatives. When this examination is couched in the context of the program environment and practical constraints, the choice of a classical randomized design is frequently the exception rather than the rule. The conditions under which most evaluations are conducted unavoidably relegate the "ideal" research design to a lesser position in favor of a more feasible yet, perhaps, less rigorous approximation.*

In this chapter, Professors Anthony S. Bryk and Richard J. Light survey these evaluation designs and the salient issues associated with their selection, use, and interpretation. They begin by tracing the developments that have contributed to the expansion of program evaluation activities and, consequently, the complicated nature of designing evaluations. This is reflected in the need for evaluators to consider the kinds of questions to be asked, the relative strengths and weaknesses of alternative designs, the interests of the clients and audiences, and the availability of technical expertise and human and physical resources. Next, the authors distinguish among three types of program environments: regular school district, discretionary, and demonstration programs. The remainder of the chapter is devoted to a review of designs that can be used to assess the effectiveness of demonstration programs. The coverage includes randomized designs, nonequivalent control group designs (most common approach), time series designs, sample survey designs, single subject designs, and growth curve models. Special attention is given to designs for highly individualized programs. Examples of two popular single subject designs are the reversal and multiple baseline. Professors Bryk and

11

Light's trenchant critique of the various designs sorts out the advantages and disadvantages of each. This is followed by a discussion of issues related to the generalizability of evaluation results such as volunteer effects and the sampling fraction problem. The authors stress that generalizability of results depends largely upon our ability to identify the elements critical to the program's success. These elements can usually be described in terms of program ideas, the program's physical structure and human resources, the characteristics of the children served, and interactions among these elements. They conclude the chapter with two charges to evaluators: (1) constantly rethink evaluation procedures in light of changing conceptions and results of past efforts, and (2) focus on discovering why an educational program succeeds or fails, not just whether it does. The explanation for "why" requires the tailoring of evaluation designs to the program, social, and political environments.

INTRODUCTION

IT WAS NOT long ago that evaluation was viewed as a one-time effort to determine effects of a program. Evaluation design meant the application of experimental research techniques to assessing program effectiveness. A design consisted primarily of a set of decisions about the placement of treatments and observations, and procedures for selecting individuals and assigning them to a treatment or control group. This methodology drew heavily on the statistical principles pioneered by R. A. Fisher (1935) in agricultural research.

While impact or outcome evaluations based on such classic design procedures remain commonplace today, the field of program evaluation has broadened considerably. The scope and function of evaluation and the research techniques used have expanded dramatically. The literature on evaluation design has become voluminous and increases daily. Thus, in a chapter such as this, we must have a modest agenda. Our objectives here are twofold: first, to present a brief overview of emerging themes in evaluation design; and second, to discuss in somewhat more detail a set of particularly interesting issues focusing on evaluations of demonstration projects and highly individualized service programs.

The Times Are Changing: An Overview

In addition to impact studies, the recently proposed *Standards for Program Evaluation* (Evaluation Research Society, 1980) identifies five other categories of activities:

1. Front end analysis—activities taking place prior to the initiation of a program to determine necessary levels of support or even whether to initiate the program at all;

2. Evaluability assessment—an analysis of the feasibility of conducting future evaluation activities such as an impact study;
3. Formative evaluation—appraising the process of a program, particularly during a period of program development in order to improve its functioning;
4. Program monitoring—the periodic examination of programs that might focus on issues of program compliance (e.g., Is the Head Start center meeting the Head Start performance standards?) or the collection of basic descriptive data (e.g., What services are being delivered and to whom?) that might assist in program management;
5. Evaluation of an evaluation—this may take a variety of forms ranging from a profession critique of a report to reanalysis of original data, to the collection of new data (see Stufflebeam, chapter 7).

Concurrent to a broadening of evaluation activities, there has been a financial explosion of the research industry that is extraordinary. The National Research Council's 1978 report on social research and development found that the various agencies of the federal government invest nearly two billion dollars a year on such activities. This was three times larger than the amount invested in the early 1960s. A 1974 study by the General Accounting Office found a 500% increase in expenditures between 1969 and 1974 just for program evaluation activities.

In introducing the *New Directions for Program Evaluation* sourcebooks, Scarvia Anderson (1978) describes the expanding role for program evaluation that has enlarged the practice of evaluation in a number of ways. As the list of activities above suggests, the kinds of questions addressed by evaluators are now extremely diverse. In addition to issues of program effectiveness, questions are now being asked about *access*—are the services reaching the target population? About *equity*—are services being allocated in a fair and reasonable manner? About *efficiency*—can programs be improved to provide better services for lower cost?

With this expanding set of evaluation questions has come about the introduction of new research methods. Evaluators today draw approaches from such diverse fields as anthropology and qualitative sociology, economics and accounting, operations research, law, engineering, and art criticism (see Anderson et al., 1976). Thus, the process of evaluation design has come to involve linking appropriate research methods to particular questions of interest in a particular context. Perkins (1977) provides a nice summary of this set of concerns.

In addition, since appraising the worth of a program or some subset of its activities is a central feature of evaluation, considerable interest has been devoted to examining the role of values. Thus, another part of evaluation design is identifying whose values any particular study will attend to. Stufflebeam and Webster (1980) provide a rich and detailed analysis of various audiences for evaluation, their value frameworks, and how they interact with concerns about identifying evaluation questions and linking appropriate research methods to these questions.

Since a common purpose of evaluation is to improve the management of program decisions, much attention has focused recently on the nature of such decision making and how evaluation can help. While much of the early work on this topic found that evaluations were not used in social decision making, and suggested numerous problems in this linkage, some recent analyses are far more encouraging, pointing to significant uses of evaluation, although they are complex and subtle. Weiss (1980) provides an excellent review of the research on this topic.

Nevertheless, evaluation design has been substantially influenced by these utilization analyses. Robert Stake's responsive evaluation model (1970) and Ernest House's essay on "Justice in Evaluation" (1976) encouraged a pluralizing of the design process. Michael Patton's book on *Utilization-Focused Evaluation* (1978) describes a process where the clients for the evaluation are fully involved. More recently, we have seen the genesis of a stakeholder strategy that suggests that all parties who have a significant interest in a program (i.e., the stakeholders) should play a significant role in the design effort (see Datta, chapter 6). What was once primarily a set of technical decisions involving the linkage of research methods to evaluation questions, has taken on important political and social dimensions as well.

Conceptions about the role of the evaluator have thus changed drastically. The notion of an objective social scientist coming in from outside to assess a program's worth is no longer the obvious model. In some cases now evaluators are staff persons in support of key program managers and decision makers. They may be advocates who articulate and bolster the arguments for special interest groups. They may be social critics whose analyses challenge fundamental assumptions underlying programs and policies. Their potential roles are almost endless.

In short, program evaluation has expanded in scope and function, and this expansion has greatly complicated the design task. No longer is it simply selecting an appropriate "research recipe" from the appropriate cook book. Rather, evaluation design must blend a variety of considerations, including the kinds of questions to be asked, the relative strengths and weaknesses of alternative research designs, the interests of the clients and audiences for the study, and the availability of appropriate technical expertise and of human and physical resources. Finally, like building design, evaluation design has an artistic character that is difficult to capture in writing about the design process.

Differentiating among Program Environments: A Key Theme

Writings on evaluation design seldom distinguish among the kinds of educational programs to be examined. Yet, there is considerable diversity that has important implications for the design process. In particular, program environment influences the kinds of questions that evaluations seek to address and the methods they utilize, as well as the organizational and resource factors that affect how the evaluation develops and proceeds.

Regular school district programs. At one extreme, we have regular school district programs such as a Kindergarten through Grade 6 reading curriculum. Evaluation design for these programs has a distinctly local flavor, in that the evaluator attends exclusively to the information needs and stakeholders in that particular school district.

A fascinating issue here is the great diversity of actors and the kinds of decisions that they make, even in a relatively small district. In examining evaluation practices in some Title I programs, Bryk and Mathews (1979) organized this diversity into three broad domains of information use: LEA policy and accountability, generic program decisions, and individual child instructional decision making. LEA policy decisions deal with such issues as desegregation and minimum competency requirements. Generic program considerations relate to curriculum changes or considerations about selection policy for individual programs. Finally, decisions about children's programs range from determining next week's lesson to retaining a child for another year in the same grade.

From the perspective of evaluation design, this suggests a broad array of potential useful activities to consider. In terms of accountability-type decisions, some LEA's might find impact evaluation models, such as the proposed USOE Title I models (Tallmadge & Wood, 1978), useful. Others might find designs based on program objectives (see Popham, 1969) appealing. At the program planning level, there are management information systems that may help large LEAs obtain basic descriptive information about their programs. Also potentially useful are process-product studies, naturalistic inquiry, peer and professional reviews, all of whose purpose is to improve local practice. [For a discussion of these alternative methods and further readings, see Goodwin and Driscoll (1980) or Apling and Bryk (1980)].

Clearly, the range of potentially useful evaluation activities is enormous. Bryk and Mathews (1979) report that the kinds of evaluations that LEA staff claimed were most useful to them were activities they developed themselves, often with technical assistance from some outside resource such as the local university. In part this seems to reflect two phenomena—local pride and local relevance. If staff can generate sufficient commitment to undertake evaluation activities and if these activities are tied in to their current concerns, these should be good predictors of future use.

Discretionary programs. A second category of activities is the variety of discretionary programs funded by federal and state governments. These include programs such as compensatory education, bilingual education, and services for the handicapped. While these programs share the same local information needs and stakeholders mentioned above, they also have important external audiences such as state and federal agencies and legislatures. The accountability concerns of these latter groups often dominate the evaluation design process. This can create situations of considerable conflict where school districts are required to support evaluation activities that have little tie-in to local concerns. David's (1978) analysis of local use of mandated Title I evaluations illustrates these problems.

Demonstration programs. A third group of activities is demonstration programs whose funding is not assured beyond some trial period. The Bureau for the Education of the Handicapped, for example, funds each year a number of projects to demonstrate the delivery of special education services to children under age 5. These projects receive monies for three years to develop and deliver early childhood special education programs. Additional funds are available for program dissemination if the local project can demonstrate effectiveness.

Demonstrations are undertaken for at least two main reasons. One is simply to see if a new program or curriculum can in fact be implemented. For example, the Brookline Early Education Program was proposed as an effort to improve school performance of young children by offering families comprehensive diagnostic and educational services from the birth of their child onward. It was unknown whether public school staff could organize themselves to deliver such services, and whether families would participate. In fact, the planned services were organized, and approximately 40% of the eligible families agreed to take part, indicating that this program could at least "take hold" in the pilot community. Without guaranteeing that this program would take hold elsewhere, the pilot site demonstrated that it is *possible* with the right set of circumstances for such an effort to be mounted.

A second reason for a demonstration is to investigate whether a new program in fact "works." This requires a certain leap of faith because it will be evaluated in one or only a few sites. The hope here is usually that an effective innovation will be picked up by others and implemented elsewhere. If a new method for teaching reading to young children is tried in one school system, and carefully documented, and the children seem to read with better comprehension, other schools are likely to try this new curriculum.

This concept of demonstration, as an effort in program development that if successful will be tried in other communities, exerts strong influence on evaluation design. First, since these are program development efforts, evaluation can play an important formative role. The current evaluations for the Push/Excel demonstration projects (American Institutes for Research, 1980), for example, focus on these needs. The evaluators interact often with the staff and other stakeholders at each site, working with them by acting as a "mirror"—describing what is actually occurring and comparing this to what the various stakeholders think the program should be doing. This technical assistance role for evaluation holds considerable promise, but unfortunately it is rarely used.

Second, since demonstrations are pilot efforts, evaluation seeks to determine "does the pilot work?" This usually requires a rigorous assessment of program effectiveness. The evaluation of impact in a demonstration project, however, brings up special design issues. An impact assessment of a regular school program conducted for accountability purposes need only document program outcomes. But an impact evaluation of a demonstration program must also try to identify which features of the program influence its overall effectiveness. This latter concern is particularly important because if the pilot seems successful, we would like the evaluation to provide some insights about the generalizability of the program's effects over time and other contexts. Further, since it is likely that the process of program adaptation by a new community will result in significant alterations as it is fitted to a different local context, any data on the possible consequences of such changes would be especially useful to the new community. For the remainder of this chapter, we pursue in more detail those two concerns—designs for rigorous assessment of program impact, and procedures that might lead to greater generalizability of findings over time and context.

REVIEW OF GENERAL DESIGNS FOR ASSESSING PROGRAM IMPACT IN DEMONSTRATION PROJECTS

The Randomized Field Trial or True Experiment

The randomized field trial represents a very powerful technique for evaluating program effectiveness. If, for example, there are n people at a site, and there are two programs being compared, an "old" one and a "new" one, an evaluator can randomly assign $n/2$ people to the old and $n/2$ to the new. Through this random assignment we are assured that the two groups will be similar in all respects except for the program. If differences occur at the posttreatment point, we can attribute these differences with reasonable confidence to the effects of the program. When feasible, randomization is a good strategy for drawing causal inferences about program effects.

In order to implement a randomized trial design, several conditions must exist. First, the evaluator must be able to control the assignment of programs to people. Second, the evaluator must be sure that the two programs retain their integrity. For example, if we are comparing two curricula we would not like the students getting the old curriculum to go home in the evening and study with friends getting the new curriculum. Third, if the demonstration programs require students' informed consent to participate, problems might arise. For one, people who volunteer might be different from those who do not and, therefore, the results from the evaluation will not generalize to nonvolunteers. Alternatively, by agreeing to participate, the students clearly know they are part of an experiment. This creates the risk of an experiment reactivity—

simply by knowing that they are "in an experiment" may lead to changed behaviors for some participants.

In general, whenever a randomized trial requires an evaluator to establish and maintain a situation that seems artificial to the participants, the danger of reactivity to the experimental *situation* (rather than the program) looms large. These issues are discussed in some detail in Cook and Campbell (1979) in their chapters on randomized trials that have been effectively carried out to evaluate educational programs. While such studies are not always feasible, if a demonstration program can possibly be studied in this manner, the evaluation will benefit from the strong causal inferences that are possible.

Nonequivalent Control Group Designs

The most common approach for assessing the impact of a demonstration project is the nonequivalent control group design. This design is useful in situations where an evaluator doesn't have "control" over assignment of people to programs. Students who sign up for the old curriculum may be different in some ways from those who sign up for the new one. While we can investigate the two groups to see if we can discover in what ways they differ, and try to compensate for this with statistical adjustments, there will always be some uncertainty as to the comparability of the two groups. This is the ever present problem with an observational study.

On the plus side, these designs are usually easy to implement. While a randomized trial can provide a stronger basis for assessing causality, the mixture of students thrown together by a randomized trial may never be even roughly approximated in the real world. In a nonequivalent control group design, however, students make their "natural" choices, and then an evaluator tries to isolate program effects as cleanly as possible. The hard work for such a study comes in the analysis of data. While the uncontrolled individual choice of program creates inferential problems, it is also a major strength in that people now distribute themselves into programs as they might in real life. That in itself can be important information for the evaluation.

Time Series Designs

Although time series designs to evaluate program effectiveness have been suggested for some time (see Campbell & Stanley, 1963), they have just recently become more widely used. The basic idea behind time series designs is quite simple. We have a set of observations over time, such as average third grade reading achievement scores over ten years. We introduce a program, such as a new reading sequence, and collect additional observations over time under the new program. We can plot the time series both prior to and after adding treatment, and apply an "eyeball test"—do the series look the same? If we find that the time series after the treatment looks different from the time series prior to treatment, we can infer a program effect.

Beyond this simple time series design, there are many elegant variants on this approach, including the introduction of a nonequivalent control group time series (a design like the one described in the last section, only now we have a time series on each group). These alternatives and some of the conceptual and logistical problems that can occur with them are discussed in detail in Cook and Campbell (1979) (also see Box & Jenkins, 1976; Glass, Willson, & Gottman, 1975; McCleary & Hay, 1980). We also note that while the logic of the designs and the ''eyeball tests'' are quite appealing, estimating the formal program effect and assessing its statistical significance can become quite complicated. Nevertheless, these designs have many attractive features and certainly merit more careful scrutiny and future application.

Sample Survey Designs When Programs Have Local Control

Many innovations in education permit and even encourage local control. For example, the Experience-Based Career Education Program pioneered by the National Institute of Education encouraged different sites to create whatever specific curriculum they thought would best meet the needs of local students. These curricula varied across sites. Similarly, the Career Internship Program of the Department of Labor encouraged local variations in student activities. It is tempting to organize evaluations of such programs by collecting survey data, pooling the students who receive training across sites, and then comparing their average performance to a pooled group of similar students not receiving training.

Indeed, this was precisely the methodology that the RMC Corporation used to evaluate the Career Internship Program. Yet what might we expect such an evaluation to show? Most likely, we would find that ''on the average,'' the program wasn't very effective. But this would not be surprising. After all, in any new demonstration program, where there is a large amount of variation *among experimental centers* with respect to curriculum, staffing, and program structure, we could expect a priori that *most* new centers would not do a particularly outstanding job. Further, if an ''average'' is taken over all of the new experimental centers, the many unsuccessful ones will likely swamp the rare handful that are having a significant impact, so that ''on the average,'' the program will be judged as unsuccessful.

Evaluators must ask a different question here: which versions of a new program seem to be working, and what are the program features that characterize these successful efforts? Let us not judge a program on a first round of evaluation by lumping all the unsuccessful centers together with the few successes and taking an average. Rather, we should focus on detecting the few successful programs, and try to understand *why* they were successful. We could then in a second round of program development set up new centers that incorporate these seemingly valuable features, and see if they are, in fact, replicable and transferable.

A Special Problem: Assessing Impact When Services Are Highly Individualized

It is generally assumed that educational programs can, in principle, be delivered with a high degree of standardization, and in fact this is required for "successful implementation." Cook and Campbell and other basic evaluation design texts, such as Rossi, Freeman and Wright (1979) assume that standardizing the treatment is a desirable goal from both a research and program perspective.

However, we are witnessing increased interest in individualized instruction in education. This is particularly true in special education, where federal law PL 94-142 requires an individualized educational plan for each child. In these kinds of programs the actual sequence of activities and experiences for an individual child often cannot be defined a priori. Rather, it emerges over time out of the interaction between the program and the individual child. Nevertheless, this does not require that such program activities be idiosyncratic. Each teacher may operate within a general framework from which individual educational programs are derived. That is, although there may exist a set of implicit or explicit program objectives, the teacher has no expectation of implementing all of these objectives with every child, nor of implementing them at the same rate or in the same way.

Such highly individualized educational programs present significant problems for the standard group designs reviewed in the last section. Suppose we assume an ideal situation where there exists program success for each child in accord with that child's own needs, as well as reliable and valid quantitative assessment of these individual gains and a perfectly matched program and control group. Then it would still be unlikely that we could obtain evidence of significant program impact as defined by statistically significant mean differences across groups. A highly individualized program can be effective without all of its subjects moving in a particular direction on all dimensions within a single evaluation time frame. Yet, this uniformity constitutes the implicit assumption of all traditional univariate and multivariate analysis methods. In individualized programs the search for mean differences across groups, variable by variable, is often futile. There is usually less statistical power than might appear on the basis of total sample size since each outcome variable is only relevant for a small subset of children at any particular point in time.

Even if it were possible to measure short-term gains with perfect validity for each child on each program dimension, a serious problem of interpretation might exist. Without a detailed assessment of the needs of the individual child and an account of the program "intentionality" or focus over the recent short term, it will be hard to place *a value* on the outcomes generated by the classic statistical paradigm that compares group performances.

These concerns suggest that when programs are clearly individualized, impact is best examined on an individual case basis. The most effective way to approach this, however, is an open issue. The N = 1 research design methodology represents one promising approach to this problem. Recent efforts (Hersen & Barlow, 1976; Kratochwill, 1978) have argued for more extensive use of this approach in research on clinical and educational settings. These designs have been used in basic research on human behavior (see Baer, Wolf, & Risley, 1968; Dukes, 1965; Kazdin, 1973; Yates, 1970), and have been advocated for evaluation research in special education (Blackman, 1972; Edgar & Billingsley, 1974; Guralnick, 1973).

There are two main versions in current use: the reversal (ABA or ABAB design) and the multiple-baseline design. For evaluating regular school programs, the reversal design is inappropriate since it is highly intrusive to the instructional process. It requires teachers to alter their interactions with a child for research rather than instructional purposes, and it assumes that there is no carryover of the treatment effect across period reversals.

Multiple-baseline designs appear more promising. These involve the successive application of the treatment to a number of children thought to be similar in important ways, who are being monitored continuously on the outcome variable. A treatment effect is inferred if behavior changes occur only upon application of the experimental variable. This approach makes less intrusive demands on the instructional process. It does not require large numbers of children, and it does not require a control group of children excluded from the program. It has been suggested by some (Guralnick, 1973; Wynne, Ulfelder, & Dakof, 1975) that this approach is particularly well suited for highly individualized programming.

The multiple-baseline design builds on a time series model and requires a large number of observations over time on the outcome variable for each child. The multiple cases provide an opportunity to replicate the treatment effects and thus increase the validity of our findings. Strenio, Weisberg, and Bryk (1979) recently developed a variation of this approach based on growth-curve models and an empirical Bayes estimation strategy that extends the single-subject research model, and, potentially, uses the available data more efficiently.

The basic idea is quite simple. Assume that we have a limited number of observations (say between 3 and 10) on each child, and some additional background information. On the basis of an individual child's own data, we can derive one estimate of a growth curve. On the basis of the across-subject data, we can derive a second growth-curve estimate for each child. Our optimal estimator is a weighted combination of these two.

This growth-curve model can be used as part of either an experimental or observational strategy. In an experimental mode, we might collect data prior to the intervention, estimate a child's growth curve, and use this to predict an outcome in the absence of the intervention. By comparing the observed outcome with the predicted outcome, we have a natural measure of treatment effectiveness.

In an observational study, we might collect our case data while the child is in a program. We could use the model to develop an estimate of the growth trajectory for each child while he/she is under treatment. We could then compare the growth trajectories across individual cases, examining whatever natural variation exists in the background variables and treatment conditions.

Like the randomized study, these growth-curve and single-subject approaches require a degree of control over the research setting. Difficulties in applying them can occur from the shared control that often characterizes an instructional process. First, the multiple-baseline design assumes that an evaluator can control the onset of a program to meet data collection needs. In many situations, however, important aspects of a program (e.g., physical environment and presence of peers) are ever-present, and a child may engage himself/herself before the adults initiate it, even without their knowledge.

Second, in situations where control is shared between teachers and students, there is only limited predictability that the program as actually experienced by a child will follow any a priori pattern or sequence. In fact, the environment that a child experiences is not fully defined until the child enters that environment. The child has an impact on peers and teachers, and they have impacts on one another, in turn, creating a new set of relationships with their own boundaries and constraints. It is within this newly created organization that the child's program begins to unfold. Even if the program is highly purposeful, attempting to optimize development for the child, it is taking place within a framework whose future structure is only partially predictable.

Third, although there may be clarity and purposefulness in the long-term goal structure for these programs (e.g., developing competence in basic developmental areas), there are many short-term routes that can be followed toward the achievement of this desired end. From an educational perspective, each route may be equally valid. Thus, even if one comprehensively assesses an individual child's needs, no single instructional strategy or specific set of short-term objectives must by definition follow.

Fourth, and perhaps most important, there are substantial measurement problems with single-subject designs. Precisely because we wish to learn something about a single case, our design relies very heavily on the accuracy of the data obtained on that case. The growth-curve model provides some relief here, because it allows us to borrow some strength from the cross-sectional data. Nevertheless, we need valid growth-metric data to apply this approach. Although there is considerable current interest in developing such measures, the instrumentation now available provides adequate growth metrics for only a very limited range (usually very microlevel) of behaviors.

Finally, the single-subject designs implicitly assume that there is only one or a limited number of variables of interest, and that these data will be collected on at least a few cases. In fact, individual educational plans can involve a bewildering and varied array of very specific objectives. It doesn't seem reasonable to think about building designs and collecting data on hundreds of outcomes for each child. Rather, it would make more sense to collect data on a limited set of "marker variables" that might have relevance for most children. In doing this, however, we must remember that we are no longer fully evaluating impact, but only examining a segment of program outcomes.

Problems in Generalizing from Demonstrations

Even if a demonstration is judged highly successful, we generally don't know whether similar results would occur upon implementation of the program in other locations. Unfortunately, most past evaluations of demonstration programs seem content to confine their efforts to establishing that a pilot program works. Yet sometimes a program that looks highly promising on a small scale disappoints us upon widespread implementation. We review in this section some problems that have occurred in past cases, and suggest some possible solutions.

Volunteer effects. As was mentioned earlier, the use of volunteers in randomized studies can raise questions about the generalizability of the findings. There is a "soft" way for an evaluator to examine this problem. The basic idea is that in the early stages of a randomized trial using volunteers, the volunteers should be randomly divided into two subgroups. One subgroup should participate in the randomized trial at the demonstration site, just as they expected. The other subgroup of volunteers should be told, "Thank you for volunteering, but we have more volunteers than we needed, so you just go ahead and choose the curriculum that you prefer. Use your best judgment as a guide, rather than the flip of the evaluator's coin."

This second subgroup, then, has two known features. First, each person made up his/her own mind to choose either A or B depending upon personal preference. In other words, as a group, these "rejected volunteers" were for evaluation purposes just like the children in the nonexperimental site, where each chose a curriculum freely. But in addition we know that each of these children was a volunteer for the randomized trial, even though they didn't "get in."

Why is this knowledge valuable? By comparing this second subgroup to the original *non*volunteers (i.e., examining the curriculum A versus curriculum B comparison for each group), we can get a rough estimate of the *volunteer effect*. For example, if A outperforms B for the nonvolunteers while B outperforms A for the volunteers who were not selected for the randomized study, this would be a strong indication of a substantial "volunteer effect." On the other hand, finding similar results for the two groups would indicate *no* volunteer effect.

The "sampling fraction" problem. Suppose that a new education program is developed to train marginally employed young people. Services include vocational information, training, and financial support and counseling. This multi-service program is to be implemented as a demonstration at one site, and then evaluated using a randomized controlled field trial. From a pool of 100 applicants, 50 are randomly assigned to the services, and 50 to a control group. One year later, a comparison is made. The results of the demonstration are clear. The 50 trainees (e.g., assume they are paramedics) are all employed at good salaries, and their supervisors are highly satisfied with their performance. The control group is not nearly as well off. So the conclusion as to program effectiveness seems obvious. The vocational training is a success, as determined by a well-done randomized field trial. The next policy step is to expand the demonstration to a large scale and to give many more people in many places the same excellent training.

Next year the integrated service program is widely implemented in many cities. Fifty thousand unemployed but trainable people in these cities are prepared to ultimately become paramedics. What happens? The program is a failure. A year later, most of the trainees are unemployed. Why? Because while there was strong demand for 50 trained paramedics, perhaps there was not demand for 50,000. So the highly successful and well-evaluated demonstration effort breaks down when expanded into a large-scale program.

This example illustrates an important concept. There are some education programs or services where the benefit that the program confers on any one recipient is a function of how many other people receive the program. The value to an individual participant depends upon the program size. In this case, the more widely the program is offered, the lower the expected benefit to any one trainee. A similar comment might be made for preschool education. If all four-year-old children received preschool education, the value of preschool education as a compensatory education strategy might disappear.

If an evaluator believes that a particular program has this character, there are two steps that can be taken at the "demonstration" level. One is to make an effort to keep up with the "demand side" of the ledger. For vocational education programs, for example, it would be valuable to estimate demand for different sorts of trainees with different skills. A second step is to see whether the skills offered by a training program have the property that the market is quickly saturated, a "relative size constraint." This can be accomplished if data on program effectiveness exist at several sites with different sampling fractions, n/N. Here, n represents number of trainees receiving services, while N represents local labor force in any job category in a city. If such data are available, one can compare each site's sampling fraction with the program's demonstrated effectiveness. When those sites with larger fractions have smaller positive program effects, one should suspect that a relative size constraint may be operating for these services. The message for evaluators, then, is to try a new program of this type at several sites, including both larger cities and smaller towns.

Bumps in the tails of a distribution of program effects. It is not unreasonable for a manager of a large demonstration effort, such as Follow Through, to ask a simple "on the average" question. Is his/her program "working"? This often involves pulling together results from many evaluation studies conducted at a local level. But assuming here that the various local studies are well done methodologically, what should one expect to find? We would guess that large-scale multiple-site programs, such as the ones just mentioned, would vary considerably in their effectiveness among sites. A goal, then, would be to search for the subgroup of sites that are notably successful, and look for commonalities in how they are structuring their program. If such commonalities are found, they may be generalizable to other sites.

This information will be found, most likely, in a careful analysis of the *variation* in among sites' effectiveness. Cohen (1970) quotes a nice example from an Office of Education study of pre- and posttest scores in big city Title I programs (Piccariello, no date):

> For the total 189 observations [each observation was one classroom in a Title I program], there were 108 significant changes (exceed 2 s.e.). Of these 58 were gains and 50 were losses. In 81 cases the change did not appear to be significant.
>
> As the data in Appendix D show, success and failure seem to be random outcomes, determined neither clearly nor consistently by the factors of program design, city or state, area or grade level. (P. 4)

In fact, do such results indicate random outcomes? We think not. Even though an "on the average" analysis may show zero, a study of the distribution of outcomes shows that if outcomes were random, with no underlying program effect, we would expect about five significant gains and five significant losses using the two-standard-error criterion given in the original study.

Instead, the abundance of significant results in both directions far exceeds that expected from normal sampling variation. So, the conclusion that the program has no effect is wrong. We believe a better interpretation would be that the effects of Title I programs differ in a systematic way from school system to school system. The value of combining information across sites and examining variation is to secure an amount and kind of information that would not be available from any single site (see Cooley, Bond, & Mao's discussion of multilevel data analysis in chapter 3).

Identifying program elements critical to success. Many studies view educational programs as simple fixed entities. By this we mean a direct analogue to the pill in drug research, or fertilizer in agricultural research. In reality, an educational program can be very complex. Conducting an impact evaluation and finding that the program was effective can still leave us with the question, "What is it?" Or, more precisely, what features of the pilot program seem crucial for producing the effects we have documented? Without such information, there is no basis for dissemination to other locations.

One of the authors (Bryk) confronted exactly this question in attempting to evaluate some early childhood special education demonstration projects in the Boston area. Program descriptions were available, but such descriptions often were more statements of philosophy and objectives than what people actually do. This led to the question, "How can we describe most education programs?" The literature on educational programs suggested four major entities: ideas, physical resources, human resources, and the characteristics of the children. Each one of these entities is a system requiring description and careful analysis.

First, in the domain of _program ideas,_ these derive from values—both personal, as they emerge either from the community culture or more narrowly from the perspectives of the program developers, and professional, as they are reflected in the basic theories of child development and social science research. Taken together, these values generate a philosophy that leads to more specific program goals and objectives.

Second, any program has some _physical structure:_ the organization of the classroom environment, both physical and temporal, and the materials available. Normally included here are items such as class size and teacher to child ratio, the kinds of books and toys available, the structuring of the environment into interest centers, and the temporal plan for a day's activities. In some kinds of programs the elements of the physical structure are critical to actualizing program ideas. In others, their role is peripheral.

Third, there are the program personnel, the _human resources_. An important aspect of personnel structure is simply the number of people involved and how they relate to one another. Other important dimensions of personnel include professional training and personal characteristics of each staff person. Any observed teacher behavior will depend upon these features, and how we think about dissemination of effective practices will be influenced substantially by which characteristics produce an observed impact.

Fourth, an important component of an instructional system is the collective group of _children_ who are served. This "group" feature is often ignored, yet frequently it determines the character of the classroom in operation. For example, the presence or absence of a particular child can substantially alter a program environment. Individual children can exert influence over time on the philosophy and structure of the program and the behavior of personnel. In some programs a child's peers are a vehicle for attaining program goals and objectives.

Each of these four components and the relationships among them merge to define a particular program. The relative importance of the components, however, may vary greatly from program to program. Some of these features are easily disseminated; others are not.

Take as an example a program for language-delayed children that we recently studied. It had a reputation for being a "good" program. It consisted of one classroom with five children (all handicapped) and two adults. Our first observations suggested this was a teacher-centered context and that the head teacher dominated all aspects of the instructional effort. The character of the program seemed to be determined primarily by the teacher's character. While we could identify aspects of her behavior that might be called professional knowledge in practice (e.g., strategies for extending children's use of language), a large part of the classroom ambiance seemed to reflect the head teacher's personality characteristics (general exuberance, enthusiasm). On the other hand, the work of the classroom aide involved primarily some simple exercises in object labeling. It seemed likely that one could exchange this aide with many other people and not alter the character of the program very much.

Since this was a demonstration project, concerned about dissemination, this analysis has important consequences. We might, for example, attribute success to a set of teaching strategies (e.g., object labeling and extending children's use of language), when the critical element might really be the personality of the head teacher. Can this personality be "transplanted" to other sites? Perhaps yes. But if not, these other sites would have a program that is effectively different from this pilot site.

In general, it seems likely we will encounter these kinds of problems in generalizing from pilot programs. By its very nature, a pilot program is often extraordinarily selective in hiring staff. As a result, these "ninety-ninth percentile" instructors can produce a substantial "program effect" that will not generalize to other sites. A recent collaborative study by Lazar et al. (1977) reported long-term effects for a series of pilot preschool programs that were conducted in the middle 1960s. On the basis of this analysis, the authors concluded that early childhood education has long-term effects. A more cautious interpretation is that several small pilot programs, tightly run, with very select staff, indeed produced long-term effects. Inference that a broad federal policy of early education for all children will produce similar results is more precarious.

Similarly, the choice of community or context in which the demonstration is conducted may significantly qualify the generalizability of findings. Sometimes a demonstration is initiated because the community is particularly receptive to the innovation. While many judgments enter here, the basic argument is that a new treatment should be installed in a place that gives it every chance to work. If it doesn't work in such a receptive environment, it probably is not worth pursuing. If it does work, it will have "demonstrated" two things. First, that in an ideal setting the treatment is effective. Second, that in a certain type of setting, we know that the treatment can be implemented. In fact, seeing these two outcomes might lead a previously unenthusiastic institution to become more enthusiastic. On the other hand, it is clearly inappropriate to conclude that because it worked in the pilot site, widespread dissemination of the program is automatically warranted. A more appropriate action would be to pilot the program in some additional and different communities and then evaluate what happens.

How else might we take these factors into account? There seems to be a significant role here for qualitative or naturalistic inquiry. One might send in some experienced observers and ask them to watch on-site for a while and report back what they see. On the quantitative side, evaluations should be designed to capitalize on naturally occurring variations that exist within a program. For example, there are often many classrooms or many sites. It is possible to design data collection and analysis to estimate effects at the classroom or site level (see Cooley, Bond, & Mao, chapter 3). Are effects consistent across classrooms or sites? If a demonstration runs for more than one year, is there consistency across years? If consistency across sites and years is found, we can be more confident in our findings. If there is inconsistency, we must look more closely, perhaps using qualitative inquiry, at possible explanations for divergent results.

SUGGESTIONS FOR FUTURE RESEARCH

Throughout this chapter, we indicated at several points areas that merit further effort. We would like to stress two of these points. First, more attention needs to be paid to the characteristics of individual demonstration programs—the students served, the staffing organization, and the community context—and the implications that these features have for interpreting results from such projects. There are important issues of generalizability in moving from a single demonstration project to a multi-site demonstration to widespread dissemination that are sometimes forgotten. Qualitative data may offer some real insight and assistance here to a generally quantitative evaluation. Building the two systematically together is an area that needs much creative work.

Our second point is that evaluation methods for highly individualized educational programs are very much needed. Although some new techniques seem promising, there are large conceptual and methodological problems remaining. In particular, adequate standards of comparison for an individual child's progress are lacking. Longitudinal norms involving growth metrics represent a potentially useful approach that probably deserves further effort (see Linn, chapter 4).

A third problem on which future research would be useful is somewhat broader. Robert Boruch, in his recent (1980) comprehensive overview of educational program evaluations at the federal, state, and local level, found only a few examples that clearly showed how evaluation results modified and improved a program. Developing ways to improve the linkage between evalu-

ation information and program management remains a major task for practicing evaluators.

Much research toward this end has been initiated recently. For example,
Marvin Alkin and his colleagues have examined the design of evaluations of
Title I and Title IVc programs of the Elementary and Secondary Education
Act in five local school sites, and how the results were subsequently used.
They were able to identify several features that seem to influence the utilization of the information. Key concerns were: (1) the evaluator's choice of role;
(2) the extent to which evaluators sought user involvement in the evaluation
process; (3) the amount of attention given to the performance of mandated
evaluation tasks; (4) the rapport between evaluators and important users; (5)
the extent to which evaluators sought to stimulate the use of information
(Alkin, Daillak, & White, 1979). Clearly, we need more research like this if
we are to improve evaluation utility.

GUIDELINES FOR EVALUATORS

A theme—the practice of program evaluation coming of age—runs through
many chapters of this book. The past decade has seen a rapid expansion of
program evaluation activities, and we all have learned a great deal from these
experiences. The task of evaluation design has become a complex effort
imposing much more than just technical decisions about fitting appropriate
methods to evaluation questions. We are now talking about a process involving important political and social dimensions, as well as technical and fiscal
resource considerations.

While there has been much criticism of past evaluation practice, these
criticisms have resulted in a series of developments that hold considerable
promise for future efforts. We welcome those changes. But a note of caution
is in order. In trying to link the results of evaluations more directly to decision
making about programs, we run the risk of diminishing an important feature
of evaluation—that of social critic challenging basic assumptions about programs and policies. In her reconceptualization of the terms "social science
knowledge," "utilization," and "decision making," Carol Weiss (1980) has
suggested that past evaluations have been quite influential in this way, and
that this is an important function for them to serve.

We would like to conclude with an historically true story. Just after the first
world war, the U.S. Army hired a time and motion expert to study various
phases of its military operations. When he arrived at an artillery section, he
noted that a certain number of men were assigned to each artillery group.
Finding this interesting, he watched as they carried out their practice drills.
After a while he noticed that there always seemed to be one extra man
assigned to each group. Since he couldn't understand why this was so, he

traced the history of how certain numbers of men came to be assigned to do certain tasks. Finally he found the explanation for the extra man. The artillery team had had an extra man assigned, pre–World War I, to "hold the officer's horse."

This little story has a serious moral for program evaluators. We have a responsibility to constantly rethink our procedures in light of changing conceptions and results of past efforts. In particular, our recent experiences suggest that future evaluations should focus more on discovering the *why* of an educational program's successes and failures, rather than simply toting them up. This requires tailoring evaluation designs to mesh with the program environment and the social and political context in which they are immersed.

REFERENCES

Alkin, M. C., Daillak, R., & White, P. *Using evaluations: Does evaluation make a difference?* Beverly Hills: Sage, 1979.

American Institutes for Research. *The national evaluation of the Push for Excellence Project* (Technical Report No. 1). Washington, D.C.: Author, 1980.

Anderson, S. B. The expanding role of evaluation. *New Directions for Program Evaluation,* 1978, *1*.

Anderson, S. B., Ball, S., Murphy, R. T., & Associates. *Encyclopedia of educational evaluation.* San Francisco: Jossey-Bass, 1976.

Apling, R., & Bryk, A. S. *Evaluation for improving early childhood Title I programs.* Cambridge, Mass.: The Huron Institute, 1980.

Baer, D. M., Wolf, M. M., & Risley, T. R. Some current dimensions of applied behavior analysis. *Journal of Applied Behavior Analysis,* 1968, *1*, 91–97.

Blackman, L. S. Research and the classroom: Mahomet and the mountain revisited. *Exceptional Children,* 1972, *39*, 181–191.

Boruch, R. F. Report on evaluations of education programs to the Department of Education. Evanston, Ill.: Northwestern University, June 1980.

Box, G. E. P., & Jenkins, G. M. *Time series analysis: Forecasting and control* (rev. ed.). San Francisco: Holden-Day, 1976.

Bryk, A. S., & Mathews, R. A utilization perspective on evaluation policy for early childhood Title I programs. Paper presented at the annual meeting of the American Educational Research Association, San Francisco, April 1979.

Campbell, D. T., & Stanley, J. C. Experimental and quasi-experimental designs for research on teaching. In N. L. Gage (ed.), *Handbook of research on teaching.* Chicago: Rand McNally, 1963. Pp. 171–246.

Cohen, D. K. Politics and research: Evaluation of social action programs in education. *Review of Educational Research,* 1970, *40*, 213–238.

Cook, T. D., & Campbell, D. T. *Quasi-experimentation: Design and analysis issues for field settings.* Chicago: Rand McNally, 1979.

David, J. L. *Local uses of Title I evaluations* (Report EPRC 21). Menlo Park, Calif.: Stanford Research Institute, July 1978.

Dukes, W. F. N = 1. *Psychological Bulletin,* 1965, *64*, 74–79.

Edgar, E., & Billingsley, F. Believability when N = 1. *Psychological Record*, 1974, *24*, 147-160.

Fisher, R. A. *The design of experiments* (1st ed.). London: Oliver and Boyd, 1935.

Glass, G. V., Willson, V. L., & Gottman, J. M. *Design and analysis of time-series experiments*. Boulder: Colorado Associated University Press, 1975.

Goodwin, W. L., & Driscoll, L. A. *Handbook of measurement and evaluation in early childhood education*. San Francisco: Jossey-Bass, 1980.

Guralnick, M. J. A research-service model for support of handicapped children. *Exceptional Children*, 1973, *39*, 277-282.

Hersen, M., & Barlow, D. N. *Single case experimental designs: Strategies for studying behavior change*. Elmsford, N.Y.: Pergamon Press, 1976.

House, E. R. Justice in evaluation. In G. V. Glass (ed.), *Evaluation studies review annual* (Vol. 1). Beverly Hills: Sage, 1976. Pp. 75-100.

Kazdin, A. E. Methodological and assessment considerations in evaluating reinforcement programs in applied settings. *Journal of Applied Behavior Analysis*, 1973, *6*, 517-531.

Kratochwill, T. R. (ed.). *Single subject research*. New York: Academic Press, 1978.

Lazar, I., Hubbell, V. R., Marray, H., Rosche, M., & Royce, J. *The persistence of preschool effects: A long-term follow-up of fourteen infant and preschool experiments* (Final Report). Ithaca, N.Y.: Cornell University, 1977.

McCleary, R., & Hay, Jr., R. A. *Applied time series analysis for the social sciences*. Beverly Hills: Sage, 1980.

Patton, M. Q. *Utilization-focused evaluation*. Beverly Hills: Sage, 1978.

Perkins, D. N. T. Evaluating social interventions: A conceptual schema. *Evaluation Quarterly*, 1977, *1*, 639-656.

Piccariello, H. Evaluation of Title I. Paper presented to the Department of Health, Education, and Welfare, Office of Education, Washington, D.C., no date.

Popham, W. J. (ed.). *Instructional objectives*. Chicago: Rand McNally, 1969.

Rossi, P. H., Freeman, H. E., & Wright, S. R. *Evaluation: A systematic approach*. Beverly Hills: Sage, 1979.

Stake, R. E. Objectives, priorities and other judgment data. *Review of Educational Research*, 1970, *40*, 181-212.

Strenio, J. F., Weisberg, H. I., & Bryk, A. S. *Empirical Bayes estimation of individual growth curve parameters and their relationship to covariates*. Cambridge, Mass.: The Huron Institute, 1979.

Stufflebeam, D. L., & Webster, W. J. An analysis of alternative approaches to evaluation. *Educational Evaluation and Policy Analysis*, 1980, *2*, 5-20.

Tallmadge, G. K., & Wood, C. T. *User's guide: ESEA Title I evaluation and reporting system* (rev.). Mountain View, Calif.: RMC Research Corporation, 1978.

Weiss, C. H. Three terms in search of reconceptualization: Knowledge, utilization, and decision making. Cambridge, Mass.: The Huron Institute, 1980. (draft)

Wynne, S., Ulfelder, L. S., & Dakof, G. *Mainstreaming and early childhood education for handicapped children: Review and implications of research* (Final Report). Washington, D.C.: Wynne Associates, 1975.

Yates, A. J. *Behavior Therapy*. New York: Wiley, 1970.

2 MEASURING PROGRAM EFFECTS NANCY S. COLE
AND ANTHONY J. NITKO

O nce the evaluation design has been specified along with the appropriate
independent variable(s), the next major step in the evaluation study is
to identify the dependent variables. This usually entails a consideration of
cognitive, affective, and/or psychomotor outcome measures. Inter alia, it is
highly desirable that these measures provide a valid, sensitive, and unbiased
assessment of program effects. Attaining that objective requires a strong
commitment, a formidable effort, and substantial resources. The current state
of practice in this area is not totally abysmal. Clearly, much work lies ahead.
The thrust of chapter 2 is to facilitate this work.

Professors Nancy S. Cole and Anthony J. Nitko examine the key practical
and technical issues in the choice of program outcome measures. Initially,
they recommend a set of systematic procedures for identifying and evaluating
potentially useful instruments. This section is followed by a comprehensive
review of the issues that an evaluator should consider in order to make a final
selection. The first issue pertains to specifying the intended and unintended
outcomes of the program, distinguishing between long-term and short-term
goals, and operationalizing the outcomes so that they can be measured. Two
outcome-related problems that affect the sensitivity of the measures to the
program are whether the outcomes should produce a change in a general
ability or a specific skill and whether long-term or short-term goals should be
assessed. In addition, sensitivity is influenced by the relationship of the measures to the instructional domain and to the program content that actually had
been taught. A third particularly perplexing issue deals with the tasks of
selecting unbiased tests and defending tests against charges of sex, racial, or
ethnic bias. Professors Cole and Nitko discuss bias in terms of content-based
and construct-based test score interpretations. They suggest three methods
that an evaluator can employ to eliminate bias: (1) use panels of experts to

NOTE: The authors acknowledge the helpful suggestions of R. Tony Eichelberger in the preparation
of this paper.

judge freedom from facial bias, (2) conduct statistical bias studies or locate such studies that are already available, and (3) limit test score interpretations to only those that can be justified by strong validity evidence. A fourth issue germane to the selection of standardized tests is whether students should be administered a test that covers the content associated with their present grade placement (on-level testing) or whether they should be tested on content appropriate to their actual achievement or instructional level (out-of-level testing). A final issue concerns the development of tests at the local level in lieu of or to complement the commercially developed standardized tests. Although there is a fundamental curricular relevance limitation with the latter, the authors stress that it is frequently very difficult to obtain structural quality, validity and reliability evidence, national norms, and overall credibility when attempting the former. At the conclusion of the chapter, there are some comments on the documentation of the independent variable in its actual operation during an evaluation study. A checklist of guidelines that evaluators could use in the selection of instruments completes the chapter.

INTRODUCTION

ALTHOUGH educational evaluation studies differ in type of research design used and the data analysis procedures followed, they have at least two common components—an educational practice being evaluated (the independent variable or treatment) and potential outcomes of that practice [the dependent variable(s)]. This chapter is about these two common components and the issues in operationalizing or measuring them in evaluation studies.

The first section of the chapter discusses the preliminary steps an evaluator must undertake to identify potentially useful tests for measuring program outcomes. It describes briefly a systematic procedure for searching for potentially useful tests and for preparing a general review of each test identified.

Once one or more tests are identified as potentially useful, the evaluator needs to consider each in the light of the particular needs of the evaluation study at hand. Of concern, for example, is the appropriateness or sensitivity of the measures of the outcomes for detecting the actual effects the program produces. An educational program that in fact is producing intended outcomes may appear to be failing if the measures of the outcomes are insensitive or inappropriate. Section two is devoted to this selection of program outcome measures based on considerations such as (a) identifying the intended program goals, (b) judging the sensitivity of a test to the impact of instruction, (c) matching a test to the instructional domain, (d) estimating the impact of a sex-, racial-, or ethnic-biased test on the evaluation, (e) matching the test to the general educational development level of the pupils, and (f) deciding whether to buy or build the needed tests.

While the selection of appropriate tests to measure program outcomes is the primary focus of this chapter, there are problems often neglected in the "measurement" of the independent variable (the program itself). Section three discusses briefly the concerns for documenting or measuring the nature and implementation of the program or treatment variables.

The final two sections present specific areas for further research and provide guidelines for evaluators to use when selecting tests for evaluation studies, respectively.

PRELIMINARY STEPS IN THE SELECTION OF OUTCOME MEASURES

Searching for Potentially Useful Tests

The fundamental criterion for selecting any test is its appropriateness for measuring the intended variable. This implies that evaluators must (a) specify the variable(s) they intend to measure, (b) find or develop tests purporting to measure the intended outcome(s), and (c) judge the appropriateness of each of the possible tests identified. Problems of specifying the intended variable(s) are discussed separately for outcome variables and process or treatment variables in subsequent sections.

The very practical problem of finding possible instruments is a complex one because there are available many *seemingly* appropriate tests and because there are multiple, frequently nonoverlapping, sources of information about them. In general, it is desirable to systematically search a variety of resources in order to identify several potentially useful tests from which a final selection ultimately can be made. (The final selection will require a more detailed evaluation of the tests in terms of specific questions that are of concern to evaluation studies. These are discussed in the next section.)

Table 2.1 lists some steps that can be taken by evaluators to search systematically for tests, as well as listing a few selected resources of information about tests. Two particularly helpful resources are the catalogues by Aaronson (1974) and Backer (1977) that list the many bibliographies of tests that exist.

Formulating a General Review of a Potentially Useful Test

The task of evaluating the appropriateness of possible instruments is many-faceted. Most introductory measurement texts address the crucial issues in evaluating a test in a general way. Thorndike and Hagen (1977), for example, present an especially good discussion of a number of the concerns facing evaluators in judging a test, as well as providing a guide for reviewing a test in a general way (pp. 107–110). Another possible outline for a general review of a test, adapted from Anastasi (1976), is presented in Table 2.2. The outline there illustrates both the practical and the technical considerations relevant to judging almost any measurement procedure.

If one or more potentially useful tests have been identified and information about each obtained, it is necessary to make a more detailed examination in order to reach the final choice of the test(s) to use. The specific concerns of this more detailed review are the topics of the next section.

TABLE 2.1. One Procedure for Systematically Searching for Measurement Procedures

---

  I. *Initial Preparation*
    a. *Identify the behavior to be observed and measured:* formulate purpose for testing, identify project concerns, state project objectives.
    b. *Identify working constraints:* nature of persons tested, personnel available, cost and time factors, school and community concerns, scheduling, etc.
    c. *Identify "state of the art" of the area to be tested:* broad view of area obtained from a "definitive" source or "state-of-the-art" reference (see Backer, 1977, for some suggestions).
    d. *Make a review worksheet:* a place is needed to systematically record information about practical and technical qualities of each test found (see Table 2 for an example).
 II. *Survey Specialized Test Literature*
    a. *Publications of the Buros Mental Measurements Institute: Mental Measurements Yearbooks (MMY), Tests in Print,* etc.
    b. *News on Tests* (formerly *Test Collection Bulletin*): Periodic publication of the ETS Test Collection listing tests that become available after the publication of the *MMY*.
    c. *Bibliographic references of tests:* Backer (1977) and Aaronson (1974) contain lists of over 90 of these bibliographic resources.
    d. *Review test publisher's catalogues.*
    e. *Scan textbooks on tests and measures:* Review measurement texts specializing in specific disciplines as well as general books.
III. *Survey the General Literature*
    a. *Indexes and abstracts.*
    b. *Educational Resources Information Center* (ERIC)
    c. *Professional journals:* Review articles and test reviews and look for advertisements.
    d. *Textbooks* in area under study may mention tests.
 IV. *Make Personal Contact*
    a. *Information directories:* See, for example, *Encyclopedia of Information Systems and Services.*
    b. *ETS Test Collection, Head Start Test Collection*
    c. *Universities and centers:* University's testing office, educational research and psychology departments, federal research and development centers and regional laboratories, child study laboratories, etc.
    d. *Professional organizations and special interest groups.*
    e. *Author(s) of the test or a similar test.*
  V. *Construct a Test* (if unable to locate an appropriate measure)
    a. *Contract with others:* educational company, test publisher, individual specialist in measurement.
    b. *Build your own:* use item and objectives pools commercially available or build your own without help.

Source: Adapted from Educational Testing Service (n.d.)

REVIEW OF ISSUES IN THE SELECTION OF OUTCOME MEASURES

The choice of tests depends on both practical and technical considerations. The basic practical concern centers around feasibility and cost. The fundamental technical concern focuses on the validity of the measure: Will the test(s) measure the treatment outcome(s) of interest? Within these two broad concerns of practicality and validity, a number of special issues frequently arise in evaluation studies which, if left unattended in the test selection process, may render an otherwise excellent evaluation study useless. This section

TABLE 2.2. A Suggested Outline for Evaluating a Possible Instrument

---

A. *General Information*
   Title of instrument (including edition and forms if applicable)
   Author(s) and publisher, date of publication
   Time required to administer
   Cost
B. *Brief Description of Purpose and Nature of the Instruments*
   General type, nature of content
   Population for which designed
   Subtests and separate scores, types of items
C. *Practical Evaluation*
   Qualitative features (design, ease of use, attractiveness, etc.)
   Ease of administration, clarity of directions
   Scoring procedures
   Administrator qualifications and training
   Face validity and examinee rapport
D. *Technical Evaluation*
   1. *Norms*
      Type of norm-based scores
      Standardization sample (size, representativeness)
   2. *Reliability*
      Type and procedure including size and nature of samples employed
      Scorer reliability if applicable
      Equivalence of forms
      Long-term stability
   3. *Validity*
      Specification of variable supposed to be measured
      Appropriate types of validation procedures (content, criterion-related, construct)
      Specific procedures followed in assessing validity and results obtained
      Size and nature of samples employed
E. *Reviewers' Comments*
   From *Mental Measurements Yearbooks,* journal reviews, or other sources
F. *Summary Evaluation*
   Major strengths and weaknesses across all categories

Source: Adapted from Anastasi (1976, pp. 705–706)

addresses the special issues facing evaluators when they select outcome measures to assess treatment effects.

Specifying Outcomes

Identifying intended outcomes. An early task in planning and implementing an evaluation is identifying the possible outcomes of the educational practice or program. Many authors have discussed the importance of this task as well as procedures to facilitate it, e.g., Bloom, Hastings, and Madaus (1971, pp. 19–41), Worthen and Sanders (1973, pp. 231–268), Morris and Fitz-Gibbon (1978, pp. 69–79). This section should be viewed as a brief introduction to some of the difficulties and complexities involved in specifying outcomes, and the reader should refer to the above mentioned works for more detail.

Typically, this task involves obtaining often conflicting information from various parties. Precise statements of the goals and purposes of a program (and hence the intended outcomes) often differ depending on who is asked and what they are asked about the goals. For example, it is usual to obtain statements of purpose and goals from (a) the proposers and/or developers of an educational program and to use these statements to identify specific intended outcomes. However, the goals and purposes of the developers may not completely coincide with the goals of (b) the program's funding agency, or (c) the evaluator's funding agency. Such conflicts are common in many federal or state programs, in which legislators fund a program primarily for one purpose, but developers of the actual programs have different goals and purposes. The general goals specified at some levels may bear only minor resemblance to (d) the classroom instructional objectives that provide yet another critical source of information for identifying outcomes. Thus, evaluators can typically expect all the different parties involved in a program (Congress, state legislatures, taxpayers, school boards, school administrators, teachers, parents, students) to have different goals for a program. The task then is one of specifying at least the most important of these goals or outcomes in order to provide a credible study of whether the program accomplished its various goals.

Identifying unintended outcomes. It is important to identify not only the intended outcomes, but also the unintended, incidental outcomes. The sources of information about such possible incidental outcomes are not as clearly identifiable as is the case with intended outcomes and, consequently, the burden for identifying such variables lies largely with the evaluator. For example, (a) critics of a program may have warned of undesirable unintended outcomes, suggesting the need to examine such outcomes, or (b) educational theory may suggest possibilities to be examined (e.g., time spent in a new area of learning may result in decreased learning in areas with decreased time). Discussions with (c) program participants may suggest possibilities of positive or negative "side effects" such as parental attitude change following participation on a guiding committee for the program. (It should be noted that if not handled properly, discussing such unintended negative side effects with project personnel may result in the evaluator being perceived as an unpopular Jeremiah.)

Long-term and short-term goals. Yet another part of the task of specifying outcomes involves separating long-term, ultimate goals from short-term, immediate goals. It will probably not be feasible for an evaluation study to collect data on all the long-term ultimate goals. At the same time such ultimate goals may represent a major justification for the program. Cooley and Lohnes (1976) provide an excellent discussion of the types of links that need to be made between long-term and short-term goals in order for an evaluation study to be convincing. Evaluators will want to note their discussion of the kinds of evidence needed to substantiate the different linkages.

Operationalizing the outcomes. Once the important variables are identified or lists of instructional objectives are in hand, the question remains as to how those variables are to be measured or how the accomplishment of those instructional objectives is to be ascertained. The specification of outcomes occurs at a conceptual level: they are concepts or constructs (e.g., reading comprehension, attitude toward mathematics). To study these constructs, however, the evaluator must find ways to operationalize and measure them. In a particular evaluation study constructs are defined by describing the operations that will be used to measure them. This is part of the task of developing or finding tests to measure the possible outcomes. Logically, this must follow the specification of possible outcomes.

Sensitivity of Measures to Instructional Treatments

When studying the effect of any type of program, evaluation researchers try to locate measures that are sensitive to treatment effects—logically, theoretically, and on the basis of past research. Operationally, the purpose of the evaluation study is to see if, in fact, the particular program under scrutiny affects the measure. It is always possible in a particular study, of course, that the treatment will not produce the expected effect. However, a measure is selected so that there exists at least the possibility of detecting changes resulting from the treatment. In such research it would be less reasonable to perform the study using a measure that is known not to change as a result of the general type of treatment being investigated. Using such an insensitive measure stacks the deck against being able to show a treatment effect.

Educational evaluators are faced constantly with the task of finding measures potentially sensitive to the instructional intervention being studied. Their task is made somewhat more difficult by two problems that exist in the goals of most instructional programs: (a) whether the real goal is to effect change in a global, general ability or in a more specific skill and (b) whether ultimate, long-term goals of the program or more immediate, short-term goals should be examined.

Impact of programs on global abilities. Suppose a test measures a global ability that develops over a long period of time in response to varied types of learning conditions both within and outside of formal instructional settings. That test is not likely to detect growth in response to a relatively short-term instructional program focusing on various subskills of the more global ability. Now, suppose that the goal and expectation are that the program itself will result in important and immediate changes in the particular global ability. In this case, the test described above still may be appropriate to evaluate this expectation. In other words, the instrument may be appropriate whether or not it is, in fact, sensitive to that particular program. On the other hand, suppose that the program's goal is the more limited one of producing improvement in some specific skills that, when coupled with various longer-term efforts, *may* eventually affect the global ability. In this second case, where there are no expectations of immediate changes in global ability, the issue of the sensitivity of the tests used in the evaluation of the specific instructional treatment becomes a very important one.

Consider as an example the many instructional programs designed ultimately to affect students' global reading comprehension skill. The most commonly used tests of global reading comprehension are from standardized achievement batteries. Suppose that the developers of one of these programs hope that a special, intensive, fifth-grade program for poor readers lasting from September through December (four months) will improve students' global reading comprehension. What might be expected if no special program were implemented? The typical growth of students in those four months of fifth grade is estimated to be about 5% of the test items, as shown in Table 2.3. (The relatively small change in tests of the global ability shown in Table 2.3 is for average students and would likely be even smaller for poor readers.)

By contrast, a test directed specifically at the immediate instructional objectives of a program (e.g., a typical classroom test) would usually be expected to have pupils answer a much larger percentage of items correctly after the program than before it.

An instrument selection dilemma. The above example illustrates a dilemma often faced by an evaluator when choosing an outcome measure: Is the appropriate goal of the program the short-term, immediate one of having pupils attain the particular skills that were directly taught or is the appropriate goal the developing of the longer-term, more global ability? This dilemma comes home to roost when an evaluator is called upon (1) to operationalize a reasonable goal for the program (Is an immediate and direct effect on the global ability too much to expect?) and (2) to select an instrument that is sensitive to the impact of the treatment on this operationalized goal.

The following points should be kept in mind when an evaluator addresses this issue: (a) Just because a skill (or ability) is difficult to instruct in a relatively short time does not mean it is not important to try to influence (or hasten) its development; (b) Just because a skill (or ability) is instructible in a short time does not mean that it is automatically important to evaluate.

It should be noted, too, that when the short-term learning goals on which instruction has been directly focused are not identical with the long-term or ultimate learning goals, there is a need to defend those short-term goals as important for the acquisition of the ultimate goals. (A minimum requirement would be to prominently note the limitations of the evaluation study.)

Other factors affecting sensitivity. In addition to these major concerns affecting sensitivity of measures to treatments, other factors affecting scores are related to the sensitivity issue. They will be discussed next. Note, in particular, the discussions on the correspondence of the test to the instructional objectives and on the actual opportunity given to pupils to learn (time spent on) the tasks comprising the test.

Factors Affecting Results on Outcome Measures

In this section we address a number of factors that affect pupil performance on outcome measures and hence are important when selecting tests to assess effects of instructional programs.

Specification of an instructional domain. When a goal of the evaluation is

TABLE 2.3. Grade 5 Average Growth in Percentage of Items Answered Correctly

	Sept.–Dec.			Sept.–June		
	% Correct GE = 5.0	% Correct GE = 5.4	Growth	% Correct GE = 5.0	% Correct GE = 5.9	Growth
Iowa Tests of Basic Skills[a]	46%	53%	7%	46%	59%	13%
Metropolitan Achievement Tests[b]	46%	50%	4%	46%	56%	10%
Stanford Achievement Test[c]	45%	50%	5%	45%	57%	12%

[a]Based on data from the *Teacher's Guide for Administration, Interpretation, and Use* (p. 87) for the 1970 *Iowa Tests of Basic Skills* for the Reading Test (74 items), Level 11, Form 6, designed for use in grade 5, Hieronymus and Lindquist (1971).
[b]Based on data from the *Teacher's Handbook* (pp. 6–7) for the 1971 *Metropolitan Achievement Tests* in Reading (45 items), Intermediate Level, designed for use in grade 5, Durost et al. (1971).
[c]Based on data from the *Manual Part II, Norms Booklet, Form A* (p. 18) for the 1972 *Stanford Achievement Test* for the Reading Comprehension Test (72 items), Intermediate Level I Battery, designed for grades 4.5 to 5.4, Madden et al. (1973).

to determine whether the intended performances were learned or acquired by students, then the correspondence of the test to the domain implied by the instruction becomes a crucial consideration. This is a concern of content validation—of validating inferences from test scores to a content (or instructional) domain. In this situation we want to be sure that the items on the test adequately represent the learning represented by the domain.

To judge the match of the test to an instructional domain we must begin by specifying the domain. Several schemes have been developed for specifying some instructional domains in very precise ways. A general review of these schemes in the context of criterion-referenced testing has been conducted by Millman (1980) and Popham (1980). A broader discussion of domain specification can also be found in Nitko (1980). In practice, definitions of content or instructional domains take on any of several forms ranging from the specifications of possibly hundreds of detailed behavioral objectives to specification of only a few global content areas. An adequate content domain definition is specific enough that any qualified judge can determine whether a particular test task is in the domain. Consider, for example, the two content domain definitions for fourth-grade spelling in Table 2.4. For fourth-grade spelling, it is possible to determine if any particular word is or is not in the domain described in Definition A (with the particular reference noted) but not with Definition B. However, even Definition A is incomplete because it does not specify the type of spelling skill included in the domain and the type of response format (e.g., whether the student should write the word in response to its oral presentation, select the correct spelling from among several printed versions, or perform some other task).

Content match. Once the domain of interest is thoroughly defined, the appropriateness of a test to measure that domain can be examined. That appropriateness basically concerns the extent to which the test adequately represents the domain—in emphasis of content and skills *and* in format of the questions. The overlap of test content with the domain defined by an instructional program is typically the central focus of curricular relevance judgments. This terminology may be somewhat unconventional: *Curriculum relevance* as used here means the extent to which the items of a test adequately sample the

TABLE 2.4. Two Incomplete Content-Domain Definitions

FOURTH-GRADE SPELLING

Definition A	*Definition B*
All spelling words at the fourth-grade difficulty level according to the word lists of some particular reference.	Fourth-grade spelling words.

performance domain *defined by the program* being evaluated. *Content validity* seeks to judge the extent to which the items of a test adequately sample the *test publisher's* definition of the domain. Traditionally, these two concerns have been confused.

Clearly, the evaluator must be concerned with curricular relevance. Content and curriculum experts are asked to judge the extent to which the content areas covered in a proposed test are appropriate to the domain of the instruction. However, such content overlap is only one part of the necessary considerations. Just as a complete domain definition addresses the type of skill development to which the instruction is addressed and the type of performance necessary to demonstrate accomplishment of the instructional objectives, so, too, judgments about the curricular relevance of a potential measure must address the same issues about the representativeness of the measure. When the instructional domain is defined by specific behavioral objectives, the procedure described by Mager (1973) is one practical way to judge the relevance of the test's items.

It is likely that just about any test developed outside the context of the particular instructional program being evaluated will lack some degree of curricular relevance. Even if every item on a test can be matched to the various instructional objectives of a program, it is likely that the items (a) will not cover all the instructional objectives and (b) will not be representative of the objectives and instructional emphasis given them. There are usually more objectives than are measured by a test and frequently the emphasis given the skills on the test is not proportionate to the classroom emphasis (see "opportunity to learn," below).

Problems of question format. The problem here is that the format of a test task can result in "things" other than the intended domain being included in the measure. For example, one can see this problem when the domain concerns basic addition but the test task requires the student to read directions or even to read the problems themselves before the addition can be attempted. Such a test format would result in a measure of reading as well as addition, at least for poor readers. If reading were not an intended part of the definition of ability to add, the interpretation of test results as reflecting only the ability to add would not be appropriate.

The problem is illustrated further by referring back to Table 2.4. The fourth-grade spelling domain described under Definition A addressed only the content and not the form of response. Thus, we do not have an adequately defined domain. Suppose, however, the domain is defined as written responses by students to dictated spelling words. Then the form of the response on the test must be this same form. When we consider using a test perhaps with each question involving one correct and three incorrect spellings of a word, we must look for evidence of construct validity in order to justify the interpretation of a multiple-choice test score as reflecting the program's definition of spelling competence. If the intended domain is the written response to a dictated word, then the test either should have that format or evidence should be presented to justify another format of response.

Part of this concern with format is related to Mager's (1973) concern that the test tasks match the intent of the instructional objectives. Suppose an instructional objective intends students to describe characteristics of an occupation when given the name of the occupation. Then a multiple-choice question that gives a description of characteristics of some occupation and asks the student to select from four listed occupations the one that has the given characteristics is calling for a different type of pupil action or behavior from that intended by the specified objective.

There are times when the format of the response is less important. These are cases where the main intent of an instructional objective is mostly a covert activity (or set of correct activities)—adding, for example (Mager, 1973). Such mental activities need to be accompanied by indicator responses—pupil responses that indicate to the observer that the correct mental activity has occurred. Frequently in these situations, the precise nature of the indicator response (e.g., circling, pointing, saying, etc.) is of little interest—*provided that such a response is within the repertoire of the pupils*. These indicator responses may be of special concern for students with particular learning problems or for students that have physical handicaps. Special tests may be needed to evaluate learning for these pupils.

These issues related to question format require more than content judgments to support an interpretation of how program participants can perform in the intended domain. They raise *construct-validity* issues. Construct-validity evidence is required for tests used in evaluations whenever the format of the test tasks (i.e., items) does not directly match the format of the responses called for in the domain defined by the program. Standard practices for claiming curricular relevance operate as though it is sufficient for most intended test score interpretations to make only general judgments about the correspondence between the typical coverage of the test and the topical coverage of the instructional domain. Too little attention has been paid to the format of the measurement procedure even though a test's format can both (a) introduce irrelevancies into the task (such as reading directions on how to mark answers) and (b) require a performance other than the one toward which the instruction is directed.

Opportunity to learn. The extent to which a test matches an instructional intent of a program is an important factor affecting scores on outcome measures. In this section, however, we move beyond the goals and intentions of the program to its actual implementation with students. The issue is the extent to which a test or outcome measure matches what has been taught in the particular program or, in other words, what the students actually had an opportunity to learn.

In studies of the various factors influencing achievement test performance, a persistent research result is that the amount of time students spend actively engaged in learning objectives measured by the tests is correlated with their test scores (Berliner, 1979; Cooley, 1977; Cooley & Leinhardt, 1978; Fisher et al., 1978a, 1978b; House et al., 1977; Kowal, 1975; Rosenshine, 1979; Walker & Schaffarzick, 1974). When a part of a standardized achievement test lacks curricular relevance, it is sometimes helpful to develop a separate score for those items corresponding to objectives on which pupils *did* receive instruction. This would allow one to make a judgment about how well students attained the relevant curricular objectives that happen to be measured by the test. Examples of analyzing reading test content can be found in Jenkins and Pany (1976) and Armbruster, Steven, and Rosenshine (1977) and for mathematics tests in Porter et al. (1977). It is possible, of course, that a test will be appropriate even though opportunity to learn is minimal. A test may be chosen because of the educational importance of the outcomes it measures; it may be important to test these outcomes even though formal instruction on them is limited. In some instances the variation between instructional objectives and actual implementation may reflect variation between goals of program developers and those of the implementing teachers. In any event, it is important to recognize opportunity to learn as an important factor affecting scores on outcome measures.

Obtaining maximal performance. Measures of educational outcomes are typically classified as measures of maximal (as opposed to typical) performance. That is, we want students to perform their very best—to perform near the upper limits of their skills and abilities. Any factors that produce less than maximal performance will affect test scores. Factors of special concern to evaluators include general motivation, test anxiety, and familiarity with the testing process. The latter two factors are of general concern in test use and usual procedures to familiarize students with the form of the test, to teach test-taking skills, and to reduce undue anxiety are part of the recommended standard testing procedure for many tests. (One shouldn't assume, however, that this is going to be done routinely.)

Motivation is also a concern of typical test users, but it may be especially important in evaluation studies since how well students perform does not directly affect the students themselves—it affects directly only the program being evaluated. There is a suspicion afoot that some evaluation studies may be affected by unmotivated students exhibiting forms of behavior that negatively affect the evaluation results, such as filling in answer sheets without reading test questions. All the factors affecting maximal performance, especially student motivation, deserve the attention of the evaluator.

Bias of a Test and Its Effect on Evaluation

Issues of racial, ethnic, or sex bias have been prominent ones for over a decade. In evaluation, such issues arise in program content, program target groups, program advisory or other input roles, as well as in measures of program outcomes. Tests of various types have served as lightning rods for many bias issues. Consequently, evaluators are regularly faced with the task of selecting unbiased tests and of defending the tests selected against charges of bias.

Meanings of bias. One of the difficulties in dealing with the notion of bias is the fact that there are disagreements over what bias is. However, there is a common theme that has dominated discussions of bias: an item or test is thought to be biased if it measures different things (skills, thought processes, prior experiences) in different groups. Thus, if an outcome measure is designed to measure performance on a content domain, then it would be considered fair if the test items measured performance in that domain in the same way in every group of examinees for whom it is intended. However, if the test scores of one of the groups were differentially and systematically influenced by a factor other than that intended, we would label the results biased. Similarly, if an outcome measure is designed to measure a construct and it measures the construct in the same way in different groups, we label the measure fair. If, on the other hand, factors extraneous to the construct differentially affect the groups measured, we speak of bias.

Bias in content-based interpretations. According to Ebel (1975), a content-valid achievement test cannot be biased if it "1) is composed of tasks which sample representatively some clearly defined domain of tasks; and 2) yields reliable scores" (Ebel, 1975, p. 12). However, such a statement assumes at least three conditions that do not in fact always exist: (1) it assumes that the interpretation includes all relevant aspects of the content domain; (2) it assumes that students perform at their best; and (3) it assumes that interpretations do not extend beyond the fully defined content domain. When such assumptions are incorrect (and they often are), issues of possible bias in content-based interpretations of test scores arise.

A major problem in content-based interpretations is that we so often are unable to define all of the crucial and limiting aspects of the content domain and this may lead to bias. Consider, as an example, the Mathematics Concepts subtest of the *Stanford Achievement Test* (Primary Level). Note that the problems of the content domain discussed here for the *Stanford Achievement Test* are common to all standardized achievement tests and this discussion does *not* imply that there are any special problems with the *Stanford Achievement Test* that others do not share. Figure 2.1 gives slightly altered versions of three items from the Mathematics Concepts subtest. What are the crucial dimensions of the content domain from which these items were

FIGURE 2.1. Simulated items from the Mathematics Concepts Test of the *Stanford Achievement Test* (Primary Level).

1. Directions read aloud to students: "Which word tells how many dots are in the box?"

	four	five	two	NG	DK
	○	○	○	○	○

2. Directions read aloud to students: "Which of the things shown would be sold by the bushel?"

			NG	DK
○	○	○	○	○

3. Directions read aloud to students: "Which figure shows three dots in an interior space?"

			NG	DK
○	○	○	○	○

selected? We can recognize some general number concepts to which the items are addressed, but what are the crucial aspects of the question formats, the language required, the time allowed, etc.? How do we specify the level of reading and vocabulary included in the domain? The questions take a variety of formats. What format characteristics define the domain?

A complete description of a well-defined content domain of which these items provide a representative sample seems quite elusive, especially when we recognize that any domain-referenced interpretation that is made must carry with it all the important features of the domain. This inability to completely specify the domain has serious implications in terms of bias: If, in a domain-referenced interpretation, we fail to include a feature of the actual complex domain that does influence scores, then our interpretation in terms of the simpler domain will be in error to some unknown degree and further, if the ignored feature affects performance differentially across groups, our error will be a systematic one of measuring different things in different groups. In short, our measures will be biased. On the Mathematics Concepts subtest, scores might be interpreted in terms of a simplified domain, for example, math items covering a variety of concepts presented in a multiple-choice format. But perhaps the important characteristics of the domain that affect the performance of some groups (or of some individuals) are the (a) listening required in the test administration, (b) vocabulary used, or (c) familiarity with the different question formats used. If some group was systematically lower on one of these abilities, we would be making a biased interpretation of lower mathematics concept skills when, in fact, the differences were due to other skills.

 This consideration of a domain definition suggests the need to know much more about the effects of item formats, reading ability, vocabulary, speed of performance, answer formats, and so on, in order to be able to recognize critical aspects of domains that must be retained in interpretations to avoid bias. This is a logical extension of what Bormuth (1970) has called the need for an item-response theory.

Inferences beyond the operational description of the domain. Consider again the Mathematics Concepts subtest. In practice, it seems likely that a test interpreter rarely, if ever, remembers the particular types of item on this test when interpreting scores. There is no reminder in the reported score of the complexity of the actual content domain, only the label "Mathematics Concepts" scores. But the notion of "math concepts" is an inference beyond the content domain and is, in fact, a construct interpretation of test scores that requires evidence for justification.

As another example, consider the science achievement tests of the International Association for the Evaluation of Educational Achievement for which sex differences in science achievement have been reported (Comber & Keeves, 1973; Husén, Faterlind, & Lilijefors, 1974). On the basis of content categorizations of items in terms of science subject (e.g., biology, physics) and process (e.g., factual knowledge, understanding), these studies reported that girls perform more poorly than boys on physics items and on "understanding" items. A domain-referenced interpretation would delineate the characteristics of the content domain on which the boys did better. The construct interpretation, which seems much more prevalent, is that boys have achieved higher levels of "understanding" of science than girls. Additionally, a judgment is sometimes made that girls do not have the capability for high levels of science performance. But in a study of the items of the test, Carlson (1976) found that at least a few of the "understanding" items involved sex-differentiated practical experience: Boys did better on an "understanding" item involving how to put batteries in a flashlight; girls did better on an "understanding" item about how to place a jar under hot water to get the lid off.

A carefully, delineated domain-referenced interpretation of the scores would have retained this information of the types of items involved on which one sex did better. It would not be a biased interpretation that boys know better than girls how to put batteries in flashlights. However, when this skill is given the construct interpretation "understanding," the possibility of an incorrect and, in this case, biased interpretation arises. Here, as in many other cases, domain-referenced interpretations are often too clumsy and too complex in practice. Instead, people use shorthand—sometimes misleading—constructs in their place.

If one interprets performance on a content domain as what a student "can do" or "has learned" instead of simply what the student "did," one moves again to a new set of concerns. Now one has to be certain that the student tried his or her best to do the tasks. If some group was generally less motivated to perform on a test, one could reach the possibly incorrect conclusion that the group had learned less well. The test would then be measuring a different "thing" in the unmotivated group: lack of motivation rather than failure to learn the content domain. As a consequence, the evaluator's interpretation of what had been learned would be biased. Of course it is possible that poorly motivated students have also failed to learn the content. (But failing to identify motivation as an influencing factor may lead to attributing failure to the wrong aspect of the program being evaluated.) This suggests that to examine possible bias, even in seemingly straightforward content-based interpretations, we should consider aspects of the testing situation that could produce less than maximal performance—aspects such as differential motivating effects, anxiety effects, effects of familiarity with testing, etc.

The implication for test inferences beyond the content domain is that to examine possible bias of such construct interpretations we must examine the applicability of the construct itself to each group being tested, and whether the construct is being measured appropriately in all groups—a requirement well beyond that for content validity.

Bias in construct-based interpretations. If a test measures a construct like the understanding of mathematics concepts, reading comprehension, or understanding of science and we apply that same interpretation to a second group, but for them the test measures something else like breadth of vocabulary, familiarity with and motivation on timed tests, or experience with flashlights, then we should conclude that the first interpretation is incorrect or biased for the second group. Essentially, all of the proposed statistical indices

of item bias come from the construct-based interpretation perspective that defines an item as biased if it does not measure the same construct in the same degree in different groups. Methodology at the level of the total test score includes the factor analysis of subparts (and other procedures) done separately in different groups—procedures typical of construct-validity approaches. At the item level, we can distinguish two general categories of methodological approaches to identifying whether items measure different things in different groups: the item-by-group interaction approaches and the item characteristic curve approaches. These item-level approaches are discussed below.

The first attempts to find item bias statistically involved the examination of item-by-group interactions (in the analysis of variance sense) (Cardall & Coffman, 1964; Cleary & Hilton, 1968). The logic here was that if item-by-group interactions were prominent, it would mean that the items were operating in different ways in different groups and were therefore potentially biased. One could see the same type of effect in the correlations of item difficulties or p-values (or some transformation of item difficulties) across different groups. The approach could say nothing about the presence or absence of consistent bias over all the items of the test but it could judge the extent to which large numbers of items worked differently in different groups.

This general approach was extended to the consideration of delta plots

(Angoff & Ford, 1963; Angoff & Sharon, 1974). Deltas are inverse normal transformed p-values (i.e., Delta = 4z + 13, where z is the standard normal deviate corresponding to p, the proportion passing an item). A scattergram is then plotted, group against group, to detect outlier items on the test favoring one group more than the other. Other researchers (e.g., Fishbein, 1975) have compared the p-values directly, looking for discrepancies greater than the average item differences on the whole test. Still others (Veale & Foreman, 1975) have compared the proportion of wrong answers, ignoring the correct responses. Each of these approaches was designed to identify items unusual in the extent of group differences produced. Such items might be considered to measure "different things" in different groups. These authors turned to the content of the items in attempts to determine whether the group differences were relevant to what the tests were supposed to be measuring. If scrutiny of an item's content led to a judgment that it seemed to be measuring the intended "thing" in spite of unusual group differences, it was assumed to be fair. When scrutiny of an item's content suggested that an irrelevancy was being measured (e.g., vocabulary on a math test; an unfamiliar item format on an ability test), the item was considered biased.

Recently, several authors have noted the confounding influences in the above item bias approaches that make the intended bias interpretations difficult to substantiate and have suggested using latent trait theory to detect item bias. Green and Draper (1972) examined the percentage of correct responses for each total score separately by group (test-on-item regression curves) in very large samples. Lord (1977) and Rudner (1977) formally applied a three-parameter logistic model to compare the item characteristic curves in different groups, again with very large samples. Durovic (1975) and Wright, Mead, and Draba (1976) proposed the use of the simpler one-parameter Rasch model to examine bias.

These direct examinations of the item response curves seem to be promising approaches to answering the question of whether items measure the same thing in different groups. In cases in which more than one parameter seems necessary to describe the items in a test, the procedures are very complex, requiring special computer programs, long tests, and very large samples (probably over 1,000 per group). Such analyses are typically possible only after the tests are in use so that data are available on large samples. The one-parameter (Rasch) model approach seems possible on smaller samples, but little is known about what is lost by assuming all items have the same discrimination. Much more study needs to be made of these potentially useful approaches.

Scheuneman (1979) proposed a rather quick procedure of item analysis that approximates some aspects of the item characteristic curve approaches. Her proposal was to tabulate, separately for each group, the frequency of a correct response to an item at each of several total score levels. Then she suggested comparing these observed frequencies with the expected frequencies (based on the proportions of correct responses in the combined group). The discrepancy between observed and expected frequencies can be examined statistically by using a chi-square statistic, which should be sensitive to differences between groups in proportions correct at each total score level. (Intasuwan [1979] proposed a correction on the statistic to achieve the desired chi-square distribution.) Groups equal on total score may not be properly equated on true score when known group-mean differences exist, but this procedure seems at least to approximate the latent trait approaches for small samples typically encountered in item tryouts. Here, too, more study is needed of the proposed statistic to see how well it mirrors latent trait approaches in detecting biased items.

What a practicing evaluator would hope to find from examining the item bias research literature is an indication of the types of items or types of content that are likely to show statistical bias. Unfortunately, however, the research results have not provided this badly needed practical information. The statistical procedures create difficulties, for example, in distinguishing (when applied repeatedly to many items) Type I errors from bias. Further, the necessary links of statistical indices to content and construct interpretations have not been easy to make. Thus evaluators are left without clear statistical evidence of bias or lack of it for most existing tests: They are left only with "a number of concerns" to keep in mind when using outcome measures.

Facial bias. One area of interest to evaluators is labeled here "facial bias." This is a category of bias corresponding to the idea of face validity. Green (1975) called this same characteristic content bias and differentiated it from other types of bias. Facial bias would occur when particular words or item formats *appear* to disfavor some group, whether or not they, in fact, have that effect. Thus, an instrument using the male pronoun "he" throughout or involving only male figures in the items would be facially biased regardless of whether such uses affected the scores of women. Facial bias is not the same type of bias as the other types discussed previously. However, to evaluators, facial bias is often of great practical and political concern, even if it does not actually create a biasing result. But perhaps this is as it should be: an appearance of bias (facial bias) should put the burden of proof on the defender of the test. Regardless of the actual biasing effects, it makes good political and social sense to eliminate such appearances. Facial bias has received considerable, much-needed attention in recent years by major test publishers, and publications such as Buros's (1978) *Mental Measurements Yearbook* now often have discussions of facial bias in test reviews.

Methods of eliminating or reducing bias in tests. The methods that can be used to eliminate bias in tests follow from the general discussion of bias and the problems and issues associated with the topic. Basically, three major types of actions are open to the evaluator: (1) using panels of experts to judge freedom from facial bias; (2) conducting statistical studies of bias in the instruments or finding such studies already available; and (3) limiting the interpretations of the measures to only those interpretations justified by strong validity evidence—being especially careful of the content-justified and the construct-justified interpretation distinctions. Special consideration should be given to the use of panels of judges representing various racial-ethnic groups and sexes to determine freedom from facial bias. Such panels can identify and help evaluators to avoid potential problems of facially biased tests. However, the evaluator should be aware that any reviewer of any item anywhere might find some problem with it. A difficulty in dealing with such a panel is in accommodating legitimate concerns while diffusing trivial concerns.

Regardless of the method used, the results of item bias studies are not easily implemented by the evaluator. Changes in the items, for example, often cannot be made without affecting the data base of the test. Thus, information from previous research and development of the test in its "biased condition" may not be applicable to the revised or altered version. Norm-referenced interpretations, for example, would need to be altered if several items were made easier by the alterations. It should be kept in mind, however, that if a statistical study is not conducted, then it will not be possible to determine whether the bias in an item has been, in fact, corrected. Changes in items judged to be facially biased, may be simply "cosmetic changes" that do not in fact reduce unwanted bias, but instead, cover it up.

Issues and judgments about bias, therefore, should be addressed at the test selection stage of the evaluation study. If it is decided that a locally developed test is needed, then test development plans should include procedures for studying and eliminating biased items. Already developed instruments should be reviewed for potential bias before a final decision is made to select the test because of its content coverage. This may necessitate conducting at least a pilot study of several seemingly useful tests in order to gather information about possibly biased items.

Testing On Level or Out of Level

A fifth concern evaluators face when selecting outcome measures arises when standardized tests are to be used. Such tests are available in various "levels": each level is designed to cover content typically taught at one or two grades. Users select the level of the test to be administered. Most commonly, the test level selected coincides with the current grade placement of the students. This is called on-level testing. However, not all students in a particular grade placement are achieving in a way typical for that grade; some students may be receiving instruction that is ahead of or behind their present grade placement. The concern of the evaluator, then, is whether such students should be given a test that covers the content identified with their present grade placement (e.g., on-level testing of third graders with third-grade math content) or should be tested on content appropriate to their actual achievement and/or instructional level (e.g., out-of-level testing of third graders with second-grade math content).

This aspect of test selection is especially acute for evaluators of educational programs designed for students whose achievement is below that typical for their grade placement. Several federal programs, for example, provide funds specifically for students achieving below grade level. When evaluating such programs, several things need to be considered before making the choice of whether the students should be tested on level or out of level: the reliability of the test scores, the instructional level of the program, interpretation of grade-equivalent results of on-level tests, and various other limitations of out-of-level scores.

Reliability problems of on-level testing. Students whose achievement is well below their present grade placement are the low scorers on an on-level achievement test. In fact, students achieving as much as two grade levels below their grade placement are often scoring near the expected chance score for the on-level test, depending, of course, on the particular test and content area. (*The expected chance score* is the average score students would be expected to obtain if they were to guess blindly on all of the items. For a multiple-choice test of 36 questions, with four alternatives per question, the expected chance score is 9 ($= .25 \times 36$). In general, for a multiple-choice test with k alternatives per item, the expected chance level is 1/k times the number of questions on the test. On the average, we would expect students to get 1/k of the items correct if they guessed blindly on all of them.)

For examinees near the chance level, a test typically cannot distinguish different levels of achievement as well since chance factors play a much larger role in determining the scores. As a result, the scores are expected to be much less reliable for low scorers. Some writers have suggested, further, that the use of an on-level test may be especially frustrating to low-achieving students. Such frustration could decrease the reliability of the scores even more because frustrated students may take less care, may not read many questions, or may give up and fill in the answer sheet without even reading the questions.

There is the very real possibility then that the results of on-level testing in low-achieving groups produces much less reliable scores in these groups (Fisher, 1961). The possible consequence for an evaluation study is that a test may not be sensitive to what has been achieved by the program. For example, pretest to posttest changes on an on-level test may be masked by these chance factors. It has been suggested that out-of-level testing may help to correct some of these problems of the unreliability of scores for low-achieving students.

Interpretations of on-level scores. One additional problem of using an on-level test with below grade level students is the traditional problem of identifying the meaning of grade-equivalent scores markedly different from present grade placement. Basically, this is the problem of estimating the content a student has learned from a test based on different content (the on-level content). Many writers have noted this problem of interpreting grade-equivalent scores (see Linn, chapter 4), although again the magnitude of the problem depends on the particular procedures used in the development of grade-equivalent scales—procedures that differ markedly among major test publishers. Information about how grade-equivalent scales have been developed can be obtained by special request to test publishers; the details are typically not included in the usual "specimen set."

The safest and soundest interpretation of a grade-equivalent score occurs when the grade level of a test's content and the grade level of a student's score coincide. Even aside from issues of reliability, the meaning of a discrepant grade-equivalent score is difficult to establish. Consequently, it is sometimes desirable to minimize these discrepancies by selecting out-of-level tests where appropriate.

Role of instructional level. Following the earlier discussion of determining the intended outcomes and seeking valid measures of those outcomes, the choice of an on-level or out-of-level test logically should depend upon the instructional level of the program being evaluated. Again, the concern is the match of the test to instructional intent. If instruction is directed at the typical content of the present grade level, then an on-level achievement test may have curricular relevance for that intended outcome. If, on the other hand, instruction is directed to the actual achievement level of the student (as educational theory suggests it should be and experience suggests is often the case), then the level of the test would have to be chosen to match that instructional content. This determination of curricular relevance must be made by matching the items of different test levels to the instructional objectives of the program.

Problems of out-of-level testing. Although several factors point to the potential use of out-of-level tests, there are, nevertheless, several considerations involved. Given that it has been decided to use out-of-level testing, one of the first considerations is to determine the appropriate test level to use for each student. Two basic procedures for determining the appropriate level have been proposed: (a) using a judgmental decision made by the teacher or (b) using a locater test. Teacher judgments require knowledge of each student's achievement level and instructional level as well as a thorough knowledge of the content of the test. In practice, the decision is often cumbersome and not straightforward. For example, a student may be at very different levels in mathematics and reading, but the mathematics and reading *tests* are packaged together at the same level. Teachers may not feel qualified or may not have the time to make these decisions for each pupil. Locater tests have their perils as well, since they are necessarily short and, consequently, less reliable than longer tests. Much more research is needed on the issue of selecting the appropriate level at which to test the student for purposes of program evaluation.

A second problem concerns the type of normative information typically available for out-of-level scores. Norms for standardized tests are developed using students at a particular grade level who have been given an on-level test. Consequently, we can determine the relative standing among fourth graders of a fourth grader taking a fourth-grade test. But if that fourth grader takes a *second-grade* test, no direct empirical norms usually are available for fourth graders on second-grade test content. What is available for the second-grade test is data from second graders. The difficulty, then, is to whom do we reasonably compare this fourth-grade student's score? Do we compare the fourth grader to second graders?

This problem is helped somewhat by the grade-equivalent score scale (or other growth scale). Such a scale allows the computation of a grade-equivalent score from any level test and then the linking of that grade-equivalent score to an estimated percentile rank for fourth graders. However, such percentile rank scores are much farther removed from empirical norms than are the on-level percentile ranks.

A practical problem encountered is giving different tests to the same group of students in which some students are to be tested on level and some out of level. This presents problems of logistics (e.g., assuring the directions are the same for both, assuring that each student gets the correct test booklet, etc.), as well as potential problems of student feelings. (What are the implications of students knowing they are being tested out of level?)

Equivalence of on-level and out-of-level scores. An additional consideration in the choice of on-level versus out-of-level testing is the apparent fact that the one that is chosen will have a systematic effect on the scores of low-scoring students (Ayrer & McNamara, 1973). This problem is the same as discussed in the section on reliability—a low-achieving student's performance on an on-level test may be near the chance level. The chance level provides a type of floor below which even a very poor student will not be expected, on the average, to fall. Consequently, this artifact may result in higher grade-equivalent scores on an on-level test than on the out-of-level test. The out-of-level test, being closer to the student's actual achievement level, will yield scores that are well above chance. This possibility has political ramifications: Even if the out-of-level score in such an instance is more meaningful, it may be very difficult politically for a school to shift to out-of-level testing and then explain to the public the small decline in average performance over previous years.

Commercially Developed versus Locally Developed Instruments

Much of the above discussion of selecting curricularly relevant tests of the domain of a program's instructional objectives suggests the need for locally developed instruments. However, there are some severe difficulties with developing instruments at the local level that push the evaluator toward seeking instead published or commercially available instruments. Further, there is the concern over construct interpretations of the measures that push the evaluator in the same direction.

The most fundamental problem of commercially available tests is the extent to which they measure the intended outcomes of instruction. Such tests are frequently developed from the instructional elements common to most schools across the nation. Unusual content is not typically covered and content that is used is tested at a general level in order to be as broadly applicable as possible. While this is a readily achnowledged fact for norm-referenced, standardized tests, it is apparently a major consideration for criterion-referenced test developers too (e.g., Popham, 1972, 1978). This makes it very likely that a good part of the focus of instruction in a particular program may not be tested by a commercially available test. As has been indicated, even when the content from the program and the test overlap superficially, it is very important to examine the actual questions on the commercial test and the type of skill to which they are addressed in order to determine the test's correspondence to the program's instructional domain.

Although it would be possible to start to build a test locally from the instructional objectives of the program, there are numerous pitfalls with this approach as well. When one buys a nationally standardized norm-referenced test, one is paying presumably for time, quality, supporting evidence, and norms. Such a test takes several years to develop. Even with an abbreviated process of local test development, considerable time may be required to develop a suitable set of tests—time which the evaluator seldom has. So, with an already developed commercial test, one is buying time.

Second, one expects to be buying quality test construction. Some publishers employ only highly qualified item writers or test authors and maintain editorial staffs to assure the basic quality of the test items. But this is not always true, and evaluators should not assume that all commercially available tests have been written by professional item writers. Examine the item quality for yourself. It is highly unlikely, however, that funds will be available in a single school or school district to develop a test having a quality comparable to that obtained from professional item writers. Instead, locally developed tests are frequently subject to a myriad of test construction flaws that are far less common on a high-quality, commercially available test.

Third, one expects to be paying for evidence of the validity and reliability of a test when a nationally distributed test is purchased. Test manuals of major tests provide much information of this type, often from studies involving thousands of students in many parts of the nation. Such information is not always available for commercial instruments, especially for many criterion-referenced or objectives-based tests (Hambleton & Eignor, 1978), but it should be. This information will not automatically be available for a locally developed set of tests, and much money and time may have to be spent on smaller studies to even approximate such information.

Fourth, when buying a published, norm-referenced test, one is buying information on how students from around the nation perform so that comparisons can be made. Such normative information (and the scores derived from it such as grade equivalents, percentile ranks, normal curve equivalents, etc.) is clearly beyond the realm of possibility for a local test.

A related factor that must be considered in the choice of a locally developed or commercially produced instrument involves the credibility the instrument will have to the people to whom the evaluation is addressed. Usually a nationally distributed instrument provides greater credibility whether or not it is actually the more intellectually appropriate choice.

"MEASURING" THE TREATMENT

Evaluators have always been concerned with measuring outcome variables but have only recently become aware of the importance of "measuring" the treatment or independent variable as well (e.g., Cooley & Lohnes, 1976; Cooley & Leinhardt, 1978; Leinhardt, 1976). Educational research texts tell us that the independent variable is manipulated and we describe the independent variable by the operations by which the conditions producing a treatment are manipulated. The special problem with this experimental model for evaluation studies is that the evaluator's role is not identical to that of the experimenter. Evaluators often have little to do with the implementation of a treatment. They may not even begin an evaluation until after implementation, or the study itself may involve many implementations of programs in widely varying places (see Bryk & Light, chapter 1). Even when experimenter control is exercised, experimenters are expected to report in detail the nature of the manipulation. When evaluators have less control, it becomes even more imperative to identify and document the independent variable in its actual operation during the study as well as describing the procedures and manipulations used to initiate it.

Identifying the Independent Variable

The apparently simple problem of specifying the independent variable is not as simple as might at first appear. Many federal- or state-sponsored programs begin with the availability of funds for a (usually) generally stated purpose. So at the legislative or governmental level the manipulation is often "making funds available" and the research question is, "Do those funds produce the desired (or desirable) effects?" Some national evaluations have been carried out with "funding versus lack of funding" as the explicit, primary independent variable of the study (e.g., Coulson et al., 1974). More commonly, however, educational evaluation studies treat the instructional program as a type of independent variable. In either case we must be able to identify the appropriate independent variable before we can "measure" or document it.

Documenting the Treatment

Whatever the independent variable is, its implementation must be documented so that the nature of the actual treatment can be known. For example, even when "funds available" was viewed as the independent variable in the evaluation study cited above, the implementation of these funds was documented. [It was found, incidentally, that school districts were supplementing control school funding; this wiped out most of the funding differential that was supposed to be the identifying characteristic of the treatment (Coulson et al., 1974.).]

When the independent variable or treatment is a type of educational or instructional program, it is critical to the accumulation of knowledge about instruction from evaluation studies that the treatment be documented. Such documentation is traditionally required of any researcher but poses special problems for evaluators. First, the operations performed to cause a program to be started (such as, how proposed, controlled by whom, how implemented at the local instructional level, how were instructors trained, materials and objectives prepared for use, etc.) must be specified, since all together they determine the character of the treatment. Thus, any effect of the treatment could possibly be due to some feature of the set of procedures used to implement the program. An evaluation study cannot be properly interpreted and judged without documenting the procedures used to bring the program into being.

A second important step goes beyond that usually required in traditional research. This is the step of documenting not only the operations creating a program, but the actual instructional implementation of the program. This second step has become important in evaluation because evaluators have discovered a common pitfall: A program being evaluated was supposed to be of a certain type, but it was discovered, perhaps by accident, that the actual instructional activities bore little resemblance to the initial plans of the program developer. Such pitfalls can lead to the rejection of types of instructional procedure when, in fact, the intended procedure may never have been implemented very well. Two aspects of this problem to note are: (1) difficulty in implementing a program may of itself be a potential weakness, but (2) for the accumulation of knowledge about the effects of types of instruction, it is important that we do not judge a potential instructional method as a failure without having actually implemented it.

Documenting an actual implementation at the classroom level may involve several types of new and difficult measures for evaluators. For example, it may not be sufficient to ask teachers what they have done when instructing students; in many cases, it may be necessary for the evaluator to observe directly the instructional process. This suggests classroom observation procedures as possible methods of measuring the treatments, and several large-scale evaluations are including such measures (Cooley & Leinhardt, 1978). Of course, the more distant from the evaluator and less controlled the implementations are, the more important such observation procedures become. However, it is not uncommon for a single program in a single school district to bear little resemblance in practice to the supposed nature of the program.

Variables in Implementation

When observing a variety of implementations of programs in several settings, it will often be helpful in understanding the results of the evaluation study to identify variables in the implementation observed and to try to relate those variables to the results achieved. Such variables as characteristics of the teachers, the students, or the school, or support given to the implementation efforts by the local school district, may suggest reasons for variable achievement of instructional outcomes. By considering such variables, the evaluator may be able to suggest possible explanations for the variation in results that are almost certain to occur in a large-scale implementation.

SUGGESTIONS FOR FUTURE RESEARCH

This chapter has addressed a number of complex and difficult issues facing evaluators in the selection of measuring instruments for evaluation studies. However, for many issues discussed, we need more information and better procedures in order to do justice to the concerns they raise.

Tittle (1979) noted three important areas of priority for future research:

1. procedures and instruments to describe the degree of overlap between the outcome instrument and the treatment (curriculum analyzed as to content, process or operations, and learning and response formats);
2. procedures and instruments to describe the degree of opportunity to learn (classroom implementation); and
3. procedures and instruments to describe prior familiarity with school-related tasks—the socio-cultural environment of students. (Pp. 12–13)

To these needs could also be added the need for study of the links between highly specific, instructionally related educational outcomes and the more general, more global, and perhaps more generalizable competencies that represent the ultimate goals of the educational process. These links are important not only to evaluators when choosing outcomes to measure, but to educational theorists as well. In addition, of course, the same issues have important implications for educational policy.

Finally, we need further work in the area of bias. We need a better understanding of why some item content or format produces greater racial, ethnic, or sex differences than others, and we need better procedures for examining the content of texts for facial bias toward racial, ethnic, or sex groups.

GUIDELINES FOR EVALUATORS

The decisions evaluators make about instrumentation will usually have important effects on the conclusions reached by the evaluation study. Consequently, it is crucial that the evaluator be aware of major decisions being made and the implications of those decisions for the evaluation. Table 2.5 presents, in summary form, a guide to major decisions about measuring instruments addressed in this chapter. This guide could also serve as a checklist through which evaluators could proceed in the selection of instrumentation to assure that the major questions have been considered.

TABLE 2.5. Summary Guide and Checklist for Instrumentation Decisions in Evaluations

CONSIDERATIONS WHEN SELECTING OUTCOME MEASURES

1. *Specifying Outcomes*
   Decisions: What outcomes should be measured? Will unintended outcomes be detected? Are the appropriate outcomes short-term or long-term?
2. *Sensitivity of Measures to Instructional Treatments*
   Decisions: Do goals involve global or specific skills? Are the measures sensitive to potential treatment effects?
3. *Factors Affecting Results on Outcome Measures*
   Decisions: Do measures match the instructional domain? Does measure format match instructional intent? Has there been the opportunity to learn? Have procedures encouraged maximal performance?
4. *Bias of a Test and Its Effect on Evaluation*
   Decisions: Are score interpretations limited to those for which validity evidence exists? Are empirical data on bias available? Have measures been reviewed for facial bias?
5. *Testing On Level or Out of Level*
   Decisions: Which test level relates best to the instructional level of the program? Can practical and political problems of out-of-level testing be overcome?
6. *Commercially Developed versus Locally Developed Instruments*
   Decisions: Does a commercially available instrument adequately match local objectives? Is it feasible to develop instruments locally?

"MEASURING" THE TREATMENT

7. *Identifying the Independent Variable*
   Decision: What variables are the independent variables for the purposes of the evaluation?
8. *Documenting the Treatment*
   Decision: What actually occurred in implementation of the program?
9. *Variables in Implementation*
   Decision: Can variables in the program implementation be identified that will help explain evaluation results?

The area of bias deserves special mention here since it is an area with which evaluators will need to deal routinely in evaluation reports. It is also an area about which research has not yet provided all the answers needed. Even so, it is clear that in order to select unbiased tests for use in evaluations, and in order to defend those tests selected, evidence on bias is required. That evidence should include analyses of facial bias including issues of language and familiarity with situations depicted in the test as well as checking whether the test presents a ''positive, nonstereotyped representation of ethnic and sex groups (Tittle, 1979, p. 10).'' The evidence should also include item level studies of bias as well as the construct issues of bias discussed.

One key feature of the guide in Table 2.5 is that it raises the crucial questions but does not provide the crucial answers. In a real-world evaluation situation, the evaluator is under a variety of conflicting pressures (of different purposes, of time and money, etc.) and is forced to make a number of decisions, either explicitly with direct consideration of the decision being made or implicitly (by default) by actions taken or not taken. For evaluators in a variety of situations and under a variety of different pressures, there are not always the same best answers to the questions raised in the guide. The purpose of this chapter has been to discuss the complexities and implications of the answers to the questions. It is not important that all evaluators come to the same answers on all issues. It is important that evaluators, aware of the complexities and consequences of answers, explicitly address the questions raised in the guide and seek the best answers for the particular local circumstances, pressures, and practicalities.

REFERENCES

Aaronson, M. *Childhood mental health measurements sources*. Rockville, Md.: Early Child Care Research Center for Studies of Child and Family Mental Health, National Institute of Mental Health, 1974.

Anastasi, A. *Psychological testing* (4th ed.). New York: Macmillan, 1976.

Angoff, W. H., & Ford, S. F. Item-race interaction on a test of scholastic aptitude. *Journal of Educational Measurement*, 1973, *10*, 95–106.

Angoff, W. H., & Sharon, A. L. The evaluation of differences in test performance of two or more groups. *Educational and Psychological Measurement*, 1974, *34*, 807–816.

Armbruster, B. B., Steven, R. O., & Rosenshine, B. V. *Analyzing content coverage and emphasis: A study of three curricula and two tests* (Technical Report No. 26). Urbana: Center for the Study of Reading, University of Illinois, 1977. (ERIC Document Reproduction Service No. ED 136 238).

Ayrer, J. E., & McNamara, T. C. Survey testing on an out-of-level basis. *Journal of Educational Measurement*, 1973, *10*, 79–84.

Backer, T. E. *A directory of information on tests* (TM Report 62). Princeton: ERIC Clearinghouse on Tests, Measurement, and Evaluation, Educational Testing Service, 1977.

Berliner, D. C. Tempus educare. In P. L. Peterson and H. J. Walberg (eds.), *Research on teaching: Concepts, findings, and implications*. Berkeley: McCutchan, 1979.

Bloom, B. S., Hastings, J. T., & Madaus, G. F. *Handbook on formative and summative evaluation of student learning*. New York: McGraw-Hill, 1971.

Bormuth, J. R. *On the theory of achievement test items*. Chicago: University of Chicago Press, 1970.

Buros, O. K. (ed.). *Tests in print*. Highland Park, N.J.: Gryphon Press, 1974.

Buros, O. K. (ed.). *Eighth mental measurements yearbook*. Highland Park, N.J.: Gryphon Press, 1978.

Cardall, C., & Coffman, W. E. *A method for comparing the performance of different groups on the items in a test* (Research Bulletin 64-61). Princeton: Educational Testing Service, 1964.

Carlson, M. Sex differences in performance on the IEA science test items. Unpublished doctoral dissertation, University of Pittsburgh, 1976.

Cleary, T. A., & Hilton, T. L. An investigation of item bias. *Educational and Psychological Measurement*, 1968, *28*, 61–75.

Comber, L. C., & Keeves, J. P. *International studies in evaluation I: Science education in nineteen countries: An empirical study*. Stockholm: Almqvist & Wiksell, 1973.

Cooley, W. W. Program evaluation in education. Invited address at the annual meeting of the American Psychological Association, San Francisco, August 1977.

Cooley, W. W., & Leinhardt, G. *The instructional dimensions study: The search for effective classroom processes*. Pittsburgh: Learning Research and Development Center, University of Pittsburgh, 1978.

Cooley, W. W., & Lohnes, P. R. *Evaluation research in education*. New York: Irvington, 1976.

Coulson, J., et al. *Evaluation of 1972 ESAA Pilot Program*. Santa Monica: System Development Corporation, 1974.

Durost, W. N., Bixler, H. H., Wrightstone, J. W., Prescott, G. A., & Balow, I. H. *Teacher's handbook: Metropolitan Achievement Tests, Intermediate*. New York: Harcourt Brace Jovanovich, 1971.

Durovic, J. J. Test bias: An objective definition for test items. Paper presented at the annual meeting of the Northeastern Educational Research Association, Ellenville, N.Y., October 1975.

Ebel, R. L. Constructing unbiased achievement tests. Paper presented at the National Institute of Education Conference on Test Bias, Annapolis, Md., December 1975.

Educational Testing Service. *Suggested procedures for a systematic search for tests and assessment devices*. Princeton: Author, n.d.

Fishbein, R. L. An investigation of the fairness of the items of a test battery. Paper presented at the annual meeting of the National Council on Measurement in Education, Washington, D.C., March 1975.

Fisher, C. W., Filby, N. N., Marliave, R., Cahen, L. S., Dishaw, M. M., Moore, J. E., & Berliner, D. C. *Teaching behaviors, academic learning time and student achievement: Final report of Phase III-B, Beginning Teacher Evaluation Study* (Technical Report V-1). San Francisco: Far West Laboratory for Educational Research and Development, June 1978. (a)

Fisher, C. W., Berliner, D. C., Filby, N. N., Marliave, R., Cahen, L. S., Dishaw, M. M., & Moore, J. E. *Teaching and learning in the elementary school: A summary of the Beginning Teacher Evaluation Study* (Technical Report VII-1). San Francisco: Far West Laboratory for Educational Research and Development, September 1978. (b)

Fisher, J. A. The use of out-of-grade tests with retarded and accelerated readers. Unpublished doctoral dissertation, University of Iowa, 1961.

Green, D. R. What does it mean to say a test is biased? Paper presented at the annual meeting of the American Educational Research Association, Washington, D. C., March 1975.

Green, D. R., & Draper, J. F. Exploratory studies of bias in achievement tests. Paper presented at the annual meeting of the American Psychological Association, Honolulu, September 1972.

Hambleton, R. K., & Eignor, D. R. Guidelines for evaluating criterion-referenced tests and test manuals. *Journal of Educational Measurement,* 1978, *15,* 321-327.

Hieronymus, A. N., & Lindquist, E. F. *Teacher's guide for administration, interpretation, and use: Iowa Tests of Basic Skills.* Boston: Houghton Mifflin, 1971.

House, E. R., Glass, G. V., McLean, L. D., & Walker, D. F. No simple answer: Critique of the "Follow Through" evaluation. Urbana: Center for Instructional Research and Curriculum Evaluation, University of Illinois, 1972. (mimeo)

Husen, T., Faterlind, I., & Lilijefors, R. Sex differences in science achievement and attitudes. *Comparative Education Review,* 1974, *18,* 292-304.

Intasuwan, P. A comparison of three approaches for determining item bias in cross-national testing. Unpublished doctoral dissertation, University of Pittsburgh, 1979.

Jenkins, J. R., & Pany, D. *Curriculum biases in reading achievement tests* (Technical Report No. 16). Urbana: Center for the Study of Reading, University of Illinois, 1976. (ERIC Document Reproduction Service No. ED 134 938).

Kowal, B. Location in a curriculum hierarchy and performance on three standardized achievement tests. Unpublished master's thesis, University of Pittsburgh, 1975.

Leinhardt, G. Observation as a tool for the evaluation of implementation. *Instructional Science,* 1976, *5,* 343-364.

Lord, F. A study of item bias using item characteristic curve theory. In N. H. Poortinga (ed.), *Basic problems in cross-cultural psychology.* Amsterdam: Swits & Vitlinger, 1977. Pp. 19-26.

Madden, R., Gardner, E. F., Rudman, H. C., Karlsen, B., & Merwin, J. C. *Manual part II, norms booklet, form A: Stanford Achievement Test.* New York: Harcourt Brace Jovanovich, 1973.

Mager, R. F. *Measuring instructional intent: Or got a match?* Palo Alto, Calif.: Fearon, 1973.

Millman, J. Computer-based item generation. In R. A. Berk (ed.), *Criterion-referenced measurement: The state of the art.* Baltimore: Johns Hopkins University Press, 1980. Pp. 32-43.

Morris, L. L., & Fitz-Gibbon, C. T. *Evaluator's handbook.* Beverly Hills: Sage, 1978.

Nitko, A. J. Distinguishing the many varieties of criterion-referenced tests. *Review of Educational Research,* 1980, *50,* 461–485.

Popham, W. J. *Procedural guidelines: Developing IOX objectives-based tests* (Technical Paper No. 8). Los Angeles: Instructional Objectives Exchange, 1972.

Popham, W. J. *Criterion-referenced measurement.* Englewood Cliffs, N.J.: Prentice-Hall, 1978.

Popham, W. J. Domain specification strategies. In R. A. Berk (ed.), *Criterion-referenced measurement: The state of art.* Baltimore: Johns Hopkins University Press, 1980. Pp. 15–31.

Porter, A. C., Schmidt, W. H., Floden, R. E., & Freeman, D. J. Impact on what? The importance of content covered. Paper presented at the first annual meeting of the Evaluation Research Society, Washington, D.C., October 1977.

Rosenshine, B. V. Content, time and direct instruction. In P. L. Peterson and H. J. Walberg (eds.), *Research on teaching: Concepts, findings, and implications.* Berkeley: McCutchan, 1979.

Rudner, L. M. An approach to biased item identification using latent trait measurement theory. Paper presented at the annual meeting of the American Educational Research Association, New York, April 1977.

Scheuneman, J. A method of assessing bias in test items. *Journal of Educational Measurement,* 1979, *16,* 143–152.

Thorndike, R. L., & Hagen, E. P. *Measurement and evaluation in psychology and education* (4th ed.). New York: Wiley, 1977.

Tittle, C. K. Comments on "Instrumentation and bias: Issues in selecting measures for educational evaluations." Discussant paper presented at the second annual Johns Hopkins University National Symposium on Educational Research, Washington, D.C., November 1979.

Veale, J. R., & Foreman, D. I. *Cultural validity of items and tests: A new approach.* Iowa City, Iowa: SCORE Statistics Unit, Westinghouse Learning Corporation/ Measurement Research Center, 1975.

Walker, D. F., & Schaffarzick, J. Comparing curricula. *Review of Educational Research,* 1974, *44,* 83–111.

Worthen, B. R., & Sanders, J. R. *Educational evaluation: Theory and practice.* Worthington, Ohio: Charles A. Jones, 1973.

Wright, B. D., Mead, R. J., & Draba, R. E. *Detecting and correcting test item bias with a logistic response model* (Research Memorandum No. 22). Chicago: Statistical Laboratory, Department of Education, University of Chicago, 1976.

3 ANALYZING MULTILEVEL DATA WILLIAM W. COOLEY, LLOYD BOND, AND BOR-JIIN MAO

*A*fter the evaluation design and the appropriate instrumentation have been determined, the types of data analysis necessary to address the different levels of decision making—student, classroom, school, district— must be specified. For example, state-level evaluation decisions typically require district-level analyses, and district-level decisions typically require school-level analyses. Unfortunately, differential analyses for multiple levels in the educational system is a topic that heretofore has been virtually ignored by evaluators. The issues surrounding this topic need to be confronted before statistical methods are selected, particularly for quasi-experimental and non-experimental designs.

In this chapter, Drs. William W. Cooley, Lloyd Bond, and Bor-Jiin Mao tackle the critical issues in the analysis of multilevel data from evaluation studies. Their presentation is restricted to explanatory observational studies where the statistical methods usually involve the analysis of relationships among variables (e.g., multiple regression). The review of the issues is organized into four sections. The first section focuses on the importance of choosing a causal model prior to choosing a method of analysis. The authors indicate that the structured equation implied by the model will suggest the appropriate data analysis scheme. In this discussion it is emphasized that the question of which unit of analysis is appropriate is the wrong question. If the causal models are multilevel, then analyses will have to be conducted at several different levels to acquire a more thorough understanding of the data. The next section examines aggregation bias, or the effect that the level of aggregation exerts upon the correlation and regression coefficients. Two reasons are offered for why relationships at one level of analysis differ from relationships at another: grouping effect and specification error. The choice between the use of standardized and unstandardized regression coefficients,

NOTE: The research reported herein was supported by the Learning Research and Development Center, supported in part by funds from the National Institute of Education (NIE), United States Department of Health, Education and Welfare. The opinions expressed do not necessarily reflect the position or policy of NIE and no official endorsement should be inferred.

which is associated with the aggregation bias problem, is also dealt with in the second section. The authors prefer unstandardized coefficients in multilevel analyses. In the third section of the chapter the implications of the variation that might occur in within-group coefficients are discussed. It is stressed that such variation must not be overlooked in estimating a variable's effect. The fourth section proposes some general strategies for analyzing multilevel data. One recommendation is to begin with an understanding of relationships among the lowest level variables and then proceed to investigate the relationships among the lower level and higher variables. The authors conclude the chapter with a few suggestions/caveats for evaluators: (a) do not make inferences about relationships at one level using data aggregated at another, (b) make the causal model explicit; then base the selection of a statistical procedure on that model, (c) when analyzing multilevel data, note whether the estimate of effect size varies from group to group, and (d) to establish causal links across levels, specify and measure the variables at one level that might influence variables at another level.

INTRODUCTION

THIS CHAPTER considers issues surrounding the unit of analysis in educational evaluation studies. Our primary objective is to show how to analyze data that involve observations at several different levels in the educational system: students, classrooms, schools, and districts. To simplify the presentation, we shall focus upon studies done within school districts, but the general principles apply as well at state and national levels, at which the difference is simply an increase in the number of possible levels.

One way to suggest the significance of this topic is to quote Cronbach, who has written an important monograph on this general problem. In his preface to that monograph, Cronbach (1976) says: "If any fraction of the argument herein is correct, educational research . . . is in serious trouble" (p. 1). He goes on to claim that "the majority of studies of educational effects . . . have collected and analyzed data in ways that conceal more than they reveal" (p. 1). He deplores the fact that educational researchers have virtually ignored unit-of-analysis issues. Fortunately, the problems inherent in the multilevel nature of educational data are becoming more widely recognized, and some progress has been made easier by the degree of attention that these problems have received in sociology and economics.

The specific topics that will be considered in this chapter are:

1. the role of causal analysis and structural equation models in considering issues surrounding the unit of analysis;
2. the effect of aggregation and standardization on relationships among variables;

3. the implications of variation in structure coefficients among schools or classrooms;
4. a general approach to multilevel analysis.

As you might infer from these topics, we are concerned about the unit of analysis problem in the context of explanatory observational studies (Cooley, 1978), and shall not deal with these problems as they relate to true experimental designs. In those rare cases where randomized experiments are possible and desirable in evaluation studies, unit of analysis questions are easily answered by knowing the unit of randomization (see, for example, Glass & Stanley, 1970, pp. 501–508, for a discussion of this point). If the evaluation study is a quasi-experiment (no randomization to treatment), then the issues addressed in this chapter are directly relevant.

REVIEW OF THE MAJOR ISSUES

Unit of Analysis and Causal Models

A data bank found in a school district's evaluation and research department might contain variables that are observed at the student level (e.g., standardized test scores), classroom level (e.g., class size), and school level (e.g., sex of principal). Table 3.1 illustrates some of these possibilities. A student level variable is observed for each student and its values vary from student to student. Variables observed at the classroom level have the same value for all students in that classroom. Variables observed at the school level have the same values for all classrooms and students in that school. In other words, a higher-level variable is constant within each lower-level category. This property is important in the analysis of multilevel data as we will see later.

Notice that it is also possible to create variables at a higher level that are

TABLE 3.1. Variables Observed at Different Levels

Level	Variable	
Student	Sex	Grade level
	Race	Disciplinary actions
	Standardized test scores	Free-lunch eligibility
	Attendance record	
Classroom	Number of students	Number of Title I eligibles
	Curriculum in use	Hours per week in reading
	Grade level	Teacher characteristics
School	Number of students	Principal characteristics
	Number of paraprofessionals	Building capacity
	Grade organization	

based upon observations made at a lower level but aggregated to that higher level. Examples are: school achievement means, classroom sex ratio, percent free lunch in school, percent white teachers, etc.

Let us assume that in this data bank it is also possible to link data on students to data on their particular teachers and classrooms, and data on teachers and classrooms to data on principals and schools. Now, what if one should ask: What unit of analysis do you use—the student, the classroom or the school? The answer, of course, depends on the research question. Let's examine some simple questions one evaluation department has been asked:

1. What proportion of the district's fifth-grade students who are scoring one year below grade level in reading are also doing so in mathematics?
2. Are the experienced teachers getting the smaller classes?
3. Are the larger elementary schools organized as K–5 or K–8?

The choice of unit of analysis for these descriptive questions is simple indeed. The analyses should be at the student, the classroom, and the school level, respectively.

Now let's turn to a more complex question recently asked by a concerned taxpayer. Is class size related to student achievement in the primary grades? Interpreting this question literally, you could link the size of each student's class to his/her test score, and compute the correlation at the student level, or aggregate achievement within classroom and link the class mean on the achievement test to the class size and compute the correlation at the classroom level. The absolute magnitude of the latter correlation will be larger, depending upon the amount of within-classroom variability in reading achievement.

However, the concerned taxpayer who asked the question meant more than was said. The taxpayer knew that increasing average class size by only one student could save the large school district millions of dollars, and he/she wanted to know if smaller classes were producing higher achievement. No worthy evaluation department would offer a simple bivariate relationship, based upon either of these units of analysis, to answer that complex question.

Once we move beyond simple descriptions to causal inference, the task of choosing an appropriate analytical procedure becomes subordinate to the task of choosing an appropriate causal model. Offering the negative correlation between class size (C) and achievement (A) as evidence for the importance of smaller classes assumes the causal model indicated in Figure 3.1.

In that diagram, the structure coefficient b represents the extent to which C influences A, and u represents influences upon A not included in the model. It is assumed that u is unrelated to C. If it is not, then we have misspecified the model and we would obtain an incorrect estimate of the degree to which C influences A from the resulting coefficient b. (Readers unfamiliar with causal modeling and structural equations should study an introduction to this important topic (e.g., Duncan, 1975, or Kenny, 1979.)

FIGURE 3.1. Relationship between class size (C) and achievement (A).

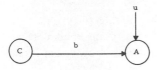

One way to detect specification error is to identify other factors that are related to class size and also affect achievement, such as teacher experience (T) and prior student achievement (P). Including those two variables results in a different model. The model in Figure 3.2 assumes that P, T, and C all directly influence A. The model does not attempt to explain the relationships among P, T, and C; nevertheless, b_1, the estimate of the degree to which C influences A, will be different from b in the previous model, unless, of course, P and T are unrelated to C.

Now let's assume that the evaluation department has established that, over time, the teachers in this district tend to migrate into the schools serving higher SES neighborhoods. That would explain the observed P and T relationship, given the dependence of P on SES. Also, they know that class size has been manipulated by principals in such a way that within a school the lower-ability students tend to be placed in smaller classrooms. They also discover that several studies conducted in other large urban districts have found that smaller classes are more effective for low-ability than for high-ability students. Now the model looks like Figure 3.3, where P × C represents the interaction between prior achievement and class size. The relationship between P and T is explained by the assortative mating that is going on in the district. That is, higher-ability students are showing up in schools serving higher SES neighborhoods, the same schools the more experienced teachers are moving into when they get the chance.

Once a plausible causal model has been defined, the structural equations implied by that model determine the appropriateness of a particular data analysis scheme. As one learns more about the phenomena under investigation, the model changes, and the appropriate statistical procedures change as well. In the context of causal modeling, the question of which unit of analysis is appropriate is the wrong question. If the causal models are multilevel, then analyses will have to be done at the several different levels represented in the causal model for a more complete understanding of the phenomena under investigation. Later in this chapter we explain how that is done. Next, let us examine another example of causal modeling.

The attempt to identify a school principal effect seems to be another one of those cases in which everyone knows the effect exists, but quantitative verifi-

FIGURE 3.2. Relationships among prior achievement (P), teacher experience (T), class size (C), and achievement (A).

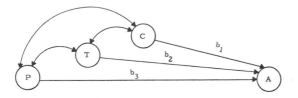

FIGURE 3.3. Relationships among prior achievement (P), socioeconomic status (S), teacher experience (T), class size (C), the interaction between prior achievement and class size (P × C), and achievement (A).

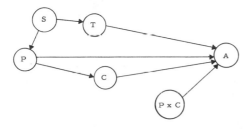

cation has been elusive. One reason is the manner in which the search has been conducted. An important variable among principals is the instructional leadership provided by the principal (L). If one wants to show the effect of L on student achievement, the important question is not whether the analysis should be done at the student level or at the school level, but rather, what is a credible causal model for explaining how L might influence student achievement? Through what mediating variables does it operate?

For example, an elementary school principal may have assigned a high priority to reading instruction. One result of this might be that the teachers tend to allocate more time (T) to reading. This in turn might increase the amount of time a given child is likely to be engaged in direct instruction in reading (E), and more E will increase reading performance. Given a pretest (P) and a posttest (A) in reading, the resulting model might look like Figure 3.4. Here L is observed at the school level, T at the classroom level, and E, P, and A at the student level.

Even though one might find an effect for L on T, for T on E, and for E on A, a direct effect for L on A, as in the model of Figure 3.5, is not at all probable.

FIGURE 3.4. Relationships among the principal's instructional leadership
(L), allocated time (T), engaged time (E), prior achievement (P),
and achievement (A).

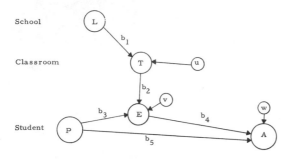

Since other factors (u) will affect T besides L, and others (v) will affect E
besides T, and still others (w) will influence A besides E, and since all
variables are imperfectly measured, it is quite easy to see how b_1 of Figure 3.4
could be nonzero, yet b_2 of Figure 3.5 be zero.

It should be noted that the common practice of analyzing a multilevel set of
predictors using a single multiple regression equation makes it extremely
unlikely that one will find an effect for the higher-level variables. For example, if L does indeed operate through T and E to affect A, including all three
predictors in a single multiple regression will not reveal an effect since it will
be masked by its mediating variables. That would be true no matter what unit
of analysis one might choose for computing that multiple regression.

It is also important to note that variables observed at the school level (for
instance, leadership qualities of the principal) can explain only the variation in
student-level observations that occurs among school means. The within-
school variation cannot be explained by school-level variables, and within-
classroom variation cannot be explained by classroom-level variables. Also,
school-level variables affect student-level measures through mediating variables at some intermediate level (teachers, classroom, peer groups). To show
school effects on student behavior, one must identify and directly measure
those mediating variables because the linkages are so weak.

Volume 4 of the *Evaluation Studies Review Annual* (Sechrest et al., 1979)
(and also volume 13 of *Health Services Research,* 1978) contains a very
interesting exchange between Brooks (1978a, 1978b) and Anderson (1978a,
1978b, 1978c) that illustrates the critical role of model specification in establishing causal effects and how the model under investigation should determine
the analytical procedures to be used. The substantive problem was the extent
to which infant mortality depends upon the availability of medical resources
and upon family socioeconomic status. The Anderson-Brooks debate con-

FIGURE 3.5. Relationships among the principal's instructional leadership (L), prior achievement (P), and achievement (A).

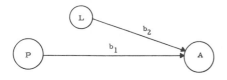

cerns the appropriate unit of analysis (county or standard metropolitan statistical area) and the adequacy of the causal models which guided the contrasting analyses. Intelligent discussion of different approaches to the infant-mortality study would not have been possible without competing structural models to guide it. For example, in considering the credibility of the Brooks model, Anderson (1978a) pointed out that one had to believe "that a large percentage of blacks in an area caused the supply of physicians to rise and that physicians, after weighing all the advantages and disadvantages of their location decisions, prefer areas with large black populations" (p. 323). We need debates about causal models in education if we expect to develop credible ones.

Effects of Aggregation and Standardization

A very important aspect of the unit of analysis problem is aggregation bias. This is the effect that level of aggregation exerts upon correlation and regression coefficients. Aggregation bias helps to explain why the results of educational research vary so much from study to study. What, for example, is the correlation between socioeconomic background and achievement test scores? Is it .3? .6? .9? All three are possible. The correlation depends upon the unit of analysis, the population sampled and the way the two constructs are measured. If you take these three factors into account, the results are fairly consistent.

Using national samples of high school students, family income correlates about .3 with achievement test results at the student level. Aggregating to the school level, the correlation is between .5 and .6 among school means nationally. If, however, one looks within large urban districts, the school-level relationship is between .8 and .9. The district-level relationship varies from state to state (.2 to .6), and at the state level the correlation between 1975 poverty rates and state achievement estimates is .63 (N = 50 states). Table 3.2 summarizes these results.*

*A review of the relationships between these two constructs was prepared by Wolf (1977), as part of NIE's Compensatory Education Study.

Other differences are found when looking at different grade levels, or when indicators other than poverty are used to represent home background. For example, in Project TALENT, an indicator of socioeconomic environment based upon home variables that exert a more direct effect on achievement (mother's education, books in the home, child has own desk, etc.) correlated .5 at the student level for high school students (Flanagan & Cooley, 1966).

Now, what is the *appropriate* unit of analysis? It depends, of course, on the question being asked. Inferring, from the within-district school-level correlation of .9, that most low-achieving students come from poor homes is an excellent example of what sociologists call the *ecological fallacy:* the error of using relationships at one level, such as school, to describe relationships at a lower level, such as student. However, aggregation bias works the other way, too. If legislators are considering procedures for distributing Title I funds to schools within districts, and are trying to decide whether it makes much difference to allocate money to schools on the basis of achievement level or poverty level, the .9 school-level correlation is the relevant one, not the .3 at the student level.

There are two reasons why relationships at one level of analysis differ from relationships at another. One is the grouping effect. This occurs when membership in the group (e.g., class or school) is related to either one or both of the variables being correlated. For example, the socioeconomic homogeneity of neighborhoods produces a relationship between SES and school building, and that relationship produces the larger correlation between SES and achievement at the school level than at the student level.

Another reason why relationships differ at different levels of aggregation is specification error. If one is attempting to show the degree to which one variable influences another, and the causal model that guides such an analysis is inadequately specified, then relationships will change from one level of analysis to another. It is also possible that different models are required to explain variation in achievement at the student level and variation in school-achievement means. If the models are different, we would expect to obtain

TABLE 3.2. Socioeconomic Background and Achievement

Level	Population Sampled	SES Indicators	Correlation
Student	National	Income	.2 to .4
Student	National	Home environment	.5
School	Large Urban District	Income	.8 to .9
School	National	Income	.5 to .6
District	Within State	Income	.2 to .6
State	National	Income	.6

different estimates of the degree to which a school variable influences achievement.

An issue that is intimately related to the problem of aggregation bias is the choice of which measure of relationship (standardized or unstandardized) to use in a given analysis. For unstandardized coefficients, if a student-level model is properly specified, the consequences of aggregation depend only upon the grouping process. Two forms of grouping—grouping by the independent variable or simple random grouping—will result in no systematic bias of unstandardized coefficients. However, two other forms of grouping— grouping by the dependent variable and grouping by a variable related to both the independent and the dependent variable—will generally result in the kinds of inflated estimates of student-level parameters noted earlier for correlations.

Aggregation biases in the estimation of student-level relationships are even more severe in the case of standardized measures of relationship such as correlations. Grouping by either the independent or dependent variable will result in systematic overestimation of the absolute value of the student-level correlation between the two measures. As noted earlier, grouping by a variable related to both the independent and dependent variable will generally result in highly inflated estimates of student-level correlations.

A more serious shortcoming of standardized measures of association is that in more complicated causal models, that is, in models where multiple causal agents are present which may have both direct and indirect effects, the standardized measures of relationship between two variables in the model (unlike their unstandardized counterparts) vary not only with the standard deviations of the two variables involved, but also with the standard deviations of other causal variables in the model. This undesirable property of standardized measures is why some authors (e.g., Richards, 1979) claim that percentage of variance accounted for by the variables in an analysis is of questionable scientific value.

Another shortcoming of standardized measures is one emanating from strictly measurement issues. Standardized coefficients are significantly reduced by errors of measurement in *both* the independent and dependent variables, while the unstandardized coefficient is reduced only by errors in the independent variable.

The major reason some researchers prefer standardized approaches is the belief that there is some underlying relationship between two variables that is unvarying across situations and levels. This is quite unlikely. A second reason often cited for the use of standardized coefficients is that different units of measurement dictate that standardized measures be used in order to get a "unit-less" measure of relationship. Note, however, that this is simply a restatement of the earlier reason, i.e., a search for a "pure" measure of relationship, independent of different units of measurement. In general, unstandardized weights are to be preferred in multilevel analyses.

A more detailed discussion of aggregation effects and the advantages and disadvantages of standardized and unstandardized measures of relationships can be found in Burstein (1978) and Langbein and Lichtman (1978). The two major implications are (1) that one must avoid the fallacies of inferring relationships at one level from estimates computed at another, because given the nonrandom ways in which students are grouped into classrooms and schools, they are almost always different, and (2) that unstandardized coefficients are generally to be preferred in analyses of multilevel data. Now let us turn to another aspect of the problem of analyzing multilevel data.

Variation in Within-Group Coefficients

One reason why Cronbach feels that educational researchers have revealed less than they might in multilevel studies is that they have tended to ignore the variability in within-group coefficients. For example, an empirical examination of the plausibility of the model in Figure 3.4 requires data on students within classrooms, and on classrooms within schools. Thus, the structure coefficients b_3, b_4, and b_5 might be estimated within each classroom, within classrooms pooled, among classrooms, or on all students without regard to classroom. If there is significant variation from classroom to classroom among estimates of the within-classroom effect for engaged time (E) upon achievement (A), that indicates that there are other important differences among classrooms that influence A and are related to E or prior achievement (P). Differences between b_4 estimated at the classroom level, using class means for P, E, and A, and b_4 estimated at the student level could be due either to a grouping effect (e.g., assignment to classroom was based upon student ability) or to specification error (i.e., the causal model is incorrectly specified). The point is that we must not ignore the possibility of variation among groups (e.g., classrooms or schools) in estimating a variable's effect. Examining this variation can reveal grouping effects or specification errors; ignoring it will conceal them.

Burstein (1978) has suggested using the within-classroom slopes as educational outcomes. That is, the regression coefficient for posttest on pretest within each classroom is computed and then the resulting variation in slopes from classroom to classroom is explained by regressing it on teacher characteristics and classroom process measures. One can view the search for predictors of slope variation as a way of looking for classroom practices which make spring posttest scores less dependent upon fall pretest scores.

To illustrate this general problem of slope variation, it might be useful to examine some multilevel data collected during the course of the Instructional Dimensions Study (Cooley & Leinhardt, 1980), a research project on classroom processes affecting achievement that involved students within classrooms, classrooms within schools, and schools within districts. This data set is particularly suited for our purposes since it involves the kind of multilevel complexity that is inevitable in studies of student achievement. Data were collected at both the student level and the classroom level. Table 3.3 gives the correlations among classroom means and standard deviations on the *Comprehensive Tests of Basic Skills* (reading and math) pretest and posttest, as well as the within-classroom standardized and unstandardized regression coefficients for 195 third-grade classrooms. In each case, the standardized coefficients (i.e., the within-classroom correlations between pretest and posttest) are highly dependent upon the mean and standard deviation of the class on both the pre- and post-measures. The unstandardized regression coefficients, on the other hand, appear to be affected only by the posttest variance. (Note: Highly similar patterns of relationship were obtained for first grade as well.) The Burstein suggestion, then, involves finding differences in classroom practices that explain the variation in within-classroom regression coefficients not explained by variation in test means and standard deviations.

Another approach is to consider heterogeneity in within-classroom regression equations (for a given causal model) as indicating misspecification of that model. An example will be helpful in illustrating this important point. Figure 3.6 is a simple model for explaining end-of-year achievement in reading. Variable D is a measure of the amount of direct instruction in reading that each child received between pretest and posttest. Let us assume that this model is properly specified, and consider what might happen if an investigator omitted D from the analysis of data from several classrooms. The investigator might find classrooms with pretest-posttest distributions as shown in Figure 3.7. Let us consider these classrooms, "knowing the true state of affairs." (That is, assume that the simple model of Figure 3.6 represents a valid model.) Looking first at the within-classroom slopes, the lack of dependence of posttest on pretest for classrooms A and C indicates that within those two classrooms, students with the same pretest varied in how much D they re-

TABLE 3.3. Correlations of r_{yx} and b_{yx} with Four Classroom Parameters (N = 195 Classes)

MATH

	M_x	S_x	M_y	S_y	r_{yx}	b_{yx}
M_x		.55	.76	.16	.39	−.08
S_x			.49	.61	.59	.02
M_y				.16	.28	−.10
S_y					.48	.54

READING

	M_x	S_x	M_y	S_y	r_{yx}	b_{yx}
M_x		.67	.85	.21	.09	.06
S_x			.59	.65	.71	.17
M_y				.17	.48	.05
S_y					.64	.53

FIGURE 3.6. Relationships among the amount of direct instruction in reading (D), prior achievement (P), and achievement (A).

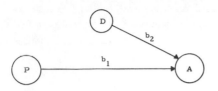

ceived. For example, in classroom A, student S_1 received more D than student S_2, resulting in different posttests even though they began with the same pretest. The degree to which posttest depends upon pretest within classrooms is in part a function of the variability in D within classroom, and in part a function of the D and pretest relationship within classroom.

On the other hand, the students in classroom B, as a group, received more D than did the students in classroom A, thus explaining the higher posttest mean for classroom B relative to A. Within classroom B, there was less variability in the amount of D each child received; thus, posttest depended more on pretest in classroom B than in classroom A.

The among-classroom regression (b_a) is affected by the variation in class means in D relative to their pretest means. For example, if classroom G were added to the analysis, that would decrease b_a. The slope b_a will depend upon the variation among classrooms on D, and upon the relationship between D and pretest among classrooms. If all students in all classrooms had the same amount of D, then the within-classroom slopes (b_i) would be homogeneous, and the pooled within-classroom slope (b_w) would not be significantly different from the among-classroom slope (b_a), or from the total regression (b_t). (Keep in mind that all of this discussion assumes that Figure 6 represents the true state of affairs.)

Now let us imagine what would happen if an investigator computed the within-classroom pre-post slopes for the Figure 3.7 classrooms, and tried to use classroom means on D to explain the variability in those slopes. It would appear as though D were irrelevant. What the variation among classroom means on D *would* explain is the classroom mean posttest residuals from b_a. The variation in b_i would be explained by the variation in the relationships between D and pretest. A teacher who tended to give more D to students with lower pretests than to those with higher pretests would reduce the within-classroom pre-post regression.

A General Approach to Multilevel Analysis

Having reviewed some of the major aspects of multilevel analysis, let us turn now to a general approach in the analysis of multilevel data. To do so we

FIGURE 3.7. Within-classroom slopes for six hypothetical classrooms.

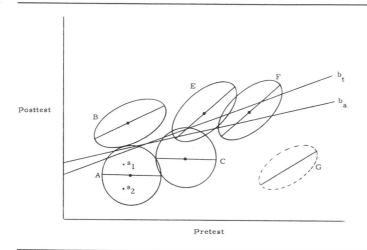

Pretest

shall return to the example represented in Figure 3.4. In Figure 3.4, A, P, and E are student variables representing final achievement in reading, pretest performance, and engaged time in reading, respectively. T is a classroom variable indicating time allocated to reading by the teacher. L is a school-level variable indicating the instructional leadership of the principal.

The model in Figure 3.4 can be represented by the following set of structural equations:

STUDENT	$A = b_5 P + b_4 E + w,$	(1)
STUDENT	$E = b_3 P + b_2 T + v,$	(2)
CLASSROOM	$T = b_1 L + u.$	(3)

Since the interest is on the degree of influence from one variable to another, the intercepts in equations (1), (2), and (3) are omitted for simplicity. Equation (1) represents the relationships among student variables, equation (2) represents the relationships among student variables and a classroom variable, and equation (3) represents the relationship between a classroom variable and a school variable. The level for a given structural equation will depend upon the level of the dependent variable. Hence equations (1) and (2) are called student-level equations and (3) is called a classroom-level equation. Note that a structural equation may include variables at one level higher than the dependent variable. For example, the student-level equation (2) includes the classroom variable T as an independent variable. However, it is less likely for student-level equations to have variables at levels higher than the classroom level as independent variables.

The hierarchical nature of multilevel data forces researchers to choose between two general research strategies. One preference might be to understand relationships at higher levels (between, say, principals and teachers) and then to "work down" to an understanding of how these relationships in turn affect teacher behaviors toward students. The opposite approach is to first understand relationships among the lowest-level variables and, subsequently, to find the relationships among lower- and higher-level variables.

Now let us return to the notion that heterogeneous regression coefficients are suggestive of model incompleteness. For any given structural equation, there are several ways to estimate its parameters. If the equation is a student-level equation, one has the choice of estimating a given parameter within each classroom and then pooling these estimates across classrooms, or one could simply consider all students as one group ignoring classroom boundaries.

As a general strategy, we recommend examining the homogeneity of coefficients at the classroom level (if classrooms are the next highest level of interest). As indicated earlier, we view the homogeneity of regression coefficients as crucial to an understanding of relationships in naturally occurring multilevel data. Let us consider this point in more detail.

Suppose, in Figure 3.4, that instead of (2), the student-level equation for explaining E is the following:

$$\text{STUDENT} \quad E = b_6 P + e. \tag{4}$$

Equation (4) can be estimated within each classroom, and there are as many estimates of b_6 as there are classrooms. The hypothesis that these regression equations are homogeneous can then be tested. If it is rejected, then it is probable that equation (4) is not properly specified, if it is accepted, then a combined estimate of b_6 is obtained from the pooled within-classroom estimate.

If the hypothesis is rejected, this indicates that there are variables missing from this student-level equation. The missing variables contain information about variation within classrooms. Because all the higher-level variables are constant in each classroom, it is obvious that the within-classroom regression coefficient, b_6, would not change with the addition of any higher-level variables as independent variables. The effect of the addition of any higher-level variables is to change the intercept of the regression equation. The missing variable or variables must be student-level variables. If a student variable Z has homogeneous within-classroom variances and homogeneous within-classroom correlation with P and A, and if Z is added to equation (4) as an independent variable, i.e.,

$$\text{STUDENT} \quad E = b_7 P + b_8 Z + f, \tag{5}$$

then the heterogeneity of b_6 implies the heterogeneity of b_7, because Z does not contain any additional information about the variation among the

classrooms. In other words, adding Z to the structural equation would not
reduce the heterogeneity of the influence of P on A. Thus the possible candidates for the missing student variables are those having heterogeneous
within-classroom standard deviations and/or heterogeneous within-classroom
correlations with the student variables already in the student-level equation.

With the within-classroom homogeneity established, a comparison between
the pooled-within estimates and those obtained from all the students ignoring
the classroom boundaries should be made. If the hypothesis that they are the
same could be accepted, then there is no indication that this equation is
inadequately specified. Should the hypothesis be rejected, then it indicates
that classroom membership affects the relationships among these student variables. There should be some variables, which could be at student level or
classroom level, included in the equation to reflect the effect of classroom
membership. Then one should reexamine the adequacy of the student-level
structural equation. If some student variable can be used to explain the
classroom differences, then it should be included in the equation, so as to
reestablish the homogeneity of the within-classroom relationships. If no student variable is able to explain the classroom differences, then classroom
variables should be considered for explaining this difference. Adding
classroom variables as independent variables to the regression would not
affect the homogeneity of the within-classroom slopes. The classroom variables should be chosen so that the pooled-within estimates are the same as the
overall estimates.

In summary, the principle of the analysis is to detect differences among
different categories at the same level and the difference of each category with
the overall. One should always remember that the theoretical consideration of
the context is indispensable.

The statistical method for testing the equality of the within-classroom regression slopes is the analysis of covariance. This method is considered in
detail by Williams (1959), Rao (1965), and more recently by Timm (1975).
The procedure simultaneously tests the equality of all the partial regression
slopes irrespective of the intercept of the regression. In other words, it is the
test of parallelism. If a specific correlation among the independent variables is
assumed, one can use the LISREL program (Jöreskog & Sörbom, 1979) to
estimate the regression slopes and also to test the equality of the slopes. In
particular, LISREL can be used to test the equality of one particular partial regression coefficient, regardless of other coefficients. The test of equality of
correlations is discussed by Snedecor and Cochran (1972). The more general
test of the equality of variance-covariance matrices is reviewed by Timm
(1975).

It sounds as though we were trying to make life unnecessarily complicated
for the educational evaluator who is trying to identify differences in school
and classroom practices that influence what students learn. In fact, we have

contrived the simplest model possible for purposes of this discussion. But in spite of the complexity of the task, we are still optimistic that we can develop valid and useful quantitative approaches to the study of the effects of schooling. We are also convinced that this will depend upon our success in specifying increasingly valid causal models for explaining student achievement.

As Duncan (1975) has emphasized, "talking about causal modeling is a lot easier than doing it" (p. 149). But if we don't make the effort, there is not much hope for a quantitatively oriented contribution to the formulation of educational policy and effective practice. The only quantitative alternative to credible models is the carefully controlled randomized experiment in classrooms and schools. It is more likely that we can achieve credible causal models.

SUGGESTIONS FOR FUTURE RESEARCH

The most critical need in improving our understanding of educational phenomena is improved causal models of those phenomena. Of course, this is a kind of chicken-egg situation. The more we understand the phenomena, the better the models will be; the better the models, the better will be our understanding. The way to improve both is to *use* models in our educational research. Make them explicit. Get them out in the open so that they can be critically examined and improved as better thinking and better data are brought to bear on them. Through such an iterative process, we will finally begin to achieve the kinds of convincing models that are so desperately needed if we are to improve quantitative approaches to the study of educational phenomena.

In the past, the multilevel nature of educational data has tended to confuse researchers and obscure potentially important relationships. We believe we now see a way in which researchers can turn this multilevel nature of educational data into an advantage through the consideration of heterogeneity of effect coefficients and the resulting implications for model misspecification. Much needs to be done to develop this general approach, but we believe it holds considerable promise for educational evaluation.

GUIDELINES FOR EVALUATORS

Having reviewed some aspects of the multilevel analysis problem, let us turn now to some guidelines for dealing with it. We have made this task more difficult by placing the problem squarely within the task of developing convincing causal models. It is hard to suggest guidelines, except perhaps to quote Percy Bridgman: "do the damndest with your mind—no holds barred!"

But a few general suggestions might be useful, as long as no one takes them too seriously.

Avoid the ecological fallacy.   Do not make inferences about relationships at one level, using data aggregated at another. This is a very dangerous practice in education because of the nonrandom ways in which children are grouped into classrooms and schools. Analytical procedures are best determined by a careful consideration of the question being asked, for descriptive questions, and by the most plausible causal model, for explanatory questions.

Make the causal model explicit.   Any attempt to establish the effects of educational policies and practices in multilevel observational studies involves a causal model, whether it be implied by the statistical procedures used, or explicitly stated by the researcher. It is far better to make the model explicit, and base the choice of statistical procedures on the model, than to discover that the causal model implied by the choice you made is a completely implausible model. People cannot be expected to accept estimates of the degree to which one variable influences another from analyses based upon incredible models.

Look for variation in size of effects.   When analyzing multilevel data, always check to see if the estimate of the size of an effect varies from group to group. For example, with data from several classrooms, if the degree to which X influences Y varies from classroom to classroom, then you are operating with a misspecified model. If you do not check for this, you may be concealing more than you are revealing.

Consider who can manipulate what variables.   In the educational system, manipulable variables that directly affect student learning are those that teachers manipulate. These can vary within classroom (e.g., some students get more teacher-led instruction than others) and among classrooms (e.g., some teachers allocate more class time to reading than others). Do not expect a variable manipulated in Washington, D.C., to show a direct effect on student achievement-test scores. In trying to establish causal links across levels in the educational system, explicitly specify and directly measure the variables at one level that are expected to influence variables at another level.

In designing evaluation studies, the decision-making level of the client of the evaluation must be considered. In general, state education departments need relationships at the district level, district superintendents at the school level, school principals at the classroom level. The only decision maker who can make good use of detailed information on each student is the teacher. National funding programs and state assessment programs, for example, have run into serious trouble when they have tried to control events at the student level. If the purpose of the evaluation research is to provide information that will result in better-informed decisions, then everyone (evaluator, client, student) is better off if the questions are posed in terms relevant to the decision-making level of the client of the evaluation. Hayman et al. (1979) provide an excellent discussion of this important point. Of course, there are exceptions to this general rule, but one can find many more bad examples of attempts at cross-level decisions than good ones.

REFERENCES

Anderson, J. G. Constructing causal models: Critical issues. *Health Services Research,* 1978, *13,* 319-326.(a)

Anderson, J. G. Constructing causal models: Problems of units of analysis, aggregation, and specification. *Health Services Research,* 1978, *13,* 50-60.(b)

Anderson, J. G. Structural equation models: Their structural, reduced, and final forms. Paper presented at the annual meeting of the American Sociological Association, San Francisco, September 1978.(c)

Brooks, C. H. Infant mortality in SMSAs before Medicaid: Test of a causal model. *Health Services Research,* 1978, *13,* 3-16.(a)

Brooks, C. H. Reply to "Constructing causal models: Problems of units of analysis, aggregration, and specification." *Health Services Research,* 1978, *13,* 305-318.(b)

Burstein, L. The role of levels of analysis in the specification of educational effects. Los Angeles: University of California, 1978.

Cooley, W. W. Explanatory observational studies. *Educational Researcher,* 1978, *7*(9), 9-15.

Cooley, W. W., & Leinhardt, G. The instructional dimensions study. *Educational Evaluation and Policy Analysis,* 1980, *2,* 7-25.

Cronbach, L. J. *Research on classrooms and schools: Formulation of questions, design, and analysis* (Occasional paper). Stanford, Calif.: Stanford Evaluation Consortium, Stanford University, July 1976.

Duncan, O. D. *Introduction to structural equation models.* New York: Academic Press, 1975.

Flanagan, J. C., & Cooley, W. W. *Project TALENT one-year follow-up studies.* Pittsburgh: School of Education, University of Pittsburgh, 1966.

Glass, G. V., & Stanley, J. C. *Statistical methods in education and psychology.* Englewood Cliffs, N.J.: Prentice-Hall, 1970.

Hayman, J., Rayder, N., Stenner, A. J., & Madley, D. L. On aggregation, generalization, and utility in educational evaluation. *Educational Evaluation and Policy Analysis,* 1979, *1,* 31-39.

Jöreskog, K. G., & Sörbom, D. *Advances in factor analysis and structural equation models.* Cambridge, Mass.: Abt Associates, 1979.

Kenny, D. A. *Correlation and causality.* New York: Wiley, 1979.

Langbein, L. I., & Lichtman, A. J. Ecological inference. In E. M. Uslander (ed.), *Quantitative applications in the social sciences.* Beverly Hills: Sage, 1978.

Rao, C. R. Linear statistical inference and its applications. New York: Wiley, 1965.

Richards, Jr., J. M. *Regression weights and communication among researchers from different disciplines.* Baltimore: Center for Social Organization of Schools, The Johns Hopkins University, 1979.

Sechrest, L., West, S. G., Phillips, M. A., Redner, R., & Yeaton, W. (eds.). *Evaluation studies review annual* (Vol. 4). Beverly Hills: Sage, 1979.

Snedecor, G. W., & Cochran, W. G. *Statistical methods*. Ames, Iowa: Iowa State University Press, 1972.

Timm, N. H. *Multivariate analysis with applications in education and psychology*. Monterey, Calif.: Brooks/Cole, 1975.

Williams, E. J. *Regression analysis*. New York: Wiley, 1959.

4 MEASURING PRETEST-POSTTEST PERFORMANCE CHANGES ROBERT L. LINN

I n selecting one or more statistical methods for assessing program effects, one typically encounters the problem of how to measure student growth. It is probably the most misunderstood and sticky technical issue in data analysis. Since 1974, evaluators of ESEA Title I programs are required to choose among three evaluation models developed by the RMC Research Corporation, all of which involve some consideration of gain or change.

Professor Robert L. Linn critically reviews the major strategies and models for measuring change and tackles the related issues of the test score metric, interval between pretest and posttest, and vertical equating. He first examines difference scores and the alternative approaches of residualized change scores, estimates of true change, and standardized difference scores. Some of the limitations of two-wave data (pretest-posttest) and the advantages of multi-wave data (multiple measurements over time) are then discussed in the context of growth curve models. This is followed by an evaluation of the most common achievement test score scales including the grade-equivalent score, percentile rank, normal curve equivalent, and scaled scores. Professor Linn prefers the latter to the former derived scores for measuring growth. Latent trait scales and proportion correct are also appraised as ''absolute'' metrics compared to the other ''relative'' metrics. Among his recommendations to evaluators, four particular points are emphasized: (1) there is no need for difference scores with randomized designs and, in fact, they have disadvantages when contrasted with alternative uses of pretest scores, (2) difference scores cannot be expected to provide the correct adjustment in nonequivalent control-group designs except where the pretest is used as the sole basis for subject assignment as in the regression-discontinuity design, (3) when difference scores are applied in conjunction with the three Title I evaluation models, they tend to conceal conceptual difficulties and they give misleading results, and (4) two-wave data have substantial advantages over posttest-only data for program evaluation, but multi-wave data are crucial to adequately characterize growth curves.

84

INTRODUCTION

THE MEASUREMENT of student growth is often considered to be a necessary and fundamental part of educational evaluation studies. The major intervention programs such as Head Start, Follow Through, and ESEA Title I have involved goals that are frequently expressed in terms of gains in student achievement. Indeed, a basic impetus for Follow Through was that children in Head Start Programs "made large gains in achievement during the preschool year, but that increases in their rate of development usually were not sustained when they entered the public school system" (Bissell, 1973, p. 87). Thus, it is not surprising that many evaluation studies have focused on gain scores.

The prominence of growth in student achievement can be readily discerned by even a casual inspection of evaluation reports. For example, it is claimed in a description of one of the largest currently ongoing educational evaluation studies that the three-year longitudinal design of the study will make it "possible not only to assess student growth over a three year period, but to relate this growth to the kinds and amounts of instruction being received" (Hoepfner, Zagorsky, & Wellisch, 1977, p. xv).

Descriptions of student gains are often phrased in terms of some implicit notion of expected normal growth, typically by reliance on the infamous grade-equivalent score. Thus, the National Advisory Council on the Education of Disadvantaged Children was consistent with common practice in claiming that the recent National Institute of Education Study of Compensatory Education "indicated that first graders in the sample made average gains of 12 months in reading and 11 months in mathematics, in the 7 month period between fall and spring testing" (no date, p. 8).

Change is certainly fundamental to any notion of learning, and determining the effects of programs on student learning is one of the most commonly stated purposes of mandated evaluations of educational programs. This is clearly indicated in the descriptions of the Title I evaluation models. "The focus of all the models is to obtain as clear and unambiguous an answer as possible to the question, 'How much more did pupils learn by participating in the Title I project than they would have learned without it?'" (Tallmadge & Wood, 1976, p. 2).

Despite the prominence of change in descriptions of the purposes of evaluation studies and of the projects to be evaluated, the seemingly obvious and intuitively appealing calculation of gain scores is not necessarily the best approach to answering questions about project impact. Gain scores sometimes have disadvantages compared to other alternatives. They are often relied upon to compensate for deficiencies in experimental design by implicitly assuming that they provide the appropriate adjustment for preexisting group differences. There is no guarantee, however, that gain scores will provide the appropriate adjustment. By giving the illusion that preexisting differences have been taken care of, gain scores may merely conceal limitations that are inherent in the design (Linn & Slinde, 1977).

The purpose of this chapter is to review some of the major issues that arise in the measurement of change. Particular attention will be given to topics, such as the characteristics of scales that are frequently used with educational achievement tests, that have special importance in educational evaluation studies. Some alternative approaches, such as residualized gain scores, will also be considered. Finally, some recommendations will be offered.

REVIEW OF STRATEGIES FOR MEASURING CHANGE

Two Properties of Difference Scores

The measurement of change has intrigued psychometricians for years and has attracted some of the leaders of the field to work on problems that are associated with this special category of measurement. This effort has resulted in some rather sophisticated methods for estimating "true" change. It has also resulted in a fairly general awareness that there are problems associated with the measurement of change. Two of the most commonly discussed and best known problems are those of reliability and of a systematic relationship between measures of change and initial status. Since these problems are well known they will be only briefly described here.

When a pretest is administered at time 1 and a posttest at time 2, the most obvious measure of change is simply a difference score. If Y_{i1} is the pretest score for student i and Y_{i2} is the posttest score, then the raw difference score, D_i, is simply

$$D_i = Y_{i2} - Y_{i1}.$$

Difference scores are typically unreliable and have a nonzero correlation with initial status (i.e., with Y_{i1}).

Reliability.   Given classical test theory assumptions, the reliability of a difference score, ρ_{DD}, can be expressed in terms of the variance and reliability of the pretest, σ_1^2 and ρ_{11}, respectively, the corresponding values for the posttest, σ_2^2 and ρ_{22}, and the correlation between the pretest and posttest, ρ_{12}. This well-known formula is

$$\rho_{DD} = \frac{\rho_{11}\sigma_1^2 + \rho_{22}\sigma_2^2 - 2\rho_{12}\sigma_1\sigma_2}{\sigma_1^2 + \sigma_2^2 - 2\rho_{12}\rho_1\rho_2}.$$

A high correlation between pretest and posttest tends to produce a low difference-score reliability. This is most readily seen by considering the special case where $\sigma_1 = \sigma_2$ and $\rho_{11} = \rho_{22} = \rho$. For this special case,

$$\rho_{DD} = \frac{\rho - \rho_{12}}{1 - \rho_{12}},$$

and it is apparent that the difference-score reliability will approach zero as ρ_{12} approaches ρ. For example, for a test with a common variance and a reliability of .8 when used as a pretest and as a posttest, the reliability of the difference score would be .60, .50, .33, and .00 when the pretest-posttest correlation was .5, .6, .7, and .8, respectively.

Low reliability of a difference score is a serious problem where difference scores are used to make decisions about individuals. But decisions about individual students are not the function of educational evaluation. For groups, the reliability problem is a much less serious concern. Thus, this feature of difference scores, for which they are most frequently maligned, is not a fatal flaw within the context of educational evaluation studies.

Correlation with initial status. The second commonly cited problem with difference scores is that they generally will have a nonzero correlation with the pretest. This is viewed as a disadvantage because an implicit goal in the use of difference scores is often to remove or adjust for initial differences and thereby make it possible to compare the gains of individuals or groups that started with unequal pretest scores.

The correlation between a difference score and the pretest score, ρ_{D1}, is given by

$$\rho_{D1} = \frac{\rho_{12}\,\sigma_2 - \sigma_1}{\sqrt{\sigma_1^{\,2} + \sigma_2^{\,2} - 2\rho_{12}\,\sigma_1\,\sigma_2}}.$$

It is apparent that the correlation of the difference score with the pretest score will equal zero only under the special condition that

$$\sigma_1 = \rho_{12}\,\sigma_2.$$

If the pretest variance is equal to the posttest variance, the correlation of the difference score with the pretest will necessarily be negative because the correlation between the pretest and posttest will be less than 1.0. With a negative value of ρ_{D1}, people or groups with low pretest scores will tend to have larger gains than people with high pretest scores. Thus, in an evaluation study where comparisons are made of the gains achieved by two groups that differ in pretest performance, the initially lower scoring group has a built-in advantage.

The sign of the correlation between difference and pretest scores depends on the pretest and posttest variances that in turn depend, in part, on the scale properties of the test. Where the variance remains fairly constant, a negative correlation is to be expected. Some types of scales, most notably grade-equivalent scales, have variances that tend to increase with grade level. If the posttest variance is enough larger than the pretest variance, the correlation between the difference score and the pretest may be positive rather than negative, as is more commonly expected. A positive correlation would obviously give a built-in advantage to the initially higher scoring group when comparisons are made in terms of simple difference scores.

Alternatives to Difference Scores

The two most commonly suggested alternatives to simple difference scores for estimating student growth in achievement are ''residualized change scores'' and estimates of true change. The latter estimates involve the use of regression analysis and depend upon classical test theory assumptions about true scores and error scores underlying the observed pretest and posttest scores. The residualized change scores are motivated by the desire to obtain gain scores that are uncorrelated with initial status.

Residualized change scores achieve the goal of being uncorrelated with initial status, but as noted by several authors (e.g. Rogosa, in press) they are not really measures of change. Rather, they are simply measures of whether a person's posttest score is larger or smaller than the value predicted for that person using the linear regression of the posttest on the pretest. Expressed in terms of change, residual scores provide a way of identifying individuals who changed more or less than expected on the basis of the person's initial status (Cronbach & Furby, 1970).

Rogosa has criticized the use of residualized change scores because they do not correspond to measures of individual growth curves and because their usefulness is limited to two-wave data, i.e., measures taken at only two points in time. The latter criticism is of concern, of course, only in situations where measures are taken more than twice, which, while desirable, is not the norm in evaluation studies. The first criticism is more telling because it concerns not just the generalizability of the approach, but the conceptual interpretation of the scores.

Since residualized change scores are not in fact measures of change, it would be better to refer to them simply as residual scores (Linn & Slinde, 1977). These scores are one of several types of scores that might be considered for use in an evaluation. To call them growth measures or change scores only tends to confuse the issue.

An estimated true change score can be thought of as a ''corrected'' measure of change within the context of classical test theory. Procedures for estimating true change are described by Lord (1963) and Cronbach and Furby (1970), as well as by several other authors. A major practical drawback of this approach for most evaluators is the requirement that reliability estimates be available for both the pretest and the posttest. Good estimates of reliability for the sample involved in the study are often unavailable. It is unwise to use reliabilities based on other samples, such as the norm group, for example. It is also unwise to use the wrong type of reliability coefficient. For example, internal consistency reliabilities may yield results that are quite misleading for achievement tests that have somewhat heterogeneous content.

Kenny (1975, 1979) has presented an argument for another alternative to raw difference scores. He proposed the use of standardized change scores, which are simply difference scores between pretest and posttest scores that have been standardized, i.e., have means of zero and unit variances. Since standardized difference scores are based on pretest scores and posttest scores with variances that have been set equal, it is clear that the correlation of the standardized difference score with initial status will be negative.

Standardized difference scores are closely related to some other procedures that have been suggested for use in evaluation studies that are specifically dependent on a particular scale of measurement. In particular, they share some aspects of the rationale that has been used to support the use of Normal Curve Equivalent scores (Tallmadge & Wood, 1976) with one of the currently recommended Title I evaluation models. Thus, further discussion of the use of standardized difference scores will be postponed until after consideration of some of the scale properties of standardized achievement tests.

Models of Change

Discussions of change bring growth curves to mind almost immediately. Growth curves have been plotted to show changes in physical characteristics, such as height and weight as a function of age. Plots have also been used for many years to show growth curves in "mental age" on intelligence tests and in several other types of scores on other types of tests. Although there are important distinctions to be made in growth curves for measures such as height and ones for test scores, both types have considerable descriptive utility. It is also conceptually very appealing to imagine evaluating educational programs in terms of their effects on student achievement growth curves.

An individual's height can be measured repeatedly over a period of time with reasonable accuracy and with little or no concern that the scale is changing, that the construct that is being measured is changing, or that the process of measurement is altering the course of the growth curve. In measures of educational achievement one cannot be very sanguine about any of these concerns. Nonetheless, the notion of plotting growth curves, describing their characteristics, and evaluating programs in terms of their effects on growth curves is conceptually appealing.

A growth curve is basic to a model that represents the level of a variable as a function of time. The steepness of the curve, or rate of change, is an important property of the growth curve. The rate of change is, of course, given by the derivative of the function corresponding to the growth curve with respect to time.

The simplest type of growth model is based on the assumption that the level of the variable of interest is a linear function of time. For each individual, the growth curve for such a simple model would be characterized by two parameters, the slope and the intercept. The slope, of course, is the rate of change. As pointed out by Rogosa (in press), the slope for two-wave data is estimated by the difference between the posttest and the pretest score divided by the difference in the time points. For convenience, the time difference may be defined as one unit of time that makes the raw difference between the posttest and pretest scores equal to the estimated slope of the growth curve.

The above provides a formal rationale for the use of a simple difference score as an estimate of the rate of change of an individual's growth curve. It should be recognized, however, that this interpretation depends on a simplistic linear growth model. On the other hand, it may be argued that a linear model may provide a reasonable approximation to a more complex growth curve over the interval between the pretest and the posttest. Furthermore, with measurements at only two times, there is no data basis for evaluating more complex growth models as alternatives to a linear growth model.

The weakness of a difference score as a measure of the rate of change is merely a reflection of the weakness of two-wave data for measuring growth curves. There simply are not enough data points to adequately describe a growth curve. In keeping with this perspective, Rogosa (in press) concluded that "The difficulties with . . . [difference scores] are due to the severe limitations of two-wave data for the assessment of change especially when the data are fallible." Unfortunately, as was already noted, two-wave data is the norm rather than the exception in evaluations of program effects on educational achievement. Thus, it is important to judge the utility of measures of change within that context.

Bryk and Weisberg (1976) have suggested a "value-added" approach to estimating the effects of educational treatments. Their approach is based on the use of a growth model to estimate the amount of growth that would be expected for a group participating in an educational program if they did not participate but instead were in the "regular" or "comparison" program. The actual change of the participants is compared to the expected change and the difference is the "value added."

Several techniques that have been suggested for adjusting posttest scores for differences in pretest scores in order to compare nonequivalent control groups were investigated by Bryk and Weisberg (1977) using varying assumptions about the "natural growth" curves for program and comparison groups. They convincingly demonstrated "that the choice of an appropriate analysis method is highly sensitive to assumptions about the nature of individual growth" (Bryk & Weisberg, 1977, p. 960).

Given a model of growth, the adequacy of difference scores, analysis of covariance, or some other approach to making adjustments for preexisting

differences can be evaluated. Unfortunately, however, little is known about
the appropriateness of various possible models of growth on which the evaluations depend. The value-added approach suggested by Bryk and Weisberg
(1976) and extended and elaborated by Bryk, Strenio, and Weisberg (1980) is
promising. It is tailored to the situation that is often confronted by the educational evaluator; but it requires a good model of natural growth. Building such
models would be greatly enhanced by the accumulation of multi-wave data.
Two-wave data, as was already noted, provide too limited a basis for model
building or for the evaluation of growth models.

Multi-wave data can help resolve some issues regarding models for growth
curves. Some special difficulties that are associated with the measurement of
student achievement would also need to be confronted to make the conceptually appealing value-added approach widely applicable, however. Bryk and
Weisberg (1976; Bryk et al., 1980) mentioned two of these special difficulties. These are the difficulty of finding a suitable metric for standardized tests
and the difficulty of developing a growth model that allows for the jagged
pattern caused by shifts in growth rates during summer vacations.

Another difficulty that is encountered in the measurement of achievement
that does not arise with physical measures such as height is caused by the need
to change the level of the test as students advance through the grades. A
reading test that provides good measurement for first graders will be much too
easy to provide useful measurement for most fourth graders, much less students in higher grades. To use different test levels to measure growth requires
that scores on the different levels can be equated on a common scale. As will
be shown below, however, such equating is often problematic.

The special difficulties associated with standardized achievement tests have
implications for attempts to measure change whether or not the measures are
to be used within the context of explicit models of growth, as is required in the
value-added approach. Therefore, some of these special difficulties are considered in greater detail in the following sections of this paper.

Test Score Metrics

The raw score (i.e., the number of items that a student answers correctly)
on a standardized test is usually thought to have little direct meaning by itself.
This is so because there is usually no good basis for generalizing to a clearly
defined achievement domain. Consequently, a variety of derived scores are
traditionally used to enhance the meaning of the results of a test administration. Derived scores are transformations of raw scores that typically provide
information about a student's relative standing in comparison to the performance of a norm group. Examples of derived scores are grade equivalents,
stanines, percentile ranks, standard scores, T-scores, and more recently normal curve equivalents. In addition, most test publishers have their own special
scaled scores. No attempt will be made to review all of these. Only the salient

features of a few of the more popular ones that are relevant to the measurement of growth will be considered.

Grade-equivalent score (GES). Much has been written criticizing the GES (see, for example, Angoff, 1971; Horst, 1976; Linn & Slinde, 1977). Despite the criticisms the popularity of these scores has continued almost unabated. Much of the popularity as well as much of the criticism stems from a common characteristic, namely, the fact that the GES invites seemingly simple but misleading interpretations. One such interpretation is that the expected normal growth for a student should be one grade-equivalent unit in a year's time. This notion is so ingrained in many people's thinking that it is sometimes used as the standard for evaluating the effect of a program. David and Pelavin (1977, p. 5), for example, refer to "one grade-equivalent month gained for each month in the program" as the "unofficial Title I standard for success."

Although it is intuitively reasonable to think that a month's gain should be expected in a month's time, the amount of GES growth that is typically observed is markedly different for students with low pretest scores than for students with high pretest scores. A gain of a grade-equivalent month in a month's time may be a reasonable expectation for a student with a pretest score near the 50th percentile. But it is too high to reasonably expect as the typical result for students with pretest scores well below average and too low for students with pretest scores well above the average.

Because the standard deviation of GESs increases as a function of grade level, students who maintain a constant relative standing in comparison to the norm group will tend to gain more or less than one GES unit per year depending on whether their relative standing is above or below the 50th percentile (Coleman & Karweit, 1970; Prescott, 1973). The exact size of GES gain that is required to maintain a constant relative standing in comparison to the norm group varies a good deal from publisher to publisher and from one content area to another (Linn & Slinde, 1977). The tendency is quite clear and in the same direction regardless of content areas or publisher, however. Prescott's (1973) finding that .67 GES gain per year would be sufficient to maintain a constant percentile rank of 24 is not at all unusual. In view of this result, and the fact that most participants in compensatory education programs start the programs with pretest scores that are below the median, one should hardly be surprised that one empirically based estimate of the average annual growth rate of disadvantaged students is only .7 rather than the commonly assumed 1.0 (David & Pelavin, 1977).

Percentile rank (PR). Raw scores on a test are commonly converted to percentile ranks. The percentile rank provides information about a person's relative standing in comparison to a norm group in a direct and easily understood fashion. It has also been suggested as a means of determining if individuals or groups are changing more or less than is typical.

Separate norms corresponding to the time of measurement are needed in order to use percentile ranks for purposes of measuring change. The use of percentile ranks for this purpose is based on an assumption that under normal conditions a student or group of students should be expected to maintain the same relative standing from one testing to the next. In keeping with this assumption, the efficacy of an intervention program would be judged in terms of whether or not there was a shift in the mean percentile rank of the participants in the program. A program would be judged to have a positive effect if the participants had higher percentile ranks (defined in terms of norms appropriate to the time of testing) on the posttest than on the pretest.

Even if the assumption that normal growth is defined as maintaining a constant percentile rank is accepted, there are good reasons to prefer other metrics for purposes of analysis. By definition, a distribution of percentile ranks is rectangular in the group for which they are derived. In order to achieve this distribution, raw scores in the middle of the distribution typically must be spread out while those at the extremes are squeezed together. For example, on one widely used test of math concepts, a single additional correct answer would result in an increase from the 50th to the 56th percentile rank. On the other hand, the same increase in percentile rank would require three additional correct answers at the high and low ends of the distribution. The metric limitations of the percentile rank scale led Coleman and Karweit (1970) to the conclusion that the potential utility of this type of score is limited to indicating the direction of change compared to the norm. It was not considered appropriate for measuring the amount of change.

Normal curve equivalent (NCE). The NCE score was introduced for use in the Title I Evaluation and Reporting System. NCEs are normalized standard scores with a mean of 50 and a standard deviation of 21.06. They are allowed to range from 1 to 99 and have the same numerical value as a percentile rank at scores of 1, 50, and 99. At other scale points the two types of scores do not correspond. Indeed, one of the motivations for the NCE is to remove the metric limitation of percentile ranks that was just discussed. Unlike the percentile ranks, the NCEs are assumed to have an equal-interval scale (Tallmadge & Wood, 1976) and therefore it may be considered more appropriate to aggregate and average NCEs than percentile ranks.

The NCE scale is fundamentally the same as a normalized Z-score, T-score, or stanine, albeit considerably finer-grained than the last-named. It was selected for discussion here because it is the scale to be used in reporting Title I evaluation results. The comments apply equally to other types of normalized standard scores, however.

Three models, each with variations for norm-referenced and criterion-referenced tests, are recommended for use in the Title I Evaluation and Reporting System. The most used of these is model A, also known as the Norm-Referenced model. Model A is most germane to the present discussion because its validity rests upon an underlying assumption about student growth.

In model A the effect of a Title I project is estimated by comparing the average NCE posttest score of participants to the "no-treatment expectation." The no-treatment expectation is merely the average NCE pretest score. In other words, it is assumed that without participation in the project the group would maintain the same relative standing in comparison to the norm group on which the NCE scores are based. Except for the metric used in the calculation of the average, this assumption is equivalent to the assumption that "normal growth" means the maintenance of a constant percentile rank. It is also similar to Kenny's (1975) use of standardized gain scores to compare program participants with nonparticipants.

There is a certain intuitive appeal to the assumption that in the absence of special interventions students will tend to maintain the same relative standing in achievement. Intuitive appeal is not a very adequate basis for an evaluation system, however. Furthermore, even if the assumption were justified under idealized conditions, it still would be likely to lead to biased estimates of project effects as it is implemented in practice.

As Echternacht (1978, p. 2) aptly observed, model A "is not well regarded by psychologists, psychometricians, or statisticians although perhaps because of its simplicity, [it] is extremely popular with state departments of education and local school districts." The poor regard for model A by many technically oriented people is understandable. The model rests on a strong assumption for which there is no adequate basis. Furthermore, there is no good reason to expect that application of the model will yield positively biased estimates due to regression effects (Echternacht, 1978; Linn, 1979, 1980; Murray, 1978). When students are selected according to their standing on some indicator of achievement, whether that indicator is teacher judgment or a test, the group will regress toward the mean on any correlated measure of achievement obtained at a later point in time. The lower the correlation between the measure used for selecting participants and the subsequent measure, the greater the regression toward the mean.

Because of the regression effect, proper implementation of model A requires that the pretest be given to participants after they have been selected, or, at least, not be used in any way in the selection process.

This requirement is helpful because the pretest as well as the posttest will display a regression toward the mean. However, as Gene Glass (personal communication) has noted, the regression effect for the pretest will not equal the regression effect for the posttest unless the selection measure has the same correlation with the posttest as it does with the pretest. This is most unlikely. It is well known that correlations between tests given close together tend to be higher than those between tests given further apart in time. Thus, it is reasonable to expect that the selection measure will correlate higher with the pretest than with the posttest. Consequently, there will be more regression toward the mean on the posttest than on the pretest, which will result in an overestimate of the effect of Title I. (Linn, 1979, p. 26)

Although the regression effect leads to an expectation of bias in the direction of overestimating project effects, other factors may have the opposite effect. In general, the constant NCE approach to evaluation is considered "most appropriate where the treatment-group children are highly similar in terms of age, race, ethnic background, socioeconomic status and other educationally relevant variables to the children in the norming sample" (Tallmadge & Wood, 1976, p. 39). By their very nature, however, special programs are often designed for groups that are quite dissimilar to the usual norming sample. Due to this dissimilarity, the expectations based on the norms may be too high or too low (Linn, 1979, 1980; Storlie et al., 1979).

In summary, the constant NCE approach to defining normal growth and thereby providing a means for project evaluation lacks an adequate justification. In some applications it may be seriously defective and result in biased estimates of the effects of an educational program.

Scaled scores. Most publishers report scores that, under certain assumptions, can be assumed to be on an equal-interval scale. These scales are variously labeled (e.g. Expanded Standard Score Scale, Achievement Development Scale Scores, Growth Scale, or simply Scale Score). The most commonly used approach to developing these scales is Thurstone's absolute scaling method (Gulliksen, 1950, pp. 284–286; Thurstone, 1925). The equal-interval claim is based on the assumption that at any grade level the distribution of achievement would be normal if the scores were expressed in an equal-interval scale. The scale development procedure involves the normalizing of a series of score distributions at different grade levels on the same baseline. Once a suitable transformation is obtained, the units can be arbitrarily defined to produce some convenient scale (e.g., one with a mean of 200 and a standard deviation of 40 at a particular grade level).

Scaled scores are commonly used as the basis for expressing scores on different levels of the test on the same metric. As implied by some of the names used for scaled scores, the resulting scores, which are said to be "vertically equated," are intended to allow the measurement of growth in terms of the scaled scores across all levels of the test.

Scaled scores are generally preferable to the derived scores considered previously for purposes of measuring growth. Due to the use of arbitrarily defined units, these scales do not usually suffer from the surplus meaning that is associated with grade-equivalent scores. Although there is no reason to believe that the equal interval assumption is completely justified, it is more plausible than an assumption that either a grade-equivalent or a percentile rank scale has equal intervals. Unlike percentile ranks and normal curve equivalent scales, one need not know the time of testing or the particular norm group used in order to interpret the resulting scores.

Scaled scores, while generally the best choice for measuring growth, still lack any claim of being an absolute scale. Also, as is discussed below, there are special problems encountered when the level of the test is changed regardless of the nature of the scale.

Latent trait scales. Although it does not provide the basis for scaling and equating that is currently used with the most popular standardized achievement tests, latent trait theory is conceptually very appealing for these purposes. A number of authors (see, for example, the special issue of the *Journal of Educational Measurement* on latent trait theory, summer 1977) have suggested that latent trait models provide a means of solving many difficult measurement problems. Particularly relevant in the present context are the potential uses of these models for scaling and equating.

One of the simplest and most popular of the latent trait models is Rasch's (1960) logistic model. The Rasch model involves only one parameter per item (item difficulty or its reciprocal, item easiness) and one parameter per person (person ability). According to the model, the probability, P_{ig}, that person i will get item g correct is a function of only two parameters: one for the person's ability and one for the item's difficulty. Part of the appeal of this model comes from the properties that Wright (1967) has referred to as "person-free item calibration" and "item-free person measurement." These are invariance properties and refer respectively to the expectation that the item parameters should be invariant regardless of the group of examinees used for calibration and person ability should be invariant regardless of the set of items included on the test. This latter property is particularly appealing in the context of measuring change because different sets of commonly calibrated items could be used in repeated testings, but the estimates of person ability would be on a common scale.

If the data fit the model, it is clear that equated scores from hard and easy tests could be readily obtained and growth could be plotted over extended periods of time, using increasingly difficult subsets of items. It is also clear, however, that the model will not be completely appropriate for any given set of items. As is true of most latent trait models, the Rasch model rests upon the assumption that the items are unidimensional, i.e., that only a single latent trait is needed. The model also assumes that all items are equally discriminating and that the probability of getting an item right will approach zero for examinees of sufficiently low ability. None of these assumptions can be expected to hold exactly for achievement test items. The important question, however, is not whether the assumptions are precisely satisfied, but whether the model holds to a sufficiently good approximation to yield useful results with actual test data.

In this regard, Slinde and Linn (1979b) found that the Rasch model provided relatively good equating of pairs of tests designed for adjacent grade levels. The good equating was obtained despite a considerable lack of fit of the data to the model. On the other hand, equating for tests that differ more drastically in difficulty with groups that are more widely separated in ability is more problematic (Slinde & Linn, 1979a).

The Rasch model is only one of several latent trait models that are currently being actively researched. There is some controversy over the pros and cons of the various models and their range of applicability. A review of these models and the research related to them is beyond the scope of this paper. A relatively recent and comprehensive review is available (Hambleton et al., 1978). Their conclusion "that latent trait theory offers the promise for solving many problems that arise in mental measurement" (p. 503) seems to be well justified.

Proportion correct. Many of the problems associated with grade equivalents, normal curve equivalents, and percentile ranks result because they are all measures of relative standing. Consequently they lack some of the advantages of an absolute measure. Relative standing metrics are used with standardized achievement tests largely because absolute metrics such as number of correct answers are generally thought to lack meaning. Under special circumstances, however, absolute metrics can be quite meaningful.

The proportion of items that a student can answer correctly becomes meaningful to the extent that the content domain becomes well defined. If a domain of items exists either implicitly in the form of a set of item generation rules (e.g., Hively et al., 1973) or explicitly in an exhaustive listing of the items, then it is possible to draw random or stratified random samples of items from the domain. Computer generated tests are possible with either an exhaustive listing of the item domain or a well specified set of item generation rules. There are examples of computer generated spelling items (e.g., Fremer & Anastasio, 1969) and reading tests have been produced using randomly selected paragraphs and the cloze procedure. More recently, Millman (1980) has provided an example of computer-generated test items of higher-level cognitive skills. This approach makes it possible to draw random samples of items that may be used to construct an achievement test for which the proportion correct score "is an unbiased (and maximum likelihood) point estimate of the proportion of items in the domain which the student can handle adequately" (Harris, Pearlman, & Wilcox, 1977, p. 3). Where this is possible, the proportion correct, or some transformation of it, provides a "natural" and meaningful metric.

Given a well-defined universe of items, students can be tested repeatedly with independent random samples of items from the universe. Each sample can be used to provide an "estimate of the proportion of items that the student can handle adequately" at a given time. These estimates can, in turn, be used as the basis for obtaining growth curves. Where this process is feasible it has great advantages and avoids altogether the special problems associated with relative standing metrics. The catch, of course, is that content domains are only rarely defined in sufficient detail to permit the construction of tests by the random sampling of items. Thus, the application of this approach is currently limited to a few, typically rather narrowly defined, content domains.

Interval between Pretest and Posttest

The interval between the administration of the pretest and the posttest requires special attention when measuring change in student achievement, especially if any of the usual relative standing metrics are used. It is common for educational projects to be evaluated using a fall pretest followed by a spring posttest. This practice, however, has been called into question by several people in the past few years. David and Pelavin (1977), for example, found inconsistencies between the apparent effectiveness of programs when effectiveness was judged in terms of 12-month (fall to fall) gains in achievement rather than the more common school-year (fall to spring) gains. Programs analyzed were less likely to be judged effective in terms of 12-month gains than they were in terms of school-year gains.

There are a number of possible reasons that 12-month and school-year gains may yield disparate indications. Among the many possibilities are artifacts due to test publisher assumptions about school-year and summer growth rates, differences in level of the test used for the spring posttest and the one used for the fall pretest, and the temporary nature of the program effects. The primary concern here is with the first of these possibilities.

Traditionally, publishers normed tests through a single administration during the school year. Normatively derived scores for other testing dates were usually obtained by linear interpolation with the three summer months treated as a single month. That is, it was assumed that growth was linear for the 9-month school year and that one additional month's gain was made during the summer. In recent years, due largely to the demand for empirically derived fall and spring norms created by the requirements of the Title I Evaluation and Reporting System, more publishers are using twice a year norming. Projections are still required for other testing dates.

A comparison of projections based on once-a-year testing in the fall, once-a-year testing in the spring, or on twice-a-year testing reveal substantial differences. This can readily be seen using results reported by Beck (1975) for the *Metropolitan Achievement Test* (*MAT*). Longitudinal samples were tested in the fall and spring for a subsample of the sample that was used to create fall and spring norms for the *MAT*. The longitudinal sample at each grade ranged from 1,468 to 2,860 and was generally quite similar to the complete norming sample in terms of socioeconomic characteristics.

Fall testing was conducted in October and spring testing was conducted in April. Thus, there is approximately six months between fall and spring and an

FIGURE 4.1. Fall to Spring and Spring to Fall differences in standard score means
for the *Metropolitan Achievement Tests* (based on results reported
by Beck, 1975).

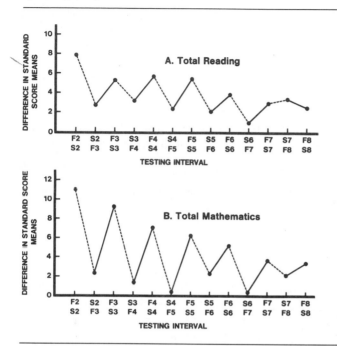

equal amount of time between spring and fall testing dates. A comparison of
mean scores on the MAT standard score scale reveals a consistent tendency
for there to be a substantially larger difference in means from fall to spring
than from spring to fall. The fall-to-spring and spring-to-fall differences in
means are plotted in Figure 4.1 for Total Reading and Total Mathematics
scores for grades 2 through 8. The zigzag effect, with larger differences
between fall and spring than between spring and fall, is apparent.

As might be expected, the zigzag pattern is somewhat sharper for mathematics than for reading. This may be the result of relatively less practice and
learning of mathematics than reading over the summer months. It should be
noted that the spring-to-fall interval includes a substantial amount of time in
school (early fall and late spring) as well as summer vacation. It should also be
noted that the spring-to-fall differences are based on cross-sectional comparisons whereas the fall-to-spring differences are based on longitudinal differences. Despite these limitations, it is evident that a linear growth model is
not very reasonable over intervals involving both summer vacation and time in
school. Even the harshest critics of schools could hardly expect that cognitive

growth would be as rapid during months spent out of school as it is during months spent in school.

Another implication of the results in Figure 4.1 is that norms projected on the basis of fall-to-fall linear interpolations would be quite different from the corresponding projections based on spring-to-spring interpolations. Neither of the once-a-year projections would be very similar to the ones based on twice-a-year administrations.

The results in Figure 4.1 also suggest that a loss in performance, especially in mathematics, might be expected during the summer. The question of whether "growth" in achievement over the summer is positive or negative, especially for relatively low scoring students participating in compensatory education programs, has become a rather controversial issue in recent years. With regard to this issue, the results in Figure 4.1 are suggestive but cannot be considered very conclusive, partially because the spring-to-fall differences are based on cross-sectional data. Thus, the apparent summer loss could be attributed, at least in part, to cohort differences.

Results for longitudinal samples with testing in fall 1976, spring 1977, and fall 1977 were reported by Hammond and Frechtling (1979). Mean fall-to-spring and fall-to-fall gains on the Reading and Mathematics tests of the *Comprehensive Tests of Basic Skills* (*CTBS*) were reported for two samples: one tested initially in the fall of grade 1 and the other in the fall of grade 3. The Hammond and Frechtling results not only have the advantage of being longitudinal over three time points, but have a somewhat smaller interval between the spring and fall testing dates than was used for the results presented in Figure 4.1. The spring-to-fall interval was approximately 20 weeks in the Hammond and Frechtling results.

The mean gains, expressed in *CTBS* Expanded Standard Scores, are plotted in Figure 4.2. As can be seen, there is essentially no difference between the spring grade 1 and fall grade 2 means for either reading or mathematics. At grades 3 to 4 there is no gain from spring to fall in mathematics but there is a noticeable increase in reading.

Results such as those shown in Figure 4.2 provide only a rudimentary basis for developing models of achievement growth. Three points are much better than two for defining a growth curve, but still very limited, especially when there are indications that the rate of growth dips during the summer and accelerates during the school year. The problem of pinning down summer and school-year rates of growth is further complicated by the fact that fall and spring measures are not taken at literally the beginning and end of the school year. In the Hammond and Frechtling study, fall tests were administered one or two weeks after the beginning of school and spring tests were administered six to eight weeks before the end of school. Thus, the spring-to-fall differences may not provide a very good indication of summer growth patterns

FIGURE 4.2. Mean gains on the *Comprehensive Tests of Basic Skills* from Fall 1976 to Spring 1977 and Fall 1977 (based on results reported by Hammond & Frechtling, 1979). Legend: O———O Reading; O----O Mathematics.

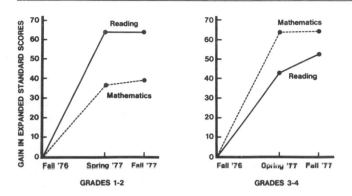

because about eight weeks of the regular school year is included in this interval.

Vertical Equating

A test designed for third- and fourth-grade students is apt to show a marked ceiling effect if administered to fifth graders. Students obviously could not continue to show much growth as measured by such a test in grade 6 and beyond. The material on the test will already have been mastered by many of the students by grade 5. Measuring growth for these students requires the introduction of new more difficult items. It is simple enough to find a more difficult test that has enough top for the students to display continued growth in grades 6 and 7. It is much more difficult, however, to be sure that scores on that more difficult test are equated with those on the easier test so that it makes sense to plot and interpret growth curves with some points based on the easier and others based on the harder test.

Equating tests that are designed to differ in difficulty is called vertical equating. Tests that are designed to measure achievement at different grade levels differ not only in the difficulty but in the content specifications for the items. Although the tests maintain the same name and are reported on a single scale, it is not always clear that the same ability is being measured, much less that the scales are, in fact, equivalent (Slinde & Linn, 1977).

Strictly speaking, equated tests should be completely exchangeable in the sense that it should be a matter of complete indifference which form of the test is administered to an examinee. It is apparent that this strict definition cannot be achieved in vertical equating. Indeed, the very purpose for having different levels is to make the test more appropriate for the examinee.

Often the goal of exchangeability is only crudely approximated, and abrupt shifts in scaled test scores can occur as the result of administering a different level of the test. For example, at one grade level the 79th percentile on a reading comprehension test (which has since been revised) was associated with a grade-equivalent score that was .6 higher on the higher-level form than on the lower-level form. At the 21st percentile, however, the higher-level form would yield a grade-equivalent score .5 lower than the one associated with the 21st percentile on the lower-level form. Shifts of this magnitude, or for that matter much smaller magnitudes, would play havoc with attempts to develop meaningful growth curves.

The anomalies caused by changing levels of the test are usually less severe than the one just mentioned, but are still apt to be of sufficient magnitude to require that test level be taken into account in evaluating growth curves. The problem is most severe when there are floor or ceiling effects for the form of a test used at one or more of the administrations (see Cole & Nitko, chapter 2).

Pelavin and Barker (1976) reported results of experimental administrations of different levels of the *Metropolitan Achievement Tests* (*MAT*). Grade 4 students were administered the Primary II *MAT Reading Test* in October. In December these students were administered both the next higher (Elementary) and next lower (Primary I) level of the *MAT Reading Test*. Half the students took the Elementary followed by the Primary I in the December administration while the other half took the tests in the opposite order. A similar pattern was followed at grades 5 and 6 but with combinations of the Primary II, Elementary, and Intermediate levels.

The means on the *MAT* Expanded Standard Score scale are plotted in Figure 4.3 for each of the administrations reported by Pelavin and Barker (1976). The numbers identifying the level of the test are connected by dotted, dashed, or solid lines for different levels. At each December administration the mean for the higher-level test is above that of the lower-level test. At grades 4 and 6 the December means on the lower-level test are also somewhat below those obtained on the higher-level test administered two months earlier. This pattern does not hold at grade 5, however.

The Pelavin and Barker results suggest that the level of the test may have an effect on the mean score obtained by a group. These results are consistent with findings reported by Slinde and Linn (1977) and by Ayrer and McNamara (1973). The magnitude of the difference in test level is apt to be greatest where there are floor or ceiling effects when a particular level of the test is administered. Even where differences due to test level are relatively small, the effects on growth curves could still be important. It is true that the differences generally are not large in comparison to the magnitude of simple errors of

FIGURE 4.3. Mean expanded standard scores as a function of test administration date for different levels of the *MAT Reading Test* (based
on Pelavin & Barker, 1976).

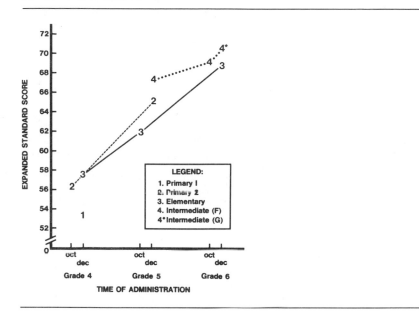

measurement. It should be noted, however, that equating errors, unlike errors
of measurement, are systematic. It cannot be assumed that they will cancel
out with large samples as is often appropriately assumed in the case of errors
of measurement.

SUGGESTIONS FOR FUTURE RESEARCH

Most work on the measurement of change has devoted little or no attention
to models of growth. But good models of growth seem crucial to measuring
and interpreting measures of change. The work of Bryk and Weisberg (1976,
1977; Bryk et al., 1980) provides a good example of the potential benefits that
can be derived from an approach that constructs a model of growth against
which the ''value added'' by an educational program can be evaluated. Developing sound models of growth, especially for growth in measured
achievement over the school years, will require considerable research.

In order to develop better models of student growth in academic achievement, measures at more than two points in time are needed. Repeated measurements over shorter time intervals are needed both before and after an
intervention. Such a possibility hardly seems feasible using conventional

standardized tests and administration patterns. The development and use of item banks, however, hold much more promise for this purpose.

Item banks will be most useful when they either (1) consist of domains of items that are completely specified through item generation rules or exhaustive listing, or (2) consist of pools of items that have been calibrated using a latent-trait model which has been demonstrated to be adequate for the pool of items. Under either of these conditions, multiple test forms can be constructed using item-sampling principles.

For estimating a group-level growth curve, frequent measures could be obtained efficiently using small independent random samples of items for each person. By keeping the number of items small for each person the measurement burden is kept to a minimum. But, by using different samples of items, the group estimate can be made reasonably precise. Frequent measurement would obviate the need for unfounded assumptions such as a linear growth curve between pretest and posttest.

Very small samples of items per individual student at each testing would limit the ability to plot individual growth curves, owing to the large sampling error associated with each measurement. Although good estimates of individual growth curves would have potential value (e.g., Bryk & Weisberg, 1976, p. 131), the price of obtaining such estimates will often be too high to pay. Just having better estimates of group-level growth curves would be an important step forward, however.

Research is also needed that will provide a better understanding of scale properties of measures used to measure achievement. In particular, the effects of changing levels of achievement tests need to be closely examined. Vertical equating is essential if sound models of growth are to be developed over extended periods of time that involve changes in levels of tests. The vertical equating of currently used achievement tests, however, is often problematic (Slinde & Linn, 1977). Approaches based on item-characteristic curve theory (e.g., Lord, 1977; Wright, 1977) are promising, but considerable research is needed to better understand the limits of applicability of these models and the practical advantages and disadvantages of alternative models for the vertical equating problem.

GUIDELINES FOR EVALUATORS

A number of issues that arise in the measurement of change have been reviewed and some of the special implications of these issues in the context of educational evaluation have been noted. Specific suggestions of what to do about measuring change, however, depend upon the nature of the evaluation and the purposes for which change is to be measured. As stated in the introduction, change scores are not necessarily the best approach to answering the questions of an evaluation.

Evaluations can have many purposes, only one of which is the assessment of program impact on achievement. Approaches to this single, relatively narrow purpose of an evaluation are often dictated by circumstances beyond the control of the evaluator. The most powerful tools for purposes of obtaining valid estimates of program impact are the design of the study and the control of the conditions of instruction. In most evaluations, however, evaluators have only limited access to these tools. Random assignment is the exception, not the rule, and control of instructional conditions is seldom within the province of the evaluator. Although obvious, these facts of life are important because they have implications for the goals that are sought when attempts are made to measure change.

Random Assignment

Random assignment assures group equivalence in a probabilistic sense. Of course, owing to sampling error, the samples cannot be expected to have the same pretest scores, but unbiased estimates of treatment effects can be obtained and the size of the sampling errors estimated. The pretest will generally be useful in increasing the power of the study, but it is not logically necessary for evaluating impact. The posttest alone is an appropriate dependent variable for comparing treatment and control conditions. Change measures are not necessary for the evaluation of impact in this situation. Difference scores are apt to yield a more precise measure of impact than the posttest alone, but generally will be less precise than other alternative uses of the pretest scores (e.g., blocking or analysis of covariance). Thus, with random assignment with a pretest and a posttest there is no necessity for change scores, and they are apt to have disadvantages in comparison to other alternative uses of pretest scores.

Nonequivalent Control Group Design

The more common evaluation situation, of course, involves the use of preformed groups rather than grouping by random assignment. The program participants cannot be assumed to be equivalent to the nonparticipant comparison group. Under these circumstances the most common motivation for using measures of change is to adjust for the nonequivalence of the groups due to preexisting differences.

Difference scores cannot, in general, be expected to provide the needed adjustment for the nonequivalence of the groups. Thus, the measurement of change cannot be justified on this basis alone. It should be noted, however, that regression analysis approaches also lack any guarantee that the right adjustment will be made. Any misspecification of the model can be expected to result in biased estimates (Cronbach et al., 1977). Except for special instances, such as the regression discontinuity design where people are assigned to conditions solely on the basis of a premeasure, there is generally no way of being sure that the model is properly specified. Thus, Lord's (1967, p. 305) discouraging conclusion that "there simply is no logical or statistical procedure that can be counted on to make the proper allowances for uncontrolled preexisting differences between groups" remains unrefuted.

Single-Group Design

The weakest design for assessing project impact is a single-group design. Model A of the Title I Evaluation and Reporting System involves collection of data for only a single group, but its use depends on comparison to another group, namely the norm group. Limitations of model A have already been discussed and will not be repeated. Suffice it to say that measuring change does not answer the need for a measure of project impact, either with or without a comparison to a norm group.

In none of the three general types of evaluation designs involving two-wave data is the measurement of change of any particular advantage for purposes of assessing project impact on achievement. On the contrary, there are disadvantages to using change scores for this purpose.

Major disadvantages in the use of change scores are that they tend to conceal conceptual difficulties and they can give misleading results. The former tendency is apparent when change scores are used to compare preexisting groups, which tends to conceal the arbitrariness of this particular form of adjustment. The latter tendency is apparent where various standardized test scales, such as grade equivalents or percentile ranks, are used to assess gains of different groups of students." (Linn & Slinde, 1977, p. 147)

Growth Curves and Multi-wave Data

Although measures of change may best be avoided in the typical pretest-posttest situation, there are still good reasons to be interested in estimated growth curves. They are fundamental to describing and understanding developmental processes. As previously indicated, adequate models of "natural" growth would provide a better basis for the analysis of the effects of an intervention (e.g. Bryk & Weisberg, 1976, 1977; Bryk et al., 1980).

Multi-wave data are critical to the adequate characterization of growth curves. Two-wave data have substantial advantages over posttest-only data for assessing the impact of interventions, but not for the characterization of growth curves. Thus, "investigators who ask questions regarding gain scores" are well advised to "frame their questions in other ways" (Cronbach & Furby, 1970, p. 80) when data are limited to only two points in time. The alternative is to invest in the collection of multi-wave data. Such an investment, while not cheap, has the potential for good returns.

REFERENCES

Angoff, W. H. Scales, norms and equivalent scores. In R. L. Thorndike (ed.), *Educational measurement* (2nd ed.). Washington, D.C.: American Council on Education, 1971. Pp. 508–600.

Ayrer, J. E., & McNamara, T. C. Survey testing on an out-of-level basis. *Journal of Educational Measurement,* 1973, *10,* 79–84.

Beck, M. D. Development of empirical "growth expectancies" for the Metropolitan Achievement Tests. Paper presented at the annual meeting of the National Council on Measurement in Education, Washington, D.C.

Bissell, J. S. Planned variation in Head Start and Follow Through. In J. C. Stanley (ed.), *Compensatory education for children, ages 2 to 8.* Baltimore: Johns Hopkins University Press, 1973. Pp. 63–107.

Bryk, A. S., Strenio, J. F., & Weisberg, H. I. A method for estimating treatment effects when individuals are growing. *Journal of Educational Statistics,* 1980, *5,* 5–34.

Bryk, A. S., & Weisberg, H. I. Value-added analysis: A dynamic approach to the estimation of treatment effects. *Journal of Educational Statistics,* 1976, *1,* 127–155.

Bryk, A. S., & Weisberg, H. I. Use of the nonequivalent control group design when subjects are growing. *Psychological Bulletin,* 1977, *84,* 950–962.

Coleman, J. S., & Karweit, N. L. *Measures of school performance* (R-488-RC). Santa Monica: Rand Corporation, 1970.

Cronbach, L. J., & Furby, L. How we should measure "change"—or should we? *Psychological Bulletin,* 1970, *74,* 68–80.

Cronbach, L. J., Rogosa, D. R., Floden, R. E., & Price, G. *Analysis of covariance in nonrandomized experiments: Parameters affecting bias* (Occasional paper). Stanford, Calif.: Stanford Evaluation Consortium, Stanford University, 1977.

David, J. L., & Pelavin, S. H. *Research on the effectiveness of compensatory education programs: A reanalysis of data* (SRI Project Report URU-4425). Menlo Park, Calif.: SRI International, 1977.

Echternacht, G. The use of different models in the ESEA Title I evaluation system. Paper presented at the annual meeting of the American Educational Research Association, Toronto, March 1978.

Fremer, J., & Anastasio, E. J. Computer assisted item writing—I (Spelling items). *Journal of Educational Measurement,* 1969, *6,* 69–74.

Gulliksen, H. *Theory of mental test scores.* New York: Wiley, 1950.

Hambleton, R. K., Swaminathan, H., Cook, L. L., Eignor, D. R., & Gifford, J. A. Developments in latent trait theory: Models, technical issues and applications. *Review of Educational Research,* 1978, *48,* 467–510.

Hammond, P. A., & Frechtling, J. A. Twelve, nine and three month achievement gains of low and average achieving elementary school students. Paper presented at the annual meeting of the American Educational Research Association, San Francisco, April 1979.

Harris, C. W., Pearlman, A. P., & Wilcox, R. R. (eds.), *Achievement test items— Methods of study* (CSE Monograph Series in Evaluation, No. 6). Los Angeles: Center for the Study of Evaluation, University of California, 1977.

Hively, W., Maxwell, G., Rabehl, G., Sension, D., & Lundin, S. *Domain-referenced curriculum evaluation: A technical handbook and a case study from the MIN- NEMAST Project* (CSE Monograph Series in Evaluation, No. 1). Los Angeles: Center for the Study of Evaluation, University of California, 1973.

Hoepfner, R., Zagorski, H., & Wellisch, J. *The sample for the sustaining effects study and projections of its characteristics to the population* (Technical Report No. 1 from the Sustaining Effects Study). Santa Monica: System Development Corporation, 1977.

Horst, D. P., *What's bad about grade-equivalent scores. ESEA Title I Evaluation and Reporting System* (Technical Report No. 1). Mountain View, Calif.: RMC Research Corporation, 1976.

Kenny, D. A. A quasi-experimental approach to assessing treatment effects in the nonequivalent control group design. *Psychological Bulletin*, 1975, *82*, 345-362.

Kenny, D. A. *Correlation and Causation*. New York: Wiley, 1979.

Linn, R. L. The validity of inferences based on the proposed Title I evaluation models. *Educational Evaluation and Policy Analysis*, 1979, *1*, 23-32.

Linn, R. L. Evaluation of Title I via the RMC Models: A critical review. In E. L. Baker and E. S. Quellmalz (eds.), *Educational testing and evaluation: Design, analysis, and policy*. Beverly Hills: Sage, 1980. Pp. 121-142.

Linn, R. L., & Slinde, J. A. The determination of the significance of change between pre and posttesting periods. *Review of Educational Research*, 1977, *47*, 121-150.

Lord, F. M. Elementary models for measuring change. In C. W. Harris (ed.), *Problems in measuring change*. Madison: University of Wisconsin Press, 1963. Pp. 21-38.

Lord, F. M. A paradox in the interpretation of group comparisons. *Psychological Bulletin*, 1967, *68*, 304-305.

Lord, F. M. Practical applications of item characteristic curve theory. *Journal of Educational Measurement*, 1977, *14*, 117-138.

Millman, J. Computer-based item generation. In R. A. Berk (ed.), *Criterion- referenced measurement: The state of the art*. Baltimore: Johns Hopkins University Press, 1980. Pp. 32-43.

Murray, S. L. An analysis of regression effects and the equipercentile growth assumption in the norm-referenced evaluation model. Paper presented at the annual meeting of the Washington Educational Research Association, Seattle, 1978.

National Advisory Council on the Education of Disadvantaged Children. *NACEDC special report on NIE study on compensatory education*. Washington, D.C.: NACEDC, no date.

Pelavin, S., & Barker, P. *A study of the generalizability of the results of standardized achievement tests* (WN-9234-NIE). Santa Monica: Rand Corporation, February 1976.

Prescott, G. A. *Manual for interpretation: Metropolitan Achievement Test*. New York: Harcourt Brace Jovanovich, 1973.

Rasch, G. *Probabilistic models for intelligence and attainment tests*. Copenhagen: Danish Institute for Educational Research, 1960.

Rogosa, D. R. Comparisons of some procedures for analyzing longitudinal panel data. *Journal of Economics and Business,* in press.

Slinde, J. A., & Linn, R. L. Vertically equated tests: Fact or phantom? *Journal of Educational Measurement,* 1977, *14,* 23–32.

Slinde, J. A., & Linn, R. L. A note on the vertical equating via the Rasch model for groups of quite different ability and tests of quite different difficulty. *Journal of Educational Measurement,* 1979, *16,* 159–165. (a)

Slinde, J. A., & Linn, R. L. The Rasch model, objective measurement, equating and robustness. *Applied Psychological Measurement,* 1979, *3,* 437–452. (b)

Storlie, T. R., Rice, W., Johnson, M. L., & Crowe, M. B. Local norms in a large urban setting for evaluating Title I programs with model A1. Paper presented at the annual meeting of the American Educational Research Association, San Francisco, April 1979.

Tallmadge, G. K., & Wood, C. T. *User's guide: ESEA Title I evaluation and reporting system.* Mountain View, Calif.: RMC Research-Corporation, 1976.

Thurstone, L. L. A method of scaling psychological and educational tests. *Journal of Educational Psychology,* 1925, *16,* 433–451.

Wright, B. D. Sample-free test calibration and person measurement. *Proceedings of the 1967 Invitational Conference on Testing Problems.* Princeton, N.J.: Educational Testing Service, 1967. Pp. 85–101.

Wright, B. D. Solving measurement problems with the Rasch Model. *Journal of Educational Measurement,* 1977, *14,* 97–116.

5 SELECTING APPROPRIATE STATISTICAL METHODS RICHARD M. WOLF

*I*n addition to the problems peculiar to the various change statistics described in the preceding chapter, there are other important issues that
*relate to the overall choice of a statistical method for analyzing evaluation
data. The decision of which method to use is probably the most crucial. While
analysis of variance (ANOVA), analysis of covariance (ANCOVA), and multiple regression constitute the primary tools, their appropriateness with nonrandomized evaluation designs has been a persistent source of confusion.
Furthermore, the interpretations and inferences deduced from the statistics
are occasionally superficial and incorrect, especially in regard to the difference between statistical significance and practical (or policy) significance.
These concerns are addressed in this chapter.*

*Professor Richard M. Wolf compares several statistical methods for analyz-
ing the results of an evaluation study. Factors that guide the selection of
ANOVA and ANCOVA are delineated in the first section. The major focus in
subsequent sections is the analysis of nonrandomized designs. The recommended reference on that topic is Cook and Campbell's (1979)* Quasi-
Experimentation: Design and Analysis Issues for Field Settings. *Special attention is given to designs based on comparable groups and to those based on
noncomparable groups. Within this context, a sharp distinction is drawn
between "evaluation" and "research." Professor Wolf stresses the increasing acceptance of quasi-experimental designs for program evaluation,
whereas many of those designs (e.g., one-group, pretest-posttest design) have
been rejected previously as scientifically worthless for research. In fact,
Overall and Woodward (1977b, p. 594) noted recently that "Random assignment is not an essential principle of good experimental design. The researcher is in a position to make strong statistical inferences, so long as he
[or she] controls the assignment to treatment groups according to any of a
variety of possible assignment rules, only one of which is random assignment."
Professor Wolf's guidelines for evaluators highlight four stages of data
analysis: (1) routine descriptive procedures (exploratory data analysis), (2)*

primary statistical procedures (ANOVA, ANCOVA, or multiple regression in one form or another), (3) secondary statistical procedures (alternative analyses), and (4) interpretation (comparison of results and internal/external meaningfulness of results). Finally, he emphasizes the value and potential of regression-discontinuity designs, but raises serious questions about the adequacy of the procedures currently employed to analyze the data from such designs.

INTRODUCTION

THOSE INDIVIDUALS who are responsible for the analysis of data in evaluation studies have a formidable responsibility. Not only must they be thoroughly knowledgeable about the substantive, organizational, and practical aspects of the studies with which they are associated, but they must also have enough statistical proficiency and common sense to deal with a data set that may be baffling and undoubtedly is troublesome in one or more ways. Given the current state of practice with regard to the design and execution of helping programs and the often sorry state of the resulting information, it is small wonder that many data analysts are prime candidates for the State Home for the Bewildered.

I want to address my remarks to data analysts who are associated with programs that are carried out on something less than a national or regional scale. The reason for restricting my remarks to the local level is that larger projects are often funded at a level that permits the purchase of a large amount of excellent statistical advice. Local programs, on the other hand, typically can't afford to. Hence, the likely payoff of whatever I have to say should be greatest for those who can't afford consultants.

To avoid redundancy with other chapters, it need only be noted that an evaluation study was designed and carried out and that instruments were carefully selected and administered. The actual design may or may not be a true experiment, but more about that later. The instruments that were used were presumably valid and administered under standard conditions to all groups involved in the evaluation. Furthermore, scores obtained from the use of the instruments are on an interval scale or have been appropriately transformed to be so, there are no great floor or ceiling effects in the instruments, and scores are reasonably reliable throughout the range of the scale. These are a lot of presumptions but, according to Tukey, "presumably means presumably."

Most conventional sources in the field of research design and statistics adopt a logical approach to the analysis of data (see, for example, Campbell & Stanley, 1966; Edwards, 1972; Hays, 1973). That is, once the design has been chosen, the study conducted and the data gathered, one selects a statistical technique that is generally a function of the scale of measurement and the number of predictor (or independent), criterion (or dependent), and control variables. The technique is than applied to the data and results obtained and interpreted. It's a tidy procedure that is well suited to the conduct of laboratory experiments but hardly pertinent to evaluation work. To be sure, analysis and interpretation are the twin goals of the specialist whose responsibility is to examine the information obtained in an evaluation enterprise. However, the evaluation worker has to contend with a number of problems that a laboratory researcher would never dream of. One set of problems centers around appropriate analytic procedures while the other involves threats to the validity of results. The two sets of problems have typically been dealt with separately. Thus, for example, some writers address the choice and use of statistical procedures while another group of writers address the issues of design considerations, instrumentation problems, and threats to validity. It is important to review both lines of work and to attempt to bring them together if evaluation workers are to adequately fulfill their potential role.

REVIEW OF STATISTICAL STRATEGIES

There are any number of works that furnish the reader with the theory and applications of standard statistical procedures (Cox, 1958; Myers, 1972; Winer, 1971). Topics covered in these works include analysis of variance (ANOVA) in all its myriad forms and analysis of covariance (ANCOVA). For the strong-hearted, there is Bock's (1975) *Multivariate Statistical Methods in Behavioral Research*. However, my later comments will urge caution in regard to the use of multivariate procedures, i.e., multiple-criterion variables, in the analysis of data from evaluation studies. While the above-mentioned standard works are useful for learning about a range of analytic procedures, they are of somewhat limited usefulness when it comes to analyzing the data from a particular study. The reason for this is that they were generally written with the experimental laboratory researcher in mind. That is, the general presumption behind the standard statistical works is that the investigator has full power to set up the levels of treatment variables, use whatever instruments are deemed necessary and, most important, to randomly assign units, whether they be individuals (usually) or groups, to treatment levels. For the methods-crazed researcher, happiness is a 24 x 24 Latin square that can actually be applied to a real problem.

While all of us were reared on the standard statistical treatises and benefited from such exposure, it is also eminently clear that such training was not sufficient to deal with evaluation problems that arise in the real world of schools, where life is anything but tidy. What was needed was guidance in dealing with the problems of a messy world. Fortunately, such help is now available. Over the past ten years there has been a fairly steady stream of articles and chapters and, now, even a book on the problems of analysis of data from evaluation studies.

One of the best single sources in the area of analysis is perhaps the one by Porter and Chibucos (1974). This fifty-page chapter addresses the issues of analyzing data that arise out of four case situations. It is a complete crossing of two cases and two situations. In the two cases, randomization has or has not been employed while in the two situations, the premeasure is either a pretest (same or parallel form) or it is something other than a pretest. Four analysis techniques are discussed in relation to each case situation. These techniques are: (1) ANCOVA with a random rather than fixed covariable, (2) estimated true score ANCOVA, (3) ANOVA using an index of response as the dependent variable, and (4) repeated measures ANOVA where one variable is the variable measured before the program gets underway and the other measure is the outcome variable.

Porter and Chibucos deal with the four case situations only in terms of a single antecedent variable and a single pretest. This, of course, is pedagogically sound and generally correct since most complex designs will probably be based on one of their four case situations. They lead the reader through a systematic and detailed set of comparisons of the various statistical procedures in relation to each of their four case situations. Their discussion includes attention to issues of statistical power and reliability of gain scores, among other matters. For example, in comparing ANOVA to ANCOVA in the analysis of data from studies where randomization is used, the authors set forth the general relationship between the expected value of the mean square error for ANOVA ($\sigma_y{}^2$) and that for ANCOVA ($\sigma_{y \cdot x}{}^2$). This is

$$\sigma_{y \cdot x}{}^2 = \sigma_y{}^2 (1 - \rho_{xy}{}^2)$$

where ρ_{xy} denotes the within-cell population correlation between pretest and posttest. It is abundantly clear from the formula that the larger the correlation between the pretest and the posttest, the greater the reduction in the error mean square in ANCOVA and the greater the likelihood of obtaining a significant F. On the other hand, if the correlation between pretest and posttest is 0, $\sigma_{y \cdot x}{}^2 = \sigma_y{}^2$, there is no gain in precision.

ANOVA versus ANCOVA

The question for the data analyst is when is it best to use ANCOVA and ANOVA. Of course, there are no hard and fast rules, but in general, it appears that if r_{xy} is less than .3, one is probably better off using ANOVA because there is little improvement in precision to be gained for the cost of one degree of freedom (Cook & Campbell, 1979, p. 157; Cox, 1957). On the other hand, if the correlation between pretest and posttest is .6 or greater, one is clearly better off using ANCOVA because of the sizable decrease in the error mean square (Cook & Campbell, 1979, p. 177; Cox, 1957). For pretest-posttest correlations between .3 and .6, blocking is the preferred method of design and analysis. The reason for this lies in the fact that the usual correlational estimate is the Pearson product-moment correlation that assumes a straight-line relationship between the pretest and posttest. The relationship may be a fairly good one but it may not be a linear one. This would probably result in a moderate moment correlation, i.e., .3 $\leq$ r $\leq$ .6, that can be fairly well accommodated by a randomized block design (Porter & Chibucos, 1974, p. 439). Of course, one would have to have some prior estimate of the relationship between pretest and posttest to plan for the use of a randomized block design. Such information should not be too difficult to obtain.

Pretest-Posttest Gain Scores

Another issue that Porter and Chibucos (1974) address is the unreliability of gain scores.* Beginning students in measurement courses learn the conventional formula for estimating the reliability of gain scores (see Linn, chapter 4).

As Linn (chapter 4) notes, the maddening consequence of this formula is that even if an evaluation worker has gone to great lengths to use highly reliable instruments, say $r_{xx} = r_{yy} = .9$, he will invariably end up with highly unreliable gain scores if the correlation between pretest and posttest is high. This, in fact, is often the case. Pretest-posttest correlations of .7 to .8 are not common over a one year period (Bloom, 1964). Given a test reliability of .9, this would result in gain scores with a reliability of .5, hardly a desirable state of affairs. Consequently, Porter and Chibucos (1974) properly conclude that "gain scores are almost never appropriate" (p. 432) in analysis. The authors do make some recommendations about an alternative measure that they term an "index of response" but admit that the use of such a measure requires the use of "some rather restrictive assumptions" (Porter & Chibucos, 1974, p. 432). The reader is encouraged to study Porter and Chibucos's thinking and recommendations on the matter. For myself, I would prefer to avoid the use of such an index and search for other ways of analyzing data from evaluation studies.

Analysis of Nonrandomized Designs

In two of the four case situations presented by Porter and Chibucos (1974), randomization is employed. The model situation in evaluation studies, in my experience, is the absence of randomization. In educational settings, students

---

*While the unreliability of gain scores for individuals is well known, the difference between pretest and posttest means can be used as a stable estimate of gain for a group. The reason for this is the balancing out of errors of measurement in the estimation of the average performance of groups (see Linn, chapter 4).

are typically placed into groups on a nonrandom basis. Of course, there is no reason not to block groups and assign the groups randomly to treatments. In other words, the idea is to use the class as the unit of analysis in a true experiment (see Cooley, chapter 3). It's a way of conducting a true experiment when class groups are formed on a nonrandom basis and it's a perfectly straightforward procedure. What I have in mind, however, is not a way around the issue of nonrandom formation of treatment groups but rather a confrontation of the issue. It's at this point that things get somewhat sticky.

Thre are two basic positions with regard to what to do about data obtained from studies that involve nonrandom assignment. The first position, stated by Lord (1967), is a counsel of despair. Lord states, ''. . . there is no logical or statistical procedure that can be counted on to make proper allowances for pre-existing differences between (treatment) groups'' (p. 305). The second position has been stated by Harnquist (1968) and is endorsed by Porter and Chibucos (1974). Harnquist (1968) wrote:

Even if the initial standing of the subjects is controlled by means of a number of relevant variables, there will always be room for uncontrolled differences that may be important. The investigator, who because of the nature of his [or her] problem cannot use random or systematic assignment of subjects to treatments, has to live with an insecurity in that respect—and try to behave intelligently within the limitations of his [or her] design—or leave the scene of nonexperimental research. (P. 57)

Once Porter and Chibucos have endorsed Harnquist's position, they go on to discuss a number of analytic issues and to suggest approaches to the analysis of data emanating from nonequivalent group designs. Their approach is properly tentative and exploratory. To initially clear the air, they state that a straightforward use of ANCOVA cannot be depended on to correct for preexisting differences between groups (see also Linn, chapter 4). This dictum probably needs repeating every time a group of evaluation workers convene. Porter and Chibucos offer ANCOVA of estimated true scores as a way of dealing with the problems of analysis of data from nonequivalent groups, but I do not find their argument to be highly persuasive. Further study along the lines suggested by Overall and Woodward (1977a, 1977b) would seem to be in order.

Comparable groups. It seems to me that there is an important distinction to be made between types of nonequivalent groups. In one type of design, groups are formed on a nonrandom basis and assigned to treatments. While randomization was not used, there may be reasonable grounds for considering that the groups are reasonably similar and, hence, comparable. For example, an elementary school may have a policy of heterogeneous grouping that results in the establishment of, say, four fifth-grade class groups. While randomization was not used in forming the groups, there is a reasonable basis for viewing the groups as comparable, i.e., equal distributions of bright, average, and slow students, roughly equal numbers of boys and girls, etc. In any study involving these groups, it would be improper to use the terms "experimental" and "control" because of the absence of randomization. However, if one substitutes the term "comparison" for "control," one can proceed along a path of analysis that is somewhat akin to that used with data from true experiments. One must, of course, proceed extremely carefully and will need to do much more investigative analysis, but that's simply the price one pays.

Noncomparable groups. In the second type of nonequivalent group design, the groups are clearly not comparable, and any attempt to regard them as being so is unwarranted. A typical example of this type of situation is when all students in a grade level who are reading below some predetermined standard are skimmed off and given a remedial treatment. Any attempt to compare the reading progress of such students as are not so deficient must be handled in a distinctly different way from the stiuation in which groups are roughly comparable.*

The best single source that recognizes this distinction between these different types of nonequivalent group designs (unfortunately called nonequivalent *control* group designs) is Cook and Campbell's *Quasi-Experimentation: Design and Analysis Issues for Field Settings* (1979). This book is perhaps the best single source of ideas and strategies for data analysis in evaluation studies. It also represents a fundamental change in point of view from that espoused by Campbell and Stanley (1963, 1966). That change is so important that it needs to be fully espoused. As you may remember from the original Campbell and Stanley chapter (1963), the one-group posttest-only design, the posttest-only design with nonequivalent groups, and the one-group pretest-posttest design were presented and discussed early on and dismissed as being scientifically worthless because of the myriad threats to internal validity. I remember reading this section of the Campbell-Stanley chapter as a graduate student and nodding affirmatively. From the standpoint of research, they were clearly correct. Today, however, quasi-experimentation has gained increasing acceptance as an approach to dealing with data arising from evaluation studies. Elsewhere (Wolf, 1979), I have distinguished between research and evaluation. If these distinctions are accepted, then the legitimacy of designs castigated for research purposes can be considered. This is precisely what Cook and Campbell do. While they are still somewhat skeptical of the three designs mentioned above, they at least do not dismiss them out of hand. Their

---

*The proper design for the analysis of data resulting from such a situation is the regression-discontinuity design. It was promulgated by Campbell (1969). The requirement in this design is that a pretest is used to separate units into two groups. One group receives a treatment while the other group receives an alternative treatment. At the end of a period of time, another measure is obtained. The regression of the posttest on the pretest for each group is used to estimate the efficacy of the treatment. This is sometimes done by comparing the intercepts of the two regression lines (or curves) at the cutting point.

discussion is under the heading, "Three Designs That Often Do Not Permit Reasonable Causal Inferences" (Cook & Campbell, 1979, pp. 95–102). The important point about the discussion is that while all sorts of caveats are issued, the designs are not rejected outright.

The importance of this shift in position should not be underestimated. Evaluation studies do not, as research studies do, attempt to produce generalizable knowledge, i.e., have external validity. What is generally important is to determine how well a program is succeeding in a particular setting. Whether the program will work well or at all in the next county is not a matter of concern. Furthermore, unlike instructional research, evaluation is not primarily concerned with determining whether one treatment outperforms another in whatever respects are chosen for study. Rather, evaluation studies are more concerned with determining how a program is succeeding in achieving its own goals. Thus, if a postsecondary program is established to train people in oxyacetylene and electric-arc welding, it is not necessary to set up an alternative program to train people in these skills. In fact, it would usually be prohibitive to do so. Thus, a single group design could be usefully employed. Furthermore, since any pretesting of performance is potentially highly dangerous, one would undoubtedly not do it. Consequently, a one-group posttest-only design could be highly serviceable.

The admissibility of such designs in special situations as the one just described open a range of evaluation possibilities that have previously been rejected. One must, of course, be extremely careful about the use of such designs and cautious in the analysis and interpretation of data resulting from their use. However, the possibility of their inclusion in evaluation work is the important point.

The chapter entitled, "The Statistical Analysis of Data from Nonequivalent Group Designs" by Charles S. Reichart in the Cook and Campbell (1979) book provides considerable guidance to evaluation workers on how to analyze data from the two types of nonequivalent group designs. Topics included in the chapter are: ANOVA, ANCOVA with a single as well as multiple covariates, ANOVA with blocking, and ANOVA of gain scores. The presentations are thoughtful and sensible. The one unsatisfying part of the chapter is the analysis of data resulting from the regression discontinuity design, the situation in which groups are clearly noncomparable, e.g., extremely deficient readers versus not extremely deficient readers. However, more about that in the next section.

This somewhat hurried tour of the literature has attempted to stress two points. First, a fair amount of attention has been given to dealing with the analysis of data arising from studies conducted in field settings where most of the elegancies of laboratory research are not present. The fact that I chose to refer to only two major works should not be taken to mean that the literature in the area is scant. Nothing could be further from the truth. The interested reader will find the references at the end of the Porter and Chibucos chapter and the Cook and Campbell book more than adequate as a jumping-off point for further reading.

The second major point that was stressed is that there has been a good deal of thought devoted to alternative analytic strategies. The fact that few dicta can be issued at this time is due to the fact that a good deal must be known about a data set before decisions about analytic strategies can be made, not to an absence of knowledge on how to proceed. I shall return to this point in the last section of the chapter.

SUGGESTIONS FOR FUTURE RESEARCH

There seems to be little need to call for further theoretical and methodological work in the area of data analysis. There is much current activity in the area, and it is reasonable to expect that it will continue. There do, however, seem to be two acute needs. The first is the necessity of exploring the consequences of different analytic strategies with real data sets; the second pertains to the use of regression-discontinuity designs.

Secondary Data Analysis

While much secondary analysis has been done with the data emanating from the Coleman and International Educational Achievement studies, we have not had much corresponding activity with data from evaluation studies (see Stufflebeam, chapter 7). The sole instance I can think of that barely qualifies as work in this area is the Cook et al. (1975) reanalysis of data from the Sesame Street evaluation. I would hope that there can be systematic secondary analysis of data from routine evaluation studies so that we can begin to assess the consequences of adopting different analytic strategies.

Regression-Discontinuity Designs

The second need for further work is more specific. I don't believe that our analytic procedures for dealing with data from studies involving regression-discontinuity designs are at all adequate. In fact, I'm not convinced that we are even asking the right questions. For example, is it more important to estimate the discontinuity between the intercepts of the regression lines at the cutting point, to estimate potential treatment-effect interactions or to estimate the shape of the regression line for each group? How much power can we expect from the analysis of data using a regression-discontinuity design? What considerations are needed in planning for studies using this design?

These are not idle questions. My own sense of educational developments is that, more and more, all learners who are eligible for a particular treatment are being assigned to it. This applies equally to learners at the low end of the scale, i.e., the disadvantaged however they're defined, and to the gifted and talented however they're defined. It is simply getting harder and harder to withhold a treatment from someone who is eligible for it even though the treatment may be wholly unproven. In such a climate, the only path to salvation I have any hope for is the regression-discontinuity design. Even then my level of hope is not boundless. I would feel much more comfortable if we had a better understanding of how to deal with data resulting from the use of this important design.

GUIDELINES FOR EVALUATORS

In this section, attention is focused on the steps to be taken in analyzing data from evaluation studies. The orientation is intended to be highly practical. Accordingly, I will set forth the procedures I would follow if I were undertaking the analysis of data resulting from an evaluation study.

Routine Descriptive Procedures

The first step, after instruments have been administered, would be to subject data to a set of routine descriptive procedures. I would be interested in obtaining frequency distributions of variables, univariate statistics (means, medians, standard deviations, skewness and kurtosis measures and the like), and scatterplots of variables I might have some interest in eventually possibly correlating. This first step is one of familiarization and is intended to educate the analyst about the nature and shape of the variables in the data set. It is at this point that one can check for possible floor and ceiling effects in instruments by inspecting frequency distributions, check out the nature of the apparent relationships between variables, and generally get the feel of the data set. I am also inclined to compare obtained score distributions to norms for standardized instruments to get an idea of the meaning of performance levels.

This first step is one that some writers describe as *exploratory data analysis*. I regard it as one of mucking about in the data. Unfortunately, it does not often receive the time or attention it deserves. My own conviction is that if evaluation workers allowed themselves a fair amount of time at this stage of analysis, they could avoid numerous problems later on.

The computations actually performed in this first step are generally simple. However, there are usually a lot of them. The general approach to work at this step is to use a routine statistical package such as SPSS (Hull & Nie, 1979; Nie et al., 1975). Subprograms CONDESCRIPTIVE, FREQUENCIES, and SCATTERGRAM will generally be adequate in providing the evaluation worker all the information needed for this first step in the analysis.

Primary Statistical Procedures

The resulting information should be highly useful in making decisions about what analytic procedures to use at the second step in the analysis. The second step in the analysis consists of formal analyses of data. Procedures that are most apt to be used include ANOVA, ANCOVA, and multiple regression analysis in one form or another. The selection of a particular technique will be based partly on the design of the study and partly on the results obtained from the first step of the analysis.

Analysis of one variable at a time. There are two general caveats to bear in mind during the second step of the analysis. First, the analysis should proceed one variable at a time. Despite the advocacy of multivariate procedures by some evaluators, the analysis of data from evaluation studies requires attention to each and every objective in a program. It may well be that a program has not succeeded in meeting 90% of its objectives but has succeeded in achieving 10%. My fear is that if a multivariate procedure such as multiple discriminant analysis is used, the fact that 10% of the objectives were achieved is likely to get lost because of a nonsignificant overall F or lambda. This would be highly regrettable. I doubt that many practicing evaluation workers have the training to identify what's significant in a pile of largely null results. My inclination is to generally avoid the use of multivariate procedures.*

Sensitivity to nonlinear relationships. The second general point to be made regarding the analysis of data during the second step is to be particularly sensitive about possible nonlinear relationships among variables. There is nothing sacred about straight line relationships. The fact that many formal procedures assume linear relationships does not restrict use in data analysis. Nonlinear relationships can be easily accommodated at this stage of analysis through the inclusion of squared, cubic, and quadratic terms. Any evaluation worker who needs guidance and/or reassurance on this matter is referred to an excellent article by Cohen (1978).

Secondary Statistical Procedures

Most evaluation workers conclude their data analysis with the second step. However, they shouldn't. A third step of data analysis would be to try out one or more alternative ways of analyzing one's data. In the second step, the evaluation worker uses a primary selected statistical procedure. As the third step, one or more secondary procedures are used. In a sense, this third step is

---

*The term multivariate, as used by statisticians, refers to the simultaneous study of multiple *outcome* variables. When there are multiple predictor or independent variables but only a single outcome variable, the analysis is often regarded as univariate. Thus, multi-factor experiments with a single dependent variable and multiple regression analysis are examples of univariate analysis (Bock, 1975, pp. 20–22).

somewhat exploratory in nature. However, it does provide the evaluation worker with alternative ways of examining his or her data.

Interpretation

Comparison of results. The fourth step of the process is one of interpretation. It consists of three stages. First, the evaluator will need to compare the results obtained from the various analyses. If the results are essentially in agreement, the first stage is quickly concluded. (The chapter by Porter and Chibucos suggests that such agreement is generally fairly likely.) If the results are not in agreement, then attention needs to be devoted to identifying the reasons for the lack of agreement and coming to reasonable conclusions. A good deal of pondering might be needed to accomplish this goal.

Internal meaningfulness of results. After concluding about the statistical significance of one's results, it is necessary to address the issue of the internal meaningfulness of one's results. If one can estimate ω^2 (omega squared) or the intraclass correlation, it is important to do so. Even a components-of-variance analysis is a worthwhile undertaking because of the importance of estimating the magnitude of an effect after its nonzero status has been ascertained. Information regarding the estimation of the strength of effects can be found in Hays (1963), Schutz (1966), and Wolf (1974, 1979).

An alternative procedure that is highly practical is to calculate an effect size. This statistic is simply the difference between the means of the treatment and comparison groups divided by the standard deviation of the comparison group in the ANOVA case (Glass, 1977). When using ANCOVA, one simply uses the adjusted treatment means of the two groups. An effect size of at least .3 is presumed to have practical importance (Cohen, 1977; Gage, 1978).

External meaningfulness of results. A third stage of the step of interpretation involves making further sense out of one's results. This can be termed external meaningfulness. This stage would apply if one was using instruments that have norms or mastery expectation. Essentially, one is interested in estimating how meaningful the effect of a treatment actually was. For example, in a further analysis and interpretation of some Sesame Street arithmetic performance data, Wolf (1979) found that students in the experimental treatment, who were encouraged to watch Sesame Street, went from an average percentage correct of 27 to 42 on the Numbers Test, while the control group who were not encouraged to watch the show went from an average of 27 to 35. The difference between the two posttest averages, 35 vs. 42, was statistically significant. The ω^2 value, the measure of relationship between group membership and test performance, was .06. However, when one notes that the Numbers Test was specially designed to measure the effects of the program, an average percentage correct of 42 is not especially thrilling. Also, outperforming a control group by 7% in the mid-range of the scale is almost trifling.

It is this kind of further interpretation of results that is vitally needed in evaluation studies. Unfortunately, it is all too often lacking. Evaluation workers frequently come from a background of research methods and statistics. They're good at manipulating data sets and drawing statistical conclusions. They're often, however, somewhat deficient in judging the meaning of their results in educational terms. Yet it is important that they do so, since the audience for their work consists largely of statistical neophytes— administrators, lay boards, and teachers. Presentations of results must not only take into account the nature of the audience but must present them in terms that are meaningful and comprehensible as well as accurate (see Datta, chapter 6). My own view is that this is one of the largest challenges facing evaluation workers today.

In summary, the way of the evaluation worker is long and hard. Data analysis must proceed through four distinct steps. The first step is one of familiarization and consists of the production of a number of routine descriptive statistics. It is needed to educate the analyst as to what formal statistical procedures to employ. The second step is the execution of the primary selected analytic procedures. These are the analyses on which the evaluation worker places his heaviest bets for estimating and evaluating treatment effects. The third step involves the use of one or more alternative procedures to analyze his/her data. This is done to check out the results obtained from the use of the primary procedures. The fourth and last step is one of interpretation. Here, the evaluation worker is concerned with the educational meaningfulness and practical importance of his/her results. My own view is that the first, third, and fourth steps in the handling of evaluation data have not received sufficient time and effort in the past. If they can receive adequate time and attention in the future, I believe the quality of evaluation work will improve dramatically.

REFERENCES

Bloom, B. S. *Stability and change in human characteristics*. New York: Wiley, 1964.

Bock, R. D. *Multivariate statistical methods in behavioral research*. New York: McGraw-Hill, 1975.

Campbell, D. T. Reforms as experiments. *American Psychologist*, 1969, *24*, 409–429.

Campbell, D. T., & Stanley, J. C. Experimental and quasi-experimental designs for research on teaching. In N. L. Gage (ed.), *Handbook of research on teaching*. Chicago: Rand McNally, 1963. Pp. 171–246.

Campbell, D. T., & Stanley, J. C. *Experimental and quasi-experimental designs for research*. Chicago: Rand McNally, 1966.

Cohen, J. *Statistical power analysis for the behavioral sciences* (rev. ed.). New York: Academic Press, 1977.

Cohen, J. Partialed products *are* interactions; partialed powers *are* curve components. *Psychological Bulletin,* 1978, *85,* 858–866.

Cook, T. D., Appleton, H., Conner, R. F., Shaffer, A., Tamkin, G., & Weber, S. J. *"Sesame Street"* revisited. New York: Russell Sage Foundation, 1975.

Cook, T. D., & Campbell, D. T. *Quasi-experimentation: Design and analysis issues for field settings.* Chicago: Rand McNally, 1979.

Cox, D. R. The use of a concomitant variable in selecting an experimental design. *Biometrika,* 1957, *44,* 150–158.

Cox, D. R. *Planning of experiments.* New York: Wiley, 1958.

Edwards, A. L. *Experimental design in psychological research.* New York: Holt, Rinehart & Winston, 1972.

Gage, N. L. *The scientific basis of the art of teaching.* New York: Teachers College Press, 1978.

Glass, G. V. Integrating findings: The meta-analysis of research. In L. S. Shulman (ed.), *Review of research in education* (Vol. 5). Itasca, Ill.: F. E. Peacock, 1977. Pp. 351–379.

Harnquist, K. Relative changes in intelligence from 13 to 18. *Scandinavian Journal of Psychology,* 1968, *9,* 50–82.

Hays, W. L. *Statistics for psychologists* (2nd ed.). New York: Holt, Rinehart & Winston, 1973.

Hull, C. H., & Nie, N. H. *SPSS update: New procedures and facilities for releases 7 and 8.* New York: McGraw-Hill, 1979.

Lord, F. M. A paradox in interpretation of group comparisons. *Psychological Bulletin,* 1967, *68,* 304–305.

Myers, J. L. *Fundamentals of experimental design* (2nd ed.). Boston: Allyn & Bacon, 1972.

Nie, N. H., Hull, C. H., Jenkins, J. G., Steinbrenner, K., & Bent, D. H. *Statistical package for the social sciences* (2nd ed.). New York: McGraw-Hill, 1975.

Overall, J. E., & Woodward, J. A. Common misconceptions concerning the analysis of covariance. *Journal of Multivariate Behavioral Research,* 1977, *12,* 171–185. (a)

Overall, J. E., & Woodward, J. A. Nonrandom assignment and the analysis of covariance. *Psychological Bulletin,* 1977, *84,* 588–594. (b)

Porter, A. C., & Chibucos, T. R. Selecting analytic strategies. In G. D. Borich (ed.), *Evaluating educational programs.* Englewood Cliffs, N.J.: Educational Technology Publications, 1974. Pp. 415–464.

Schutz, R. E. The control of "error" in educational experimentation. *School Review,* 1966, *74,* 151–158.

Winer, B. J. *Statistical principles in experimental design* (2nd ed.). New York: McGraw-Hill, 1971.

Wolf, R. M. Data analysis and reporting considerations. In W. J. Popham (ed.), *Evaluation in education: Current applications.* Berkeley: McCutchan, 1974. Pp. 201–242.

Wolf, R. M. *Evaluation in education.* New York: Praeger, 1979.

6

COMMUNICATING EVALUATION RESULTS FOR POLICY DECISION MAKING LOIS-ELLIN DATTA

T*he results of the statistical analyses along with other information pertinent to the effects of an educational program must be assembled into a
form that is meaningful and useful for decisions about that program. The
communication of this information for the purpose of choosing among decision alternatives is implicit in the definition of evaluation. If the evaluation
report is unclear or uninterpretable, such that it is useless to the decision
maker, then even the most meticulously planned and executed evaluation will
be worthless.*

*In chapter 6, Dr. Lois-ellin Datta reviews techniques and issues in com-
municating evaluation findings to decision makers. Her survey of the literature concentrates on evaluation textbooks, journals, and research reports.
The treatment of the topic by textbooks is minimal; the treatment by journals
and research reports is considerably better, including studies of techniques
such as adversary evaluation, reports of stakeholder participation studies,
and case studies of evaluation utilization. Dr. Datta's assessment of current
practices is couched within the context of evaluation reports from ten large
city school districts and five states. Despite a few exemplary reports, the
majority were characterized as descriptive statistical accounts rather than
action-oriented evaluations. Given this state of practice, Dr. Datta recom-
mends that evaluators consult the set of materials prepared by Lee and Holley
(1978; Holley, 1979, in press) that furnish specific guidelines for improving
the utilization of local evaluation reports. While systematic evidence on communicating findings is needed to determine whether communication makes a
difference in evaluation utilization, she argues persuasively that communication may be the end game, but effective communication comes at the beginning of an evaluation study as an integral part of the planning and execution.*

NOTE: Opinions expressed are the author's. Endorsement by the National Institute of Education
should not be inferred. My thanks to Robert F. Boruch and to the referees for helpful critical
reviews of earlier drafts.

INTRODUCTION

THE EFFECTIVENESS of evaluation has been questioned since at least 1969 when Guba, followed by Wholey et al. (1970) and Weiss (1972), asserted that most federally funded evaluations had little impact on programs, practices, or policy. Since then, the hunt has been up for the quick brown fox of utility. It has been sought in better design, more appropriate measurement, greater stakeholder participation, evaluation-as-enlightenment stances, and improved evaluation models. Rarely has the search centered on how the data are presented to decision influencers.

The purpose of this chapter is to see whether utility may be there, or if greater emphasis on the communication of findings would be oversell. I contend, based on scanty data, that it would not, and that more attention to the evaluation end game is warranted.

REVIEW OF ISSUES IN COMMUNICATING EVALUATION FINDINGS

During the past ten years, over 100 books have earned an evaluation listing in the Dewey Decimal Classification. A survey of these yielded little guidance on interpreting data and communicating findings. Editors and authors devote considerable space to clarifying objectives for the programs to be evaluated and the purposes of evaluation. Research design receives many chapters, and measurement, the rest.

One example is *The Handbook of Vocational Education Evaluation* (Abramson, Tittle, & Cohen, 1979). The more than 600 pages deal with vocational education history and goal setting (123 pages); evaluation approaches and special design issues including experimental and nonexperimental designs and cost/benefit analyses (121 pages); program development and evaluation concepts, including such matters as the content validity of behavioral objectives and methods of job analysis (127 pages); evaluation measures and testing issues, focused on interest measures, test bias, attitudes, and job satisfaction measures (141 pages); and politics and the evaluator's role (47 pages). On none of these pages is there discussion of report preparation and communication of evaluation findings as relevant to the matter of vocational education evaluation. The closest approach is in a summary of the evaluator's tasks, which are said to include: "the operationalization of objectives, sampling, data collection, the arrangement of data in a usable form, data processing, data analysis, the interpretation and the reporting of results" (p. 547).

A second example is the *Evaluation Studies Review Annual* (Guttentag, 1977). The more than 700 pages examine thinking about evaluation (92 pages); evaluation methodology and data integration, e.g., improvement of nonexperimental comparisons, determining optimum levels of statistical significance, and methods of aggregation across studies (217 pages); evaluation into policy, which includes a chapter on why evaluation research is not utilized (62 pages); evaluation in education, containing case studies of the quantity of schooling and the use of normative peer data as a standard for evaluating classroom and treatment effects (175 pages); studies in crime and justice (102 pages); and in human services, health, and labor (100 pages). In none of these pages is there much discussion of the nature of reports, the utilizability of their findings, or how the findings were communicated.

The closest approach in this book to such a discussion is Agarwala-Rogers's (1977) recommendation that "linkers distill and interpret this new information for the practitioners" (p. 328). This recommendation stems from the notion that people are more likely to adopt recommendations from insiders than from outsiders: "A linker is an individual who acts as liaison between two or more subsystems in a communication system. An effective research utilization system requires linkers to act as an intermediary between researchers and practitioners" (p. 332).

As part of their role, linkers are urged to provide research results according to the time schedule needed by the program officials and not that preferred by the evaluators ("The shorter the time lag between a program official's registration of a problem needing evaluation and providing him with the results, the more likely they are to be utilized" [p. 333]). Linkers also are urged to present results in a manner understandable to administrators ("Readability and the relevance of the reports would facilitate greater use of the results by administrators who typically are overworked thus do not read many research reports" [p. 332]). Multiple channels of communication are recommended ("Periodic oral presentations, short written reports and films ought to be used. Statistical tables should be accompanied with short explanation and text. Thus the heavy emphasis on receiver orientation when results of evaluation are communicated" [p. 332]). There are no references in the 600-plus citations in the book to systematic studies of communication as a factor in evaluation utilization.

A third example is Tuckman's *Evaluating Instructional Programs* (1979). The 13 chapters instruct the reader in how to define the quality of instructional programs, specify outcomes, define and measure program inputs and process, select different kinds of evaluation design (e.g., ex post facto, longitudinal, cross-sectional), assess outcomes, survey classroom inputs and process, and conduct formative, summative, and ex post facto evaluations. These chapters attend to writing objectives, constructing test items, collecting data, identifying control, comparison, and criterion groups, administering tests, analyzing prior achievement, and using growth tables and norm tables. The use of data to influence decision makers receives a few pages in the last chapter, along with discussion of individual student exit requirements, hard versus soft data, and establishing conditions for testing.

One interpretation of this brief survey is that texts, which generally provide overviews, can't dwell long on any of the many facets of evaluation. Another interpretation, based in part on the references used in these texts, is that the evaluator's role, evaluation models, measures, designs, and data analyses are perceived as more significant issues in evaluation than are communication of findings, and so the texts reflect both the extensiveness of research on better evaluation designs and the paucity of information on communicating results.

The State of Knowledge: Research Reports

A second source of knowledge about communicating evaluation findings was a survey of evaluation journals and research reports. Here the information is somewhat richer. This literature includes studies of techniques for communicating findings, such as adversial evaluation, reports of stakeholder participation studies, and case studies of evaluation utilization in education that include attention to communicating results.

Catch Their Attention

One set of reports examines ways to catch the attention of decision makers, capitalizing on the likelihood of controversy over the findings, their interpretation, and their implications for action. Windle (1979), for example, has urged evaluators to prefer socially noticeable differences in choosing outcome variables. He describes two studies in community mental health center evaluation. The first involved calling the centers' emergency numbers on weekends and evenings: most centers' numbers were out of order, and the few centers that did respond, used an answering service with almost no callbacks. Nonresponsiveness in emergencies was only one among many variables Windle could have chosen as an indicator of center functioning. Unlike other indicators, failure to answer an emergency call had such face validity that center directors to whom the findings were reported worked on correcting the situation rather than arguing about the meaningfulness of the outcome measure. Windle's second example used equity of service to the community: a comparison of the ethnic and racial composition of the clients served with the composition of the neighborhood. Disparities—and there were many—stood out sharply. Again, the face validity of the dependent variable was so socially compelling that attention focused on why and what to do, rather than on disputing the measure.

The Lawyers' Committee report on the number of children who do not attend school at all had similar consequences: the best curriculum may be debatable, and arguments can, and do, swirl about standardized achievement tests as appropriate measures of learning. Most people would agree, however, that elementary-school-age children ought to be in school in order to have the opportunity to learn.

Adversary evaluations. A second approach in the "catch-their-attention" genre capitalizes on the controversial nature of many evaluations. In this approach, individuals favoring one line of action and those opposed to it or favoring other actions debate interpretation of evaluations relevant to this action before citizen groups, their peers, and decision makers. A science-court approach has been proposed for high-technology issues such as energy policy; this has generated further controversy, part of which centers on the composition of the science court and the possibility of scientific neutrality. In educational evaluation, adversary evaluations have been reported for the adoption of Experience Based Career Education, an educational program using the community as the classroom for career exploration and academic purposes (Owens & Hiscox, 1977). A variant of this, forensic evaluation, was recommended earlier by Rivlin, in the context of the controversy over the Jensen report on the hereditability of intelligence. Rivlin described this as a situation in which individuals opposed to and favoring various interpretations of the findings use evaluative data to make the best possible case for their positions. She argued that such an approach would provide readers (or listeners) with a more honest understanding of the debaters' frame of reference for viewing the results, and that it would be most helpful for public policy to know the strongest cases that could be made for, or against, certain positions.

An approach to this model was tried for a debate on three pivotal assumptions regarding career education. These assumptions were (a) that informed choice is desirable, (b) that it was possible to predict what skills, attitudes and experiences would be useful for careers and what career opportunities the future would hold, and (c) that schools were willing to cooperate with labor unions and employers to provide career education. A debater was chosen for each side of these assertions, and the debate was held in a public forum in June 1977. The debaters spent most of their time arguing against the importance of the assertions they were to discuss and presenting papers on a related topic. The disciplined debate form apparently is not readily congenial to researchers.

In process is an elaborately planned effort to communicate findings of a study of minimum-competency testing, a controversial issue that already has reached the courts. The Judicial Evaluation or Hearing model involves (a) development of teams formed of stakeholders concerned with the use and abuse of minimum-competency testing, (b) selection of which evidentiary and hearing rules used in current legal proceedings are appropriate for the issue, (c) provision of technical assistance from experienced hearing examiners to help the teams define evidence relevant to their positions, (d) disclosure hearings, (e) collection of data needed by both teams, with equal support for analysis, and (f) hearings conducted by a senior experienced examiner that will be videotaped and made available, together with all reports, to state legislatures, to local school boards, and to other groups concerned with minimum-competency testing (Herndon, 1980). The study will be evaluated by a third party for effectiveness in communicating findings to decision-maker publics. Designed with extensive consultation from evaluators who developed models based on a hearings process, members of the legal profession, and stakeholder groups, the minimum-competency-testing study is trying harder to use the hearings approach to improve utility of evaluative findings.

Decision-theoretic approach.   Widely known as a technique to help establish what program objectives an evaluation will assess, the decision-theoretic approach also has distinctive features with respect to how the findings are reported. The results are represented according to the weights placed by various individuals or constituencies on the program features and their outcomes. A recent example of this approach was reported by Edwards (1980). The City of Los Angeles was being sued by citizens' groups for failure to desegregate. The judge called for an evaluative study of the probable consequences of the many plans put forth—and argued for and against—by various citizens' groups. Edwards identified the consequences the different groups sought through their plans and the value they placed on these consequences, as measured by the trade-offs they were willing to accept; then, using available data, he compared the probable outcomes of each of the plans recommended with the consequences sought by the various stakeholder groups. Results were reported in the form of weighted probable accomplishments of these objectives, a technique Edwards reports communicated effectively with the citizen groups, although not with the judge, who decided the approach to be used on other grounds.

Case Studies of Communicating Evaluation Results

Recommendations based on interviews with decision influencers led to the Brickell and Aslanian report, *Data for Decision Makers* (1974). Although this was begun as a study to help communicate results of a national study of career education curricula, its recommendations have been cited in other educational contexts. Among these recommendations were (a) brevity (one page of brief statements giving major findings and recommendations), (b) placing almost all technical material in appendices, (c) timeliness in relation to expectations of the people commissioning the study or to actual decision cycles, (d) use of entirely nontechnical language, (e) including action recommendations, thus merging the roles of evaluator and policy/program designer, and (f) providing as backup to the executive summary a brief report that would present the findings using charts, graphs, bullets, and other ways quickly to highlight the main points of the study. Among the other findings of interest were the concerns of policy makers at different levels. Those funding the research or evaluation were concerned primarily that important questions were being asked, and had few expectations about the definitiveness of the answers—a more sophisticated view perhaps than that with which evaluation theorists have credited decision makers. Those directly responsible for program operation wanted action recommendations backed by data. Those concerned more distantly with program policy were interested in the technical validity of the findings and more willing to leave the action implications to others, as beyond the scope of the evaluators' responsibility or role. Brickell and Aslanian concluded that a single executive summary or brief report could not be written to communicate equally effectively with different decision makers. Much work as it might be, they recommended different strokes for the different folks.

Empirically based studies. Empirical studies of evaluation utilization have grown in number and diversity. Among the more recent are the five case studies of California educational programs reported by Alkin, Daillak, and White (1979). The studies were informed by a theoretical analysis comparing mainstream and alternate definitions of utility. The mainstream definitions involved as a criterion for utilization the immediate and direct impact of the evaluation on one or more critical program decisions. The Alkin (1975) and Patton et al. (1975) definition emphasized a gradual influence on administrator perceptions of the evaluated program, which, in concert with other forces, may change slowly the course of program decision making. A second distinguishing feature was that the literature of mainstream evaluation utilization was said to concentrate on static factors influencing utilization, while the alternative perspective emphasizes "an interpersonal dynamic occurring within the evolving, ever-changing evaluation situation. It deals most significantly with the process by which individual actors deal with the unique contextual constraints in the evaluation situation and forge a workable strategy for evaluating the program" (p. 26).

All the programs examined in the case studies were funded through Title III of the Elementary and Secondary Assistance Act (the same title under which the case studies of the Rand report on educational change were supported) and Title IV-C of that Act. One involved a project to increase student retention; a second, the implementation of an individually guided instruction program (IGE, developed by the University of Wisconsin Research and Development Center for Cognitive Learning); a third, a kindergarten program intended to prevent later educational disabilities; the fourth, a career education oriented high school; and the fifth was a bilingual education program.

Alkin et al.'s analyses of these case studies required refining the definition of utilization. They distinguished three forms of consideration (dominant influence, multiple influences, multiple cumulative influences); three information purposes (making decisions, substantiating previous decisions or actions, and establishing or altering attitudes) and six issues (external funding of the program, local district funding, continuing a program component, change in curricular methods, change in administrative/personnel operations, and community acceptance). Examples of all forms of consideration, information purposes, and issues were found in the case-study data, indicating that by their definitions, utilization *did* occur.

Their second line of inquiry dealt with the factors affecting utilization. The eight factors identified were (a) preexisting evaluation boundaries, (b) orientation of the users, (c) the evaluators' approach, (d) evaluator credibility, (e) organizational factors, (f) extraorganizational factors, (g) information content and reporting, and (h) administrator styles. With regard to information content and reporting, Alkin et al. concluded that equating the contents of a final report with evaluation information is far too limited. Their conception includes multiple evaluation reports, an emphasis on qualitative as well as quantitative data, and the variety of display techniques employed to increase comprehensibility. They argue also for including oral presentations as part of dissemination.

Even with these carefully defined concepts of information content and reporting, they reported that these distinctions did not provide "any real explanatory power for potential utilization. Instead their importance only became apparent when seen within a framework that included the particular evaluation context and the people who dealt with the information. We had to ask to what extent these various content and reporting dimensions were appropriate, in terms of the substance of what was presented as well as the format, to the users and their perceived needs" (p. 253).

In addition to structural aspects of the match among content, format, and recipient, Alkin et al. emphasize the information exchange process: the evaluators' sensitivity to the people with whom they are communicating. A technically excellent evaluation, they point out, may have been inappropriate because it addressed only tangentially the concerns of local users.

The third characteristic explaining utilization variance is an information dialogue, seen as "much more than a simple exchange of information between the evaluator and the important program personnel . . . the important attribute of information dialogue is the open-ended, two-way communication in which the evaluation information and its implications are explored, rather than presented. At its most effective, information dialogue results in a more profound and shared perspective on the uses of evaluation" (p. 254). The latter finding echoes the experience of Paul Hill and his colleagues in the congressionally mandated evaluation of Title I of ESEA. Their reports, which are believed to have influenced the features of the amended legislation in 1978, were only one point in an information dialogue lasting from 1974 to 1978 among Hill, his congressional liaison, Jim Harvey, and the authorization committees in the House and Senate which had commissioned these reports in 1974 (Hill, personal communication, 1978).

According to Alkin et al., it would be an oversimplification to conclude that evaluation utilization would be assured by attention to the match between reports and audience in content and format, the sensitivity of the evaluator to the individuals in the information exchange, and the information dialogue alone. These rather are seen as one among eight factors that constitute a framework within which a theory of evaluation utilization might be formed, and in which all factors are needed to describe, and possibly predict, the course of utilization. "Evaluation is a dynamic process," they write, "and the events of an evaluation are the product of multiple influences" (p. 257).

These summaries suggest more yeasty ideas about communicating evaluation findings than the texts indicate. The studies are, however, descriptive rather than predictive: trying out the feasibility of adversial evaluation and debates, or examining case studies to derive explanatory concepts. There are few, if any, studies in which communication practice is varied systematically and changes, if any, in evaluation utilization are traced. The exceptions are studies now under way of information intermediaries, research diffusion, utilization and dissemination systems, regional education research exchanges, and other approaches based on the notion that linkage agents between researcher and practitioner are needed before evaluations or research findings will affect policy and practice (see, for example, Chelimsky, 1979; Louis, 1980).

The State of Practice

There appears to be no analysis of the state of practice in either evaluation report preparation or in the information dialogue described by Alkin et al. References to the deficiencies of evaluation reports are common, particularly lack of information on the participants, the nature of the program, its management and implementation, the ways in which the program was evaluated, and details of the analyses that are seen as necessary for interpreting the findings (see, for example, Herr, 1977, on evaluators of programs). These are, however, comments along the way to another destination, rather than a systematic analysis of the process of evaluation information communication itself (Worthen & Sanders, 1973).

As a partial proxy to such a study, evaluation directors in ten big cities and five states were asked to send any single evaluation report prepared between 1977 and 1979 with which they were reasonably satisfied. A similar request was made of Federal agencies producing educational evaluation reports (for example, the General Accounting Office and the U.S. Office of Education Office of Dissemination and Evaluation).

The resulting body of material (over 20 reports, a 90% response) is of modest value at best. Nothing is known about the context of these reports. What seems like inadequate communication, if context is studied as Alkin et al. recommend, may have been tailored admirably to the interests of a specific, significant reader. The material is thus probably biased to seem less useful than it may be. However, since the best reports had been requested, there are also probable biases in the direction of making things look better than they would have appeared to be had a nationally representative sample of educational evaluation reports been drawn and the context of their use studied. Perhaps, however, this cautious something is better than wholly speculative nothing.

The information was examined with two objectives in mind: first, a determination of how report space was used and what was emphasized, and second, a judgment about the content of the reports. Table 6.1 shows the way in which space was used in the reports, in terms of the presence/absence of an executive summary and of attention to methodology and measures; to the findings; and to interpretations, alternative interpretations, and recommendations. As the table indicates, there were few executive summaries, and these few tended to be long. There were no instances similar to the Brickell-Aslanian recommendation on one page, highlighting the study's major findings, conclusions, and recommendations. An example of a typical abstract is

TABLE 6.1. How Space Is Used in 22 Reports Evaluating Education Programs (LEA and SEA Reports)

Study	Pages	Summary	Recs.	Program	Method/ Meas.	Descr. Text	Statistics
Title IV	60	yes	yes	10	10	20	20
Special ed.	60	no	no	5	5	10	40
Special ed.	6	no	no	1	1	1	3
Sex fairness	15	yes	no	1	1	2	11
Voc. education	45	yes	no	1	4	5	35
Teachers	15	yes	no	1	1	1	12
Employees	5	yes	no	0	½	1½	3
Services	55	no	no	2	2	6	45
Parents	45	yes	yes	1	3	6	35
Migrants	90	yes	yes	20	15	35	30
Neglected	80	no	yes	10	20	10	40
Title I	140	no	no	15	15	40	70
Bilingual	515	yes	yes	----------300 mixed-----------			215
Comp. educ.	500	no	no	----------200 mixed-----------			300
Quality ind.	10	no	no	2	2	0	6
Title I	37	no	no	3	3	7	24
Title I	45	yes	yes	1	3	3	38
Bilingual	15	no	no	½	½	1	13
Title I	35	no	no	5	4	4	25
Title I	95	yes	yes	10	10	14	61
Title I	50	yes	yes	3	5	6	36
Title I	14	yes	yes	1	1	3	9

Note: Estimates, not by-the-inch analyses.

given in Table 6.2. Most of the documents dealt with measures, methodology, and findings. Comparing pages of statistics to pages of text, the median report had about 70% of all pages devoted to statistics, including copies of question-naires used and the response frequencies for each item. There were few instances of interpretation of findings and no instances in which alternative interpretations were examined. Many reports did not include conclusions, recommendations, or action implications. Recommendations for action that were presented at some length usually were urging improved evaluations, rather than program-related actions. An example of a typical set of program recommendations is given in Table 6.3, and of evaluation recommendations in Table 6.4. (In no instance was a purpose of the evaluation said to have been improved evaluation methodology.)

With regard to content, many of the evaluation reports were descriptive rather than inferential. One report, for example, was intended to assess the preparation of new teachers. The group selected consisted of recent graduates of state teacher-education programs who had been hired as regular classroom teachers during their first year out of college. The technique was a survey administered for three consecutive years to three cohorts of new graduates.

TABLE 6.2. Example of an Abstract

ESEA Title I Senior High Schools Project: Mathematics Centers
Evaluation Report

The Title I Senior High Schools project is a compensatory mathematics program that is federally funded under the Elementary and Secondary Education Act. This project at the Exemplary Unified School District was designed to meet the mathematics needs of 800 students in grades 9–10 at Good, Better, and Best Senior High Schools of the Exemplary Unified School District and 70 students in grades 5–7 attending SS. Mary and Martha Catholic School and the Ecumenical High School.

The goal of the project was to improve the students' achievement in mathematics problem solving and mathematics comprehension skills. The selection of Title I students was based on scores within stanines 1–3 on a norm-referenced test as well as teacher recommendations. Students with the greatest need for mathematics instruction were given the highest priority for participation in the Title I project.

The project objective was that after participating in the Title I project, Title I students would exceed the "no treatment expectation" as measured in Normal Curve Equivalents on the Appropriate Test of Basic Skills, Mathematics Problem Solving and Mathematics Comprehension Subtests. Title I 9th grade students gained 4.5 Normal Curve Equivalents between pre- and post-testing and 10th grade students gained 4.5 Normal Curve Equivalents. The project objective was attained.

At SS. Mary and Martha Catholic School and at the Ecumenical High School, Title I students gained 3.1 Normal Curve Equivalents in Mathematics Problem Solving and 9.5 Normal Curve Equivalents in Mathematics Comprehension. The project objective was met.

A notable accomplishment was that the 1978–1979 Title I evaluation showed greater gains in student achievement in the Exemplary Unified School District Title I Senior High Schools than in the previous three years of Title I in the Secondary Schools Project.

Note: Specifics changed slightly.

The evaluation report is limited to description of the responses to the questionnaires. For example:

One of the original concerns of the Division of Teacher Education was whether different programs of professional preparation produced teachers who could function more or less effectively in the classroom. The school means on total program characteristics were correlated with mean scores for the development of teaching skill and ability statements for the 17 schools shown in Table 1. The correlation coefficient (r = .16) obtained was so small that no relationship can be assumed.

For the 16 certification areas showing enough respondents over the three years to provide reasonably reliable means, Table 2 shows longitudinal data. As with the college means, they seem fairly stable over time. Library Science shows a five point increase from 1976 to 1977; it is the only sizeable change. The increase in Art between 1975 and 1976 may be due to the revision of items or it could be a true program change.

The percentage of teachers who said they had been able to accelerate completion of their program decreased each year. The three percent decrease from 1976 to 1977 is not a statistically significant difference (p = .14), however the five percent change from 1975 to 1977 is statistically significant (p = .01). The reader may judge whether this change is educationally significant.

TABLE 6.3. Example of Program Recommendations

The overall conduct of the Title XXX program is characterized by high quality activities and outcomes. Where impact data are available, they indicate that such activities are having a positive influence on student learning and on the overall educational program in local school districts.

Management: Consider the development of a formal assessment of the management of Title XXX. Such an evaluation should address at a minimum the following elements: planning, quality control procedures, communication, personnel management, State Advisory Council involvement, monitoring and evaluation procedures, and dissemination. Such an assessment might emphasize a particular management process from year to year, depending on available resources. If such is the case, it is suggested that the dissemination function in the Title XXX program be given consideration for early review since it appears to be a critical element in all three program areas.

Part F: Formalize the selection of Title F exemplary projects using the entire population of projects from which the selection is made. Self-nomination may be an appropriate way to narrow the field. Adapting some of the procedures used for reviewing Title XXX projects may be a means of transferring some of the clarity and accountability of the Title XXX-H process to the best Title XXX-F projects.

Broaden the dissemination effort for Part F exemplary projects. Consider using publications and presentations at orientation sessions and workshops in addition to the awards presentation at the Improved Education Conference. Disseminate information about projects that focus XXX-F monies on special projects or target populations or which are integrated with the LEA Improvement Process.

Provide LEAs with a wide range of sample objectives that are meaningful and useful. Suggest ways in which simple assessment techniques can be used to ascertain whether the money is being well spent. It is possible that appropriate evaluation procedures might be developed during FY1980 and used by those districts wishing to be considered as exemplary. At the State level, consider the use of a select number of carefully developed case studies to illustrate the variety of exemplary uses to which Title XXX-F funds can be directed.

Note: Specifics changed slightly.

Another evaluation examined delivery of services by intermediate educational units. Again, the report is limited to a description of questionnaire responses. As examples:

Total receipts increased by 5.49 percent, while total expenditures increased by 9.22 percent. This was due to the 1975-1976 balance of $14,744,280. The 1976-1977 balance dropped to $4,403,988, which would not provide enough monies to maintain a similar increase in expenditures in 1978-1979.

It is evident from this tabulation that the Intermediate Units (IUs) most successful in obtaining federal grants are IUs 3, 4, 5, 9, 11, 12, 13, 14, 15, 16, 17, 19, 21, 22, 23, and 24. The greatest percent of interest earned was by IUs 2 and 22 in 1975 and IUs 2, 12 and 33 in 1976. IU 16 was the most successful IU in receiving the greatest percentage from member districts of service users.

Insofar as accurate description goes, most of the reports seem to restate accurately in the text the statistics presented in tables, graphs, and pie charts. Inferential statistics rarely are used and these (as in the example of the test of the significance of differences in percentage of response from one year to the next) appear correctly applied. In only a few instances does zeal overwhelm common sense, as in the analyses of mean scores on an occupational knowledge measure involving about 15 items, where all data are reported to five decimal places, suggesting a degree of meaningfulness considerably exceeding the reliability of the device.

In several reports, when conclusions were reached, the relation between data and conclusions were obscure. As an example, in the evaluation of intermediate service units, all data reported related to changes in expenditures

TABLE 6.4. Example of Evaluation Recommendations That Focus on Evaluation Improvement

---

The Improved Career Guidance Project: Annual Evaluation Report

The evaluation results for 1978-1979 support the following recommendations:
1. The program should continue to be offered in its present form, with the same emphasis on parent participation and involvement.
2. Development of instruments for assessment and evaluation of the parent involvement components of ICGP should continue. These instruments reflect specifically the staff expectations, goals and objectives for parent involvement in student career decision-making in ICGP.
3. The ICGP Career Knowledge and Attitudes scale, developed by ICGP staff to reflect specific goals and activities for the student, should become the primary instrument for evaluating the student's learning and development in the ICGP program.
4. The parent participation fostered through the ICGP should be encouraged and supported throughout the senior high school grades.

Note: These are the complete recommendations for a report introduced as an evaluation of the ICGP program. Specifics changed slightly.

(e.g., "Food services had the lowest percentage of increase, .73 percent and general administration, 2.3 percent, second"), receipts and expenditures, and number of support and professional employees ("Full time support employees increased by 465 or 11.2 percent and part-time support employees decreased by 100, or 13.1 percent"). The last statement in the summary—the conclusion—is "All of the above statistics indicate that the IUs are truly service-oriented organizations, providing many essential and desirable educational services."

It was not possible, as originally planned, to discuss the reports in terms of the significance of the issues and the solidity of the conclusions, because so few reached conclusions or offered recommendations. Although titled "evaluations," an admittedly untidy word, they might be presented more accurately as uninterpreted descriptive statistical accounts of some aspects of educational programs. This does *not* mean that such information is not useful: it may be quite useful for program audits documenting services delivered, personnel hired, and expenditure flows. It does suggest that educational decision influencers could not easily read one of these reports as a way of becoming informed on what actions, if any, would be needed to maintain educational excellence or improve schools.

The Exceptions

Several reports were exceptions to these descriptive evaluations. One was a report prepared for a state education agency by a contractor with considerable experience in national evaluation. The long report (over 500 pages, single space, both sides) included an Executive Summary with recommendations. While the summary was lengthier than many full reports (over 23 pages), findings were organized around questions some decision influencers would seem likely to ask, such as, "What entrance/exit criteria are used to determine student participation in the transitional bilingual education program and are these entrance/exit criteria appropriate?" and it included both summaries of the findings and interpretations. For example:

The most commonly used procedure for determining entrance into and exit from the program is teacher judgment . . . however, teacher judgment is most frequently used in combination with a variety of other methods such as student classification on a proficiency test, parental request or approval, bilingual teacher assessment, diagnostic tests, teacher-made tests and standardized tests.
Use of a single measure or procedure would not be appropriate; current use of more than two procedures is reducing the potential incidence of misclassification.

Throughout the report, knowledge from other studies is cumulated, placing the findings from the evaluation in a context of policy, politics, theory, research, and practice. Observations and comments are blended with reports from tests, questionnaires, interviews, and reviews of student records. For example,

Some of the following comments may warrant additional investigation: The pull-out model presents some scheduling problems when attempting to ensure that all children receive all required instruction. Children may be adversely affected by a pull-out program because they miss part of the instruction in the home classroom. It is difficult to maintain the needed level of communication between teachers to effectively implement a pull-out model. The self-contained classroom model limits the interaction between students in the bilingual education program and the All-English program.

Finally, recommendations are given in actionable terms for state authorities:

Section 1.11: the five English language proficiency levels need to be reassessed in light of the multidefinitions currently being used, their number and linguistic function.

The state-wide Bilingual Advisory Council functions and composition should be reviewed to determine whether or not that body can perform their recommended role.

Section 10.01: the number of students required to warrant a teacher's aide should be reviewed in light of experience and alternative program designs.

The text is keyed to such recommendations, and the reader can find in the fuller text both data related to the conclusions and ideas for change.

A second example of different approaches to communicating evaluation findings is the now widely reported study by Holley and her colleagues on school time allocations. Prior research had indicated that amount of instruction correlates strongly with academic achievement, but observational studies have suggested that large amounts of classroom time are lost to instruction. Putting these two findings together in a detailed observational study of children in the Austin, Texas, schools, Holley and her colleagues found that students were receiving only about 3 hours and 45 minutes per day of instruction. Children in compensatory classes received less instructional time than noncompensatory children. Holley (1979) reports:

The results of this study were well publicized both internally and externally. Newspaper articles appeared. Television coverage was heavy. The Office of Research and Evaluation prepared a readable brochure that went all over the district. Graphs were used to illustrate the findings. There were some intensely negative reactions to the study. Many teachers were indignant; principals questioned the methodology; and school board members simply couldn't believe the results. Other teachers and administrators, however, confirmed the results as realistic. (P. 4)

In the following year, Holley continues, the Director of Elementary Education gave high priority to increasing instructional time and to helping teachers reduce time on management activities. A follow-up study, two years later, showed that instructional time increased by an average of 24 minutes for Title

I students, 35 minutes for non–Title I students and 23 minutes for students in non–Title I schools. This was equivalent to gaining over $2 million annually in instructional time and would amount to adding 8.4 to 13.1 additional school days a year devoted entirely to instruction. Gratifyingly, achievement in the elementary grades also increased.

Based on these and other experiences with utilization of local evaluations for school improvement, Holley has prepared a series of reports on communicating evaluation findings. Three of these seem required reading for evaluators seeking to improve utilization: "What It Takes to Win: Factors in the Utilization of Evaluation Findings for Educational Technology" (Holley, in press), "Communicating Evaluation Information: Some Practical Tips" (Lee & Holley, 1978), and "Catch a Falling Star: Promoting the Utilization of Research and Evaluation Findings" (Holley, 1979). The recommendations are summarized in Table 6.5, from Lee and Holley (1978).

Like Alkin et al., Holley places dissemination in a framework of other factors influencing utilization, which include the characteristics of the idea evaluated, the evaluation user, the organization, the evaluator, and the evaluation findings. Among her observations of factors favoring evaluation utilizations are:

the greater power of a study based on questions arising from a national body of research findings and a base of local research data.

a strong emphasis on accountability in the district, which required staff to study evaluation reports and tell the superintendent and school senior board what actions they will take as a result of the findings.

a link to research suggesting actions practitioners could take to make improvements in response to the evaluation findings.

extensive dissemination, planned to avoid striking negative buttons ("not *another* meeting!") and to lean into the most promising individual characteristics of decision influencers (openness to new information, innovativeness, reader ability to interpret data) in the formal organizational chart and in informal networks.

presentations that focus on a few, most significant findings and that avoid talking about methods, design and measures. These seem to distract practitioners from the message and its action implications.

expecting an incubation period during which the findings are related to other reports and cumulate into a body of belief.

high organizational status for the evaluation unit, including direct access to top district administrators, and high credibility, including a track record of reporting accurately negative results of superintendent and board decisions as well as positive findings.

evaluator availability to continue to push the study and its findings, and evaluator skill in speech making, interviews, press-releases and one-page information summaries.

resources to pay for graphics and for dissemination, such as individually designed brochures for students, teachers and principals.

adopting a common approach and format for all evaluation reports to speed up communication of results, particularly a format built around decision questions that link question, data, and information supporting plausible action alternatives (see Table 6.6).

avoiding the traps of (a) confusing numbers with meaning as an end of evaluation; (b) giving data at levels that are useless for individual action (such as the mean mathematical achievement scores for the district to an individual teacher); (c) using objectives for evaluation rather than only for planning since they are highly susceptible to manipulation by project staff; and (d) failing to give information about needed changes in activities.

TABLE 6.5. Practical Tips on Communicating Evaluation Information (Adapted from Lee & Holley, 1978, pp. 27–47)

Evaluation Audiences
1. Know your audiences
2. Find out what information they need and, if possible, when they need it
3. Try to understand each audience's viewpoint

Evaluation Message
4. Relate the information to action that must be taken
5. Do not give the audience more than it needs
6. Start with the most important information
7. Highlight the important points
8. Make your report readable
   a. Create an imaginary reader and keep this person in mind as you work
   b. Imagine that you are explaining the various aspects of the program to an interested but relatively uninformed person
   c. Check the vocabulary to make sure you have used familiar words
   d. Use action verbs as much as possible
   e. Cut out the deadwood
   f. Shorten your sentences
   g. Write shorter paragraphs
   h. Personalize your text
      (1) Use personal pronouns
      (2) Use contractions
      (3) Use "shirtsleeves" language

Verbal Presentations
 9. Make the presentation format interesting and varied
10. Do what comes naturally
11. Make the visuals large and simple
12. Involve the audience in the presentation

Difficult Audiences
13. Have the audience teach the content of the report to someone else
14. Have someone else deliver the information
15. Reinforce, reinforce, reinforce

Working with the Press
16. Train reporters
17. Write news releases
18. Be honest with reporters

Of more anecdotal interest, but perhaps worth a systematic study, is the way findings from the Developmental Continuity study funded by the U.S. Administration of Children, Youth and Families have contributed to turning doubt to belief, and strong negative views at least to doubt of the long-term benefits of early-intervention programs such as Project Head Start. The study, conducted under the leadership of Lazar, and reported at length by Palmer and Anderson (1979), indicates that children participating in well-designed and carefully managed preschools are less likely than nonparticipants to stay in grade without placement in special education or having to repeat a grade. These easy-to-understand results, which translate fairly readily into dollar savings, were presented over an almost three-year period by Lazar and his colleagues in almost every conceivable forum: scientific societies, profes-

TABLE 6.6. An Example from an Evaluation Report of a Format for Relating Evaluation Information to an Action That Must Be Taken

Decision Question

Should the district provide a fourth (summer) quarter for students in grades 7–12?

Information Summary

11% of the secondary students are interested in attending an additional fourth quarter, and 18% of the teachers are willing to teach an additional summer quarter.

All secondary students were surveyed about their reasons for wanting to attend a fourth summer quarter. The results:

Reasons given by students who said they would attend a summer quarter	Grades				
	7	8	9	10	11
For enrichment	26%	20%	19%	18%	27%
To graduate early	29%	22%	32%	45%	60%
To catch up	43%	57%	48%	34%	12%
Other	2%	1%	1%	3%	1%

All secondary teachers in the district were surveyed to assess their availability for teaching the fourth summer quarter. The results:

18%—would teach all four quarters
45%—could teach summer quarter if they could get off another quarter
33%—not available to teach a summer quarter under any circumstances
  4%—want more information
100%

Note: This table drawn from "Communicating Evaluation Information: Some Practical Tips" by A. M. Lee and F. M. Holley is reprinted from *How to Present an Evaluation Report* by L. L. Morris and C. T. Fitz-Gibbon, copyright 1978, p. 32 by permission of the Publisher, Sage Publications, Inc.)

sional organizations, popular magazines reaching millions of parents, national and state legislatures, and special-interest groups throughout the country and internationally. The impact of the message (as an April 15, 1980, *Washington Post* editorial describing the study makes clear) has been shown by the allocation of funds to expand Head Start and by a presidential reconvening of the original Head Start Panel with a view to using the findings of the Lazar study and other evaluations to chart a new national course for early childhood programs for all poor children.

Does Communication Make a Difference?

This chapter began with an inquiry into whether communication of findings is likely to make a sufficient difference in evaluation utilization to be worth what may be extra effort for many evaluators. The answer to this inquiry must rest on anecdote and example, because there is little systematic, let alone experimental, evidence one way or the other.

The argument is buttressed more powerfully in the negative than in the positive. Except for studies of intermediaries and linkage agents in knowledge utilization, little research attention has been given to communicating findings.* Current practice—to the extent that the 20-plus evaluation reports from schools are typical of anything besides themselves—exemplifies most often the preached against. The reports are primarily quantitiative, organized around the measures used rather than questions asked, without conclusions or recommendations, and for the most part, offer few convincing links among questions, evidence, and action possibilities, when these are given at all. The sought-for is represented primarily by case studies: by the reports of Alkin et al. (1979), documenting the impact of communications skills in the programs where evaluation seemed to make a difference, the informal reports of long-term dialogue with Congress in communicating results of the Title I national evaluation, and the extensive materials provided by Holley and her coworkers in the Austin, Texas, school district, in which communication is emphasized strongly as a factor in utilization of results.

Considerable effort is involved in conducting almost any evaluation: in identifying the evaluable question, in designing the study, in overcoming the obstacles to conducting an evaluation and protecting it methodologically from uninterpretability. It would seem worthwhile for those who carry the findings of these evaluations to decision influencers to devote the time, funds, and creativity needed to develop evaluation communications approaches that put

---

*Guidelines and manuals for evaluators are attending increasingly to communicating findings. Examples include the *Standards for Evaluations of Educational Programs, Projects, and Materials* (see Stufflebeam, chapter 7) and the Evaluation Research Society's *Standards for Program Evaluation* (see Bryk & Light, chapter 1), the General Accounting Office's guidelines, and the Morris and Fitz-Gibbon (1978) book on presenting evaluation reports. These join earlier more technical guides to clear writing such as Ewing (1974).

into action the common recommendations from almost all sources of knowledge: address the few important questions, present the evidence, and state the action implications in one page or less; back these up with a low-technology presentation of appropriate data; and repeat and repeat and repeat the message, in different forms, for different audiences. Anything worth doing well may be worth telling well, and evaluation, happily, is not without examples of both.

SUGGESTIONS FOR FUTURE RESEARCH

At least three directions for future research on communicating findings might be pursued. These are:

1. descriptive studies of how findings are communicated, including but not limited to analyses of use of the written evaluation reports;
2. predictive studies of whether features identified as likely to be effective, such as greater attention to actionable recommendations or use of a hearing model for controversial areas, actually provide more useful information than simpler or more traditional forms of communication. A useful example is Brown, Braskamp, and Newman (1978);
3. developmental research, exploring ways to deal with such possible quandaries as safeguarding accuracy of everyday language pamphlets dealing with complex phenomena.

The context in which the evaluation takes place will need thoughtful attention in such research. The models for communicating findings of management-oriented studies to local school boards (for example, a study of ways to reduce fuel costs), of instructionally oriented evaluations to a larger public (for example, percentages of Anglo, Black, Asian-American, and Hispanic youth passing state minimum competency tests), and policy-oriented evaluations to a national audience (for example, the impact of immersion, transitional, and maintenance programs for language minority students) will need to deal with considerable differences in origin of the evaluative questions, stakeholder interests, and complexity of findings. Different standards of reporting needs may surround programs that have strong political components compared with those for which effects are neutral.

GUIDELINES FOR EVALUATORS

In addition to the guidelines suggested in earlier sections and in Tables 6.5 and 6.6, evaluators concerned with communicating findings to decision makers may wish to apply to our own art and sullen craft the advice we give to others: communication may be the end game, but effective communication comes at the beginning as an integral part of the planning and conduct of technically competent, socially responsible evaluations. Attention to probable findings and how they best may be communicated can influence—and appropriately so—major features of design, measures, and study conduct. Such attention need not conflict with technical demands: for example, detailed information and statistics can be provided through microfiche attachments to the nontechnical reports. In discussions with decision makers, what can *not* be concluded and for what conditions findings *are* valid, two frequent caveats in more technical analyses, can be emphasized.

These efforts take time, sensitivity to political aspects of decision making, and the ability to communicate effectively. The first can be provided for in evaluation budgets, the second increasingly is receiving great attention in evaluation theory and practice, and the third, as evaluators such as Holley and Lazar prove, is a very possible dream.

REFERENCES

Abramson, T., Tittle, C. K., & Cohen, L. (eds.), *The handbook of vocational education evaluation*. Beverly Hills: Sage, 1979.

Agarwala-Rogers, R. Why is evaluation research not utilized? In M. Guttentag (ed.), *Evaluation studies review annual* (Vol. 2). Beverly Hills: Sage, 1977. Pp. 327–333.

Alkin, M. C. Evaluation: Who needs it? Who cares? *Studies in Educational Evaluation*, 1975, *1*, 201–212.

Alkin, M. C., Daillak, R., & White, P. *Using evaluations: Does evaluation make a difference?* Beverly Hills: Sage, 1979.

Brickell, H. M., & Aslanian, C. B. *Data for decision makers: An analysis of evaluation data needed by decision-makers in educational programs* (A report to NIE). New York: Policy Studies in Education, 1974.

Brown, R. D., Braskamp, L. A., & Newman, D. L. Evaluation credibility as a function of report style: Do jargon and data make a difference? *Evaluation Quarterly*, 1978, *2*, 331–341.

Chelimsky, E. *Proceedings of a symposium on the institutionalization of federal programs at the local level*. Arlington, Va.: The MITRE Corporation, 1979.

Edwards, W. Multiattribute utility for evaluation: Structures, uses and problems. In M. W. Klein and K. S. Teilmann (eds.), *Handbook of criminal justice evaluation*. Beverly Hills: Sage, 1980.

Ewing, D. W. *Writing for results in business, government and the professions*. New York: Wiley, 1974.

Guba, E. G. The failure of educational evaluation. *Educational Technology*. 1969, *9*, 29–38.

Guttentag, M. (ed.). *Evaluation studies review annual* (Vol. 2). Beverly Hills: Sage, 1977.

Herndon, E. *Studying minimum competency testing: A process for the clarification of issues*. Washington, D.C.: National Institute of Education, 1980.

Herr, E. What is known about career education: Concepts and findings. Paper presented at the Oregon Inter-institutional Consortium for Career Education Conference, Eugene, April 1977.

Holley, F. M. Catch a falling star: Promoting the utilization of research and evaluation findings. Paper presented at the annual meeting of the American Educational Research Association, San Francisco, April 1979.

Holley, F. M. What it takes to win: Factors in the utilization of evaluation findings for educational technology. In C. Stalford (ed.), *Evaluation frontiers*. Washington, D.C.: National Institute of Education, in press.

Lee, A. M., & Holley, F. M. Communicating evaluation information: Some practical tips. In L. L. Morris and C. T. Fitz-Gibbon, *How to present an evaluation report*. Beverly Hills: Sage, 1978. Pp. 27–47.

Louis, K. S. *Products and process: Some preliminary findings from the R & D utilization program*. Cambridge, Mass.: Abt Associates, 1980.

Morris, L. L, & Fitz-Gibbon, C. T. *How to present an evaluation report*. Beverly Hills: Sage, 1978.

Owens, T. R., & Hiscox, M. D. Alternative models for adversary evaluation: Variations on a theme. Paper presented at the annual meeting of the American Educational Research Association, New York, April 1977.

Palmer, F. H., & Anderson, L. W. Long term gains from early intervention: Findings from longitudinal studies. In E. Zigler and J. Valentine, *Project Head Start*. New York: The Free Press, 1979. Pp. 433–468.

Patton, M. Q., Grimes, P. S., Guthrie, D., Brennan, N. J., French, B. D., & Blyth, D. A. *In search of impact: An analysis of utilization of federal health evaluation research*. Minneapolis: Minnesota Center for Social Research, University of Minnesota, 1975.

Tuckman, B. W. *Evaluating instructional programs*. Boston: Allyn & Bacon, 1979.

Weiss, C. H. (ed.) *Evaluating action programs: Readings in social action and education*. Boston: Allyn & Bacon, 1972.

Wholey, J. S., Scanlon, J. W., Duffy, H., Fukumoto, J. S., & Vogt, L. M. *Federal evaluation policy: Analyzing the effects of public programs*. Washington, D.C.: The Urban Institute, 1970.

Windle, C. Searching for the JND in mental health. In L. Datta and R. Perloff (eds.), *Improving evaluation*. Beverly Hills: Sage, 1979. Pp. 131–138.

Worthen, B. R., & Sanders, J. R. *Educational evaluation: Theory and Practice*. Worthington, Ohio: Charles A. Jones, 1973.

7 METAEVALUATION: CONCEPTS, STANDARDS, AND USES   DANIEL L. STUFFLEBEAM

*T*he dominant purpose of this book is to promote quality in educational evaluations through scrupulous and perceptive planning at all stages, from design to communication of results for decision making. This is also one of the themes that permeates the preceding six chapters. The information that they provide, however, constitutes only a beginning. Criteria and standards by which the quality of evaluations can be judged are sorely needed. Although published national standards for educational and psychological testing have been available for over a decade, only within the past four years has there been any serious commitment toward devising national standards for educational evaluation. Such standards are essential to evaluate evaluations (metaevaluation) and to establish a foundation for quality control and accountability.

In this final chapter, Professor Daniel L. Stufflebeam describes the characteristics and uses of metaevaluation and reports on the production of the Standards for Evaluations of Educational Programs, Projects, and Materials. His presentation is organized into four main sections. In the first section he traces the developments in metaevaluation since the term was introduced by Scriven in 1969, offers numerous examples of metaevaluation, and outlines some of the techniques, tools, and procedures for conducting metaevaluations. This is followed by two proposed conceptualizations of metaevaluation: one for guiding evaluations (formative metaevaluation) and a second for reporting their strengths and weaknesses (summative metaevaluation). Professor Stufflebeam argues that metaevaluation can furnish valuable services by assisting evaluators in identifying possible problems in primary evaluations, by helping the public realistically appraise those evaluations, and by keeping evaluators "on their toes." The third section focuses on the Standards. As chairman of the National Joint Committee on Guidelines and Standards on Educational Evaluation, Professor Stufflebeam reviews the development of the Standards and discusses their format and content. The 30 standards that have emerged out of the four-year project are summarized in *four categories: utility, feasibility, propriety, and accuracy. The last section of the chapter is devoted to the role of metaevaluation and the* Standards *in advancing the evaluation profession through research, training, organizational development, and widespread use.*

INTRODUCTION

GOOD EVALUATION requires that evaluation enterprises themselves be evaluated. Evaluations should be checked for problems such as bias, technical error, administrative difficulties, excessive costs, and misuse. Such checks are needed both to guide the practice of evaluation and to report publicly the strengths and weaknesses of completed evaluations. Since evaluations annually consume much time by thousands of professionals and millions of dollars in public funds, efforts to assure and report on the quality of evaluation serve both professional and public interests.

The purpose of this chapter is to clarify the specialized area of meta evaluation, i.e., the practice of evaluating evaluation. Relevant developments in this area are reviewed in the first part of the chapter. An overall conceptualization of metaevaluation is presented in the second part. Standards for use in evaluating evaluations are discussed in the third part; and the concluding part considers what steps are needed to promote an ongoing profession-wide effort to develop and use metaevaluation as a means of quality assurance, self-regulation, and accountability. Since certain technical terms and definitions are used throughout this chapter, a glossary has been prepared that should help the reader avoid confusion (see Appendix).

REVIEW OF RELEVANT DEVELOPMENTS

In recent years, the concept of metaevaluation has been developed and applied extensively. There is a growing literature in the area. Several inquiry techniques have been used in metaevaluation studies. Special institutes and workshops on the topic have been conducted. And a major intersociety project to devise standards for guiding and judging evaluations and to set in motion an ongoing standard-setting process for educational evaluation has been operating since 1975. This part describes and provides references to these developments.

Michael Scriven (1969) introduced the term metaevaluation and applied the underlying concept to the assessment of a plan for evaluating educational products. Leon Lessinger (1970), Malcolm Provus (1971), Richard Seligman (1973), and others discussed the concept under the label of program auditing; they proposed procedures for: (1) monitoring evaluation studies in order to assure their quality and (2) publicly assessing the validity of their conclusions and recommendations. Campbell and Stanley (1966), Bracht and Glass (1968), the Phi Delta Kappa National Study Committee on Evaluation (Stufflebeam et al., 1971b), Krathwohl (1972), Stufflebeam (1976), Shepard (1977), and Division H of the American Educational Research Association (Schnee, 1977) proposed criteria for judging evaluations. Stufflebeam (1974, 1978) conceptualized metaevaluation, proposed a checklist of potential problems to be monitored by formative metaevaluation, listed standards for use in summative metaevaluation, and suggested procedures for both formative and summative metaevaluation. Scriven (1976) proposed two principles for assessing and controlling bias in evaluation: the first is to establish the independence of the evaluator from what is being evaluated; and the second is periodically to reestablish the evaluator's independence, since any set of arrangements is bound to deteriorate. Gowin (1978) used concept mapping to develop a model called QUEMAC for evaluating evaluations, and Millman (1979) adapted a checklist devised by Scriven (1974, pp. 85–93) for the same purpose.

Apart from the theoretical literature, there exist numerous examples of metaevaluation. A National Institute of Education (NIE) project, designed to develop a system for NIE's use in evaluating research and development institutions, illustrates the use of formative metaevaluation. This project had two teams, chaired by Michael Scriven (Scriven et al., 1971) and myself (Stufflebeam et al., 1971a), prepare alternative plans for evaluating the research and development institutions, and had a third team evaluate the two plans. An example of a summative metaevaluation was House et al.'s (1978) evaluation of Abt Associates' evaluation of the National Follow Through Program. The metaevaluation raised questions about the study's widely publicized conclusions that certain commercially available instructional materials are superior to others. Here summative metaevaluation is seen as a consumer protection device that helps the public assess published evaluations of competing products. Other examples of summative metaevaluations may be found in reports by House, Rivers, and Stufflebeam (1974), and Murphy and Cohen (1974). There are also numerous examples of formative metaevaluations, but these are seldom reported publicly.

Several techniques and devices are useful in metaevaluation work. The APA Standards for Educational and Psychological Tests (APA/AERA/NCME, 1974) and the Buros Mental Measurements Yearbooks (e.g., 1978) aid in evaluating evaluation instruments. Likewise the Campbell and Stanley (1966) and Cook and Campbell (1979) pieces on experimental and quasi-experimental designs are useful tools for evaluating alternative experimental designs. The advocate team technique, as explained by Reinhard (1972), has been used repeatedly to generate and assess competing evaluation plans. Hammond (1969) used the Delphi technique to generate and evaluate alternative national evaluation policies. Campbell, Michael, and Stufflebeam, in an unpublished metaevaluation, used a multiple classification analysis of variance framework to generate and analyze multiple judgments of various aspects of an evaluation system. Scriven (1974), Stufflebeam (1974), and Sanders and Nafziger (1977) made extensive use of checklists to evaluate evaluation plans and operations. Cook (1974) explained the use of the secondary analysis technique for reanalyzing the data from a primary evaluation; Glass and Smith (1976) explained how the metaanalysis technique was used to analyze and synthesize the results obtained from a large number of studies of psychotherapy; and Kroll (1978) performed a metaanalysis of comparative studies of the effects of desegregation on academic achievement. Wolf (1974) used administrative hearings to assess the merits of competing evaluations of a teacher training program. Finally, House (1977) and Stufflebeam (1974) argued that the writing of formal evaluation contracts helps to assure the viability and quality of evaluation projects.

Another important part of the metaevaluation scene is the essays and articles that present critical perspectives on the field of evaluation as a whole; on particular evaluation approaches, techniques, and tools; and on particular studies. Several writers, for example, have expressed doubts about evaluation and argued that their doubts are based on many well-intentioned, highly financed, but unsuccessful studies. Brickell (1974–75) and Sroufe (1977) illustrated that evaluators often are at the mercy of political forces. Egon Guba devoted an entire article to the "failure of evaluation" (1969). Gene Glass (1974) wrote of the "evaluation paradox" in which the search for excellence may inhibit the achievement of excellence through threat, disruption, and negative feedback. And Stake (1976), charging that evaluators usually promise more than they can deliver, advised practitioners not to evaluate unless some higher authority requires that they do so. He acknowledged, however, that evaluation studies are inevitable, since society will continue to require them, and recommended therefore that professional evaluators help practitioners to do the required evaluations as realistically, inexpensively, and usefully as possible.

Pieces such as those cited above reflect the philosophical bent of skepticism. As such, they are useful reminders to evaluators that: (a) they must be careful not to do disservice to their clients and to society through the improper and self-serving practice of their profession, and (b) they should constantly strive to improve their contributions.

One of the more hopeful movements in the metaevaluation area is a project designed to develop standards for educational evaluation. This project is being conducted by a joint committee, whose 17 members were appointed by 12 professional organizations. The project is being sponsored by the Lilly Endowment, the National Institute of Education, the National Science Foundation, and the Weyerhaeuser Company Foundation; is housed at the Western

Michigan University Evaluation Center; and published a book of standards in 1980. Additionally, the project will release supplementary reports that evaluate the standards and address special topics in the metaevaluation area. The project will also initiate a series of casebooks that present and analyze the procedures and results of metaevaluation studies and will present a plan for an ongoing standards-setting process. The substance of the standards is described in the third part of this chapter.

A PROPOSED CONCEPTUALIZATION

The ideas, devices, and activities referenced above demonstrate that metaevaluation is an active and rapidly developing area. To help people to understand and assess the developments occurring in metaevaluation and to promote and guide further research and development in this area, an overall conceptualization of metaevaluation is provided in this part.

A proper conceptualization of metaevaluation should meet several conditions. It should present and define all the specific concepts that are required to explain the general concept; and this presentation should be internally consistent. The conceptualization of metaevaluation should suggest hypotheses to be tested in a program of research on metaevaluation. It should give direction for developing clear guidelines for the proper conduct of metaevaluation.

The material in this part is a modest step toward meeting these conditions. Specifically, this part extends the definition of metaevaluation, describes two main roles for it, and, in doing so, proposes key assumptions. The part concludes with a basic formula that describes metaevaluation; and the implications of this formula for research and practical application of metaevaluation are discussed.

Extending the Definition of Metaevaluation

Since metaevaluation is an instance of evaluation, the definitions of these two terms must be consistent. Given that evaluation is the assessment of worth and merit, metaevaluation can be defined as the *assessment of the worth and merit of an evaluation*.

In addition to maintaining consistency between the definitions of evaluation and metaevaluation, it is desirable to extend the meaning of metaevaluation to give some idea of what is meant by the worth and merit of an evaluation. A substantive definition that serves this purpose is that:

Metaevaluation assesses the extent that an evaluation is
Useful in guiding decisions;
Practical in using resources;
Ethical in dealing with people and organizations; and
Technically Adequate.

This definition denotes categories of standards that are proposed for judging the overall adequacy of an evaluation, but the definition is far from operational.

A proposed operational definition is that metaevaluation is:

the process of delineating, obtaining, and using descriptive and judgmental information about the utility, practicality, ethics, and technical adequacy of an evaluation in order to guide the evaluation and publicly to report its strengths and weaknesses.

This definition is consistent with the prior ones, since it prescribes that an evaluation's worth and merit be judged in terms of its utility, practicality, ethics, and technical adequacy. It notes that these attributes of a good evaluation should be assessed through the use of both descriptive and judgmental information. It also refers to the activities involved in doing a metaevaluation, i.e., delineating the questions to be answered, obtaining the needed information, and putting this information to practical use. These three steps remind us that metaevaluation must be a communication as well as a technical, data-gathering process. Finally, this definition identifies two main roles of metaevaluation.

These roles are: (a) guiding evaluations, and (b) publicly reporting their strengths and weaknesses. The former role is formative metaevaluation; the latter is summative metaevaluation.

Summative Metaevaluation

Summative metaevaluation is the fundamental metaevaluation role. It sums up the overall merit of an evaluation, and usually is done following the conclusion of a primary evaluation. It holds evaluators accountable by publicly reporting on the extent that their evaluation reports meet standards of good evaluation practice. Finally, summative metaevaluations help the audiences of primary evaluations determine how seriously they should take the primary evaluation's reported conclusions and recommendations.

Symbolically, summative metaevaluation is

$$\left[\frac{\text{Evaluation Performance}}{\text{Standards}} \right]$$

The limit of this ratio is one; and the key assumption is that the quality of an evaluation can be determined through scoring and weighting evaluation performance on some known set of standards. As the ratio approaches one, the evaluation becomes more worthy. This assumption will be discussed in the final section of this chapter.

Formative Metaevaluation

Compared to summative metaevaluation, formative metaevaluation is more of a proactive, constructive application of evaluation.

Formative metaevaluations aid evaluators to make decisions about how to conceive, plan, conduct, interpret, and report their studies. Specific decisions that are served by formative metaevaluations include:

deciding whether to evaluate
defining the evaluation problem
specifying audiences
clarifying purposes of the evaluation
formulating a contract
determining information requirements
specifying data collection and analysis procedures
scheduling the work to be done
staffing
budgeting
preparing conclusions and recommendations
choosing reporting formats and media

Options are possible for each of these decisions, and formative metaevaluation helps the evaluator to identify and assess options, and thereby avoid making bad choices. Also, formative metaevaluation monitors the progress of an evaluation study and provides continuous feedback intended to help assure the quality of the evaluation. Formative metaevaluation has its foundation in evaluation guidelines and pitfalls that are believed to be linked to the meeting of the standards that serve as the basis for summative metaevaluations. Therefore, the evaluation plan and operations have to be congruent with evaluation guidelines and to avoid the pitfalls.

Symbolically, formative metaevaluation is

$$\begin{bmatrix} \text{Evaluation Plan} \\ \text{and Operations} \end{bmatrix} = \begin{matrix} \text{Meeting Evaluation} \\ \text{Guidelines} \end{matrix} + \begin{matrix} \text{Avoiding Evaluation} \\ \text{Pitfalls} \end{matrix}$$

That is, formative metaevaluation assesses the extent that the plan and day-to-day operations of an evaluation study measure up to guidelines that, if followed, will result in sound evaluation studies and avoid common pitfalls.

The main assumption underlying formative metaevaluation is that the ultimate value of an evaluation is maximized when certain procedural guidelines are met and pitfalls avoided. In other words, the summative metaevaluation is enhanced by paying attention to an appropriate, ongoing formative metaevaluation.

Symbolically, this assumed relationship between summative metaevaluation and formative metaevaluation is

$$\begin{bmatrix} \text{Evaluation} \\ \underline{\text{Performance}} \\ \text{Evaluation} \\ \text{Standards} \end{bmatrix} \begin{matrix} \text{approaches} \\ \text{1 when} \end{matrix} \begin{matrix} \text{Evaluation} \\ \text{Practice} \end{matrix} = \begin{bmatrix} \text{Meeting} & \text{Avoidance} \\ \text{of} & \text{of} \\ \text{Evaluation} & + \text{Evaluation} \\ \text{Guidelines} & \text{Pitfalls} \end{bmatrix}$$

That is, the ultimate worth of an evaluation, as determined by the summative metaevaluation, is maximized by heeding the feedback from a formative metaevaluation.

The explication of this formula should give direction for both research on, and implementation of, metaevaluation. By defining standards one is essentially developing a set of dependent variables regarding the outcomes of evaluation studies. By defining guidelines and pitfalls one is essentially developing a set of independent variables for assessing evaluation operations. Once defined, such sets of independent and dependent variables would be a good resource for deriving and testing hypotheses about how an evaluation's performance, in meeting the procedural guidelines and avoiding common pitfalls, influences the evaluation's overall satisfaction of the standards. Such guidelines and standards also constitute a basis for the actual design and conduct of metaevaluation studies. As shown in part 3, the Joint Committee on Standards for Educational Evaluation has systematically set forth its views about what standards are important and which guidelines and pitfalls apply to each standard.

Another issue for consideration in the conceptualization of metaevaluation is that of infinite regression. Whereas metaevaluation is seen to be an important means of exposing weaknesses in the primary evaluations they focus on, the metaevaluations themselves are prone to error. They may yield faulty guidance and thus compound the problems of the primary evaluation, while also consuming resources and confusing the audience.

Conceptually, this situation is problematic. If all evaluations are potentially faulty, then, theoretically, each one requires scrutiny and assistance from a metaevaluation. A primary evaluation requires a secondary evaluation, which requires a tertiary evaluation, etc. Like the facing mirrors on barbershop walls, this situation gives the prospect of successive metaevaluations with no end in sight. Michael Scriven (1976), in response to this problem, asserted that in the real world convergence among different levels of metaevaluation occurs quickly. This proposition has not been adequately tested and could serve as one useful focus for research on metaevaluation.

The general position in this chapter is that while metaevaluations—like all other forms of evaluation—are limited in what they can contribute and are prone to error, they also can provide valuable services by helping evaluators to consider possible problems in the primary evaluations, by helping the public to make realistic appraisals of primary evaluations, and by keeping evaluators "on their toes." Since the primary evaluations will be done and used, it is prudent that metaevaluations be conducted to help the primary evaluators and the public to consider relevant questions about the adequacy of these primary evaluations. *Raising such questions is sufficient reason to justify metaevaluations even if they cannot give unequivocal answers to these questions.* All evaluations are biased, and metaevaluation plays an essential role in controlling and exposing this bias.

In this part of the chapter a conceptualization and a general rationale for metaevaluation have been provided. If metaevaluation is to realize its full potential for service to evaluators, clients of evaluation, and society, the concept must be researched and developed.

Questions about metaevaluation that are implied by the foregoing material are the following:

1. To what extent does convergence of the findings of different levels of metaevaluation occur quickly?
2. What guidelines and pitfalls are most influential in meeting given standards of sound evaluation?
3. What are the costs of metaevaluations compared to those of the primary evaluations?
4. Are primary evaluations that are serviced by formative metaevaluations judged to be more useful, efficient, fair, and accurate than those that aren't so served?
5. Are the audiences for primary evaluations that have been the object of summative metaevaluations more critical and selective in their assessments of primary evaluations than the audiences of primary evaluations that have not been subjected to summative metaevaluations?

It is recommended that students and scholars who are interested in conducting research on metaevaluation consider addressing questions such as those listed above.

STANDARDS, GUIDELINES, AND PITFALLS

In addition to researching the metaevaluation process, it is also important that tools and procedures be developed to guide the process. An extensive effort in this area is the Project to Develop Standards for Educational Evaluation. The main product of this project is a book of standards for guiding and judging evaluations.

The author of this chapter was also the chairman of the Joint Committee that developed the *Standards*. A general discussion of the *Standards* is provided next.

In general, the Committee has devised 30 standards that pertain to four attributes of an evaluation: utility, feasibility, propriety, and accuracy. The utility standards reflect the general consensus that emerged in the educational evaluation literature during the late 1960s concerning the need for program evaluations that are responsive to the needs of their clients. The feasibility standards are consistent with the growing realization that evaluation procedures must be cost effective and workable in real-world politically charged settings. The propriety standards reflect ethical issues, constitutional concerns, and litigation concerning such matters as rights of human subjects and freedom of information. The accuracy standards build on those that have long been accepted for judging the technical merit of information.

Development of the Standards

To ensure that the standards in these four areas would reflect the best current knowledge and practice, the joint committee sought input from many sources. They collected and reviewed a wide range of relevant literature. They devised a list of possible topics for standards, lists of guidelines and pitfalls that they thought to be associated with the standards, and a format for writing up each standard. They engaged a group of 30 experts to expand the topics and write up alternative versions of each one. With the help of consultants, the committee rated the alternative standards, devised their preferred set, and compiled the first draft of the *Standards*. They then had their first draft critiqued by a nationwide panel of 50 experts who were nominated by the 12 sponsoring organizations. Based on the obtained critiques, the Committee debated the identified issues and prepared a second draft. The project staff critiqued this draft for correctness and effectiveness of language and developed a third draft. Based on the joint committee's review of the third draft, a fourth draft was prepared and subjected to national hearings and field tests. The results of these assessments led to the fifth draft. This final draft was published by McGraw-Hill in 1980.

Format

Each of the 30 standards is presented in a common format. It includes a descriptor, e.g., "Context Analysis," a statement of the standard, and an overview, which includes a rationale for the standard and definitions of its key terms. Also included are lists of pertinent guidelines, pitfalls, and potential conflicts with other standards. Each standard is concluded with an illustration of how it might be applied, which includes the description of a certain setting, a situation in which the standard is not met, and a discussion of corrective actions that would result in the standard being met.

A key point regarding the format is that, in order to facilitate both formative and summative metaevaluation, guidelines and pitfalls have been combined with each standard. For example, consider the Conflict-of-Interest standard. This standard states that "Conflict of Interest, frequently unavoidable, should be dealt with openly and honestly, so that it does not compromise the evaluation processes and results." One of the guidelines, included with this standard, suggests that evaluators, during initial discussions with their clients, should identify and clearly describe possible sources of conflict of interest. One pitfall included with the standard is "assuming that merely following a set of well-established 'objective' procedures will eliminate all conflicts of interest.'' On the average, four or five guidelines and about the same number of pitfalls are included in the presentation of each standard.

Content of the Standards

Utility standards.   In general, the Utility standards are intended to guide evaluations so that they will be informative, timely, and influential. These standards require evaluators to acquaint themselves with their audiences, ascertain the audiences' information needs, gear evaluations to respond to these needs, and report the relevant information clearly and when it is needed. The topics of the standards included in this category are Audience Identification, Evaluator Credibility, Information Scope and Selection, Valuational Interpretation, Report Clarity, Report Dissemination, Report Timeliness, and Evaluation Impact. Overall, the standards of Utility are concerned with whether an evaluation serves the practical information needs of a given audience.

Feasibility standards.   The Feasibility standards recognize that an evaluation usually must be conducted in a natural, as opposed to a laboratory, setting and that it consumes valuable resources. The requirements of these standards are that the evaluation plan be operable in the setting in which it is to be applied, and that no more materials and personnel time than necessary be consumed. The three topics of the Feasibility standards are Practical Procedures, Political Viability, and Cost Effectiveness. Overall, the Feasibility standards call for evaluations to be realistic, prudent, diplomatic, and frugal.

Propriety standards.   The Propriety standards reflect the fact that evaluations affect many people in many ways. These standards are aimed at ensuring that the rights of persons affected by an evaluation will be protected. Especially, these standards prohibit unlawful, unscrupulous, unethical, and inept actions by those who produce evaluation results. The topics covered by the Propriety standards are Formal Obligation, Conflict of Interest, Full and Frank Disclosure, Public's Right to Know, Rights of Human Subjects, Human Interactions, Balanced Reporting, and Fiscal Responsibility. These standards require that those conducting evaluations learn about and abide by laws concerning such matters as privacy, freedom of information, and protection of human subjects. These standards charge those who conduct evaluations to respect the rights of others and to live up to the highest principles and ideals of their professional reference groups. Taken as a group, the Propriety standards require that evaluations be conducted legally, ethically, and with due regard for the welfare of those involved in the evaluation as well as those affected by the results.

Accuracy standards.   Accuracy, the fourth group, includes those standards that determine whether an evaluation has produced sound information. These standards require that the obtained information be technically adequate and that conclusions be linked logically to the data. The topics developed in this group are Object Identification, Context Analysis, Defensible Information Sources, Described Purposes and Procedures, Valid Measurement, Reliable Measurement, Systematic Data Control, Analysis of Quantitative Information, Analysis of Qualitative Information, Justified Conclusions, and Objective Reporting. The overall rating of an evaluation against the Accuracy standards gives a good idea of the evaluation's overall truth value.

Application of the Standards

To help in the application of the *Standards,* the Joint Committee has provided a Functional Table of Contents, a standard Citation Form, and a general discussion of problems and procedures that pertain to application. The Functional Table of Contents should prove especially useful since it lists those standards judged to be most useful for each of the following tasks: Administering Evaluation, Analyzing Information, Budgeting Evaluation, Collecting Information, Contracting Evaluation, Deciding Whether to Evaluate, Defining the Evaluation Problem, Designing Evaluation, Reporting Evaluation, and Staffing Evaluation. The Citation Form, included in an appendix of the *Standards,* includes a systematic means by which evaluators and metaevaluators can report their judgments of how well a given evaluation met the standards. Completing and appending this form to evaluation documents should help those involved in the evaluation field to increase their communication about applications of the *Standards,* as well as their understanding about the state of the art of evaluation.

The preceding discussion of the *Standards* has been necessarily general. The main intent has been to convince readers that *Standards for Evaluations of Educational Programs, Projects, and Materials* constitutes a metaevaluation tool worthy of their consideration and use.

CONSIDERATIONS REGARDING THE USE OF METAEVALUATION

Thus far this chapter's treatment of metaevaluation has included review of developments, a conceptualization, and a discussion of standards. In this final part, the role of metaevaluation in regard to the professionalization of evaluation is discussed, and possible avenues for developing and using metaevaluation as a means of quality assurance, self-regulation, renewal, and accountability are explored.

Metaevaluation vis-à-vis the Professionalization of Educational Evaluation

According to *Webster's Third New International Dictionary,* a profession is "a calling requiring specialized knowledge and often long and intensive preparation including instruction in skills and methods as well as in the scientific, historical, or scholarly principles underlying such skills and methods, maintaining by force of organization or concerted opinion high standards of achievement and conduct, and committing its members to continued study and to a kind of work which has for its prime purpose the rendering of a public service.''

Given this definition there can be little doubt that educational evaluation is an emerging, though certainly not mature, profession. The methodology and literature of evaluation have been expanding tremendously. Specialization in educational evaluation usually requires graduate-level training, and a variety of universities offer masters and doctors degrees in educational evaluation. As described earlier in this chapter, a set of standards for educational evaluation is being developed for the purpose of promoting quality performance by evaluators. Also, there are several organizations—especially Division H of the American Educational Research Association and the Evaluation Network—which exist specifically to advance the theory and practice of educational evaluation and to provide continuing-education opportunities for evaluators. Finally, thousands of persons have jobs in which they evaluate educational programs, train evaluators, and/or conduct research and development in the area of educational evaluation; and these jobs are supported through millions of dollars in public funds.

Since educational evaluation is a developing profession, metaevaluation can play a vital role in advancing this field. Properly developed and implemented, metaevaluation can help by defining and applying criteria for certifying evaluators, by defining content and supplying case materials for evaluation training, by raising questions to be addressed by research on the evaluation process, by monitoring evaluations in order to assure their quality, by providing information to help the public judge evaluation plans and reports, and, overall, by helping educational evaluators to regulate their own professional activities.

Developing and Using Metaevaluation

In order to derive these contributions, people and agencies throughout educational evaluation need to sustain and increase their efforts to develop and use metaevaluation. The needed work can be grouped into four categories: research and development, training, organizational development, and use.

Research and development. There presently exist several important research and development efforts that pertain to metaevaluation. Jeri Ridings, of the Western Michigan University Evaluation Center, is studying the ongoing development and use of standards in the accounting and auditing fields, and is considering what issues and procedures, from those fields, are applicable to standard setting, metaevaluation, and self-regulation in educational evaluation. Nick Smith is leading an effort, at Northwest Regional Educational Laboratory, through which a number of scholars are studying investigative journalism, literary and art criticism, and several other evaluation-like activities in order to identify assessment techniques that might be used in educational evaluation. The Joint Committee on Educational Evaluation commissioned about 20 field tests of a draft version of their *Standards*. Francis Chase is conducting case studies of evaluation in large urban school districts, and the National Institute of Education has funded several projects that will study exemplary evaluation systems in order to devise technical recommendations for upgrading the practice of educational evaluation generally. All of these projects have important implications for improving the theory and practice of metaevaluations; and it is recommended that researchers who are interested in evaluation—especially doctoral students needing to do dissertations—review the past research and developments in metaevaluation and seriously consider contributing in this area. (Several questions that need to be addressed by research on metaevaluation were listed in the "Proposed Conceptualization" section.)

Training. As noted previously, a main requirement of a profession is that its members receive both preservice and inservice training. In recent years, the opportunities for such training in educational evaluation have expanded greatly. Graduate programs in educational evaluation are offered at UCLA, the University of Illinois, the University of Minnesota, the University of Michigan, the University of Pittsburgh, the University of Virginia, the University of Texas, Syracuse University, Cornell University, Stanford University, and Western Michigan University. Inservice training in educational evaluation has been sponsored by the American Educational Research Association, the Evaluation Network, the Association for Supervision and Curriculum Development, and the Council for Exceptional Children. Increasingly, topics such as metaevaluation, secondary analysis, and standards have been included in both preservice and inservice training for evaluators.

It is recommended that professional associations and universities continue to incorporate metaevaluation into their training programs. They can teach the content of the *Standards*. They can engage participants in evaluating completed and ongoing evaluations. And they can guide evaluation students to think critically about the philosophical and social aspects of their field. Moreover, training opportunities should be supplied to clients and audiences of evaluation, in order to help them to evaluate evaluation plans and reports. Finally, it is recommended that metaevaluation plans and reports be used to devise evaluation training materials.

Organizational development. As the profession of educational evaluation matures, it will increasingly need mechanisms by which to organize and administer vital professional functions—such as standard setting, certification of its members, quality assurance, self-regulation, and accountability. If the profession does not make adequate provisions for handling these functions, it is inevitable that government agencies will take them over since educational evaluation is so heavily supported by public funds and is so much involved in matters of public concern.

One step toward organizing the educational evaluation profession has been taken by the Joint Committee on Standards for Educational Evaluation. Specifically, this Committee has developed a plan to ensure that their *Standards* will be subjected to an ongoing program of appropriate use, research, review, and renewal. Their plan calls for a standing committee, appointed by the organizations which sponsored the development of the *Standards,* to continuously review the use of the *Standards,* to plan and conduct projects for improving them, to issue updated versions of the *Standards,* and to develop supplementary documents such as casebooks and procedural handbooks. The Joint Committee has further arranged for royalties from the sale of the *Standards* to be used to support the ongoing review and revision activities.

The Joint Committee's plan for ongoing review and revision indicates that standard setting and metaevaluation must be continuing, dynamic activities; however, the plan, so far, does not speak to issues of compliance with the *Standards,* sanctions, or other issues related to controlling and assuring the quality of educational evaluation practice. There is little doubt, however, that educational evaluation, because it uses much public money and provides public services, must sooner or later come under public scrutiny. In anticipation of this development it is recommended that evaluators begin to consider seriously what steps they, as a profession, can take toward assuring that the clients of professional evaluators are served well. Leadership for this line of inquiry could profitably be provided by the standing committee on evaluation standards mentioned above.

Use. Though research and development, training, and organizational development are all vital steps toward using metaevaluation to improve the practice of educational evaluation, the most fundamental concern is for "grass roots" employment of metaevaluation. This concept will make little difference if it is not applied conscientiously, skillfully, and systematically in planning, conducting, reporting, and applying evaluation.

It is strongly recommended that educational evaluators make metaevaluation a matter of common practice in their work. They can move in this direction by obtaining and studying a copy of the *Standards,* and by participating in inservice training programs in metaevaluation. They can apply the knowledge thus gained by conducting internal formative metaevaluations of their evaluation plans, budgets, contracts, operations, and reports. They can summarize the results of these metaevaluations in their evaluation reports. And whenever feasible, they can commission external formative and summative metaevaluations of their work and make the results available to their clients and to other evaluators.

While examining one's own evaluations and subjecting them to review by other parties is often hard on the ego, it is a sign of a true professional and is a definite step toward the upgrading of evaluation practice. Therefore, it is urged that people throughout the evaluation profession move vigorously in the direction of self-examination, regulation, and renewal.

CLOSING

This chapter has been devoted to clarifying the concept of metaevaluation and to providing some direction for its use as a means of upgrading the evaluation profession. While the chapter has undoubtedly raised more questions than it has answered, it has pointed the reader to a number of pertinent developments, to a proposed conceptualization of metaevaluation, and to a book of standards for educational evaluation. Finally, it has considered how the contributions of metaevaluation might be upgraded through relevant research, training, organizational development, and widespread use in the field. Overall, the chapter has argued that metaevaluation is a matter of vital importance to both professional evaluators and members of the public.

APPENDIX: GLOSSARY OF TERMS

Evaluation: the assessment of worth and merit

Metaevaluation: the assessment of the worth and merit of an evaluation, it includes all levels of evaluation above that of the primary evaluation; i.e., a secondary evaluation of the primary evaluation, a tertiary evaluation of the secondary evaluation, etc.

Primary evaluation: an evaluation that is the subject of metaevaluation

Formative metaevaluation: a metaevaluation that is intended to guide a primary evaluation

Summative metaevaluation: a study that judges the worth and merit of a completed evaluation

Standards: widely shared principles for the measure of the worth and merit of an evaluation

Guidelines: procedural suggestions intended to help evaluators meet evaluation standards

Pitfalls: mistakes that are commonly made by persons who are unaware of the importance of a given principle of sound evaluation

REFERENCES

APA/AERA/NCME Committee. *Standards for educational and psychological tests* (Rev. ed.). Washington, D.C.: American Psychological Association, 1974.

Bracht, G. H., & Glass, G. V. The external validity of experiments. *American Educational Research Journal,* 1968, *5,* 437–474.

Brickell, H. M. *Policy study in education*. American Educational Research Association Cassette Tape, Series 7C, 1974-75.

Buros, O. K. (ed.). *Eighth mental measurements yearbook*. Highland Park, N.J.: The Gryphon Press, 1978.

Campbell, D. T., & Stanley, J. C. *Experimental and quasi-experimental designs for research*. Chicago: Rand McNally, 1966

Cook, T. D. The potential and limitations of secondary evaluations. In M. W. Apple, M. J. Subkoviak, and H. S. Lufler, Jr. (eds.), *Educational evaluation: Analysis and responsibility*. Berkeley: McCutchan, 1974. Pp. 155-222.

Cook, T. D., & Campbell, D. T. *Quasi-experimentation: Design and analysis issues for field settings*. Chicago: Rand McNally, 1979.

Glass, G. V. Excellence: A paradox. Paper presented at the second annual meeting of the Pacific Northwest Research and Evaluation Conference, 1974.

Glass, G. V., & Smith, M. L. Meta analysis of psychotherapy outcomes studies. Paper presented at the annual meeting of the Society for Psychotherapy Research, San Diego, June 1976.

Gowin, R. D. QUEMAC value: An approach to meta evaluation. Unpublished paper, Cornell University, April 1978.

Guba, E. G. The failure of educational evaluation. *Educational Technology*, 1969, *9*, 29-38.

Hammond, R. L. Context evaluation of instruction in local school districts. *Educational Technology*, 1969, *9*, 13-18.

House, E. R. Fair evaluation agreement. Urbana: Center for Instructional Research and Curriculum Evaluation, University of Illinois, 1977. (mimeo)

House, E. R., Glass, G. V., McLean, L. D., & Walker, D. F. No simple answer: Critique of the Follow Through evaluation. *Harvard Educational Review*, 1978, *48*, 128-160.

House, E. R., Rivers, W., & Stufflebeam, D. L. An assessment of the Michigan accountability system. *Phi Delta Kappan*, 1974, *55*, 663-669.

Krathwohl, D. R. Functions for experimental schools evaluation and their organization. In G. V. Glass, M. L. Byers, and B. R. Worthen (eds.), *Recommendations for the evaluation of experimental schools projects of the U.S. Office of Education* (Report of the Experimental Schools Evaluation Working Conference). Boulder: Laboratory of Educational Research, University of Colorado, 1972. Pp. 174-194.

Kroll, R. A meta analysis of comparative research on the effects of desegregation on academic achievement. Unpublished doctoral dissertation, Western Michigan University, 1978.

Lessinger, L. M. *Every kid a winner: Accountability in education*. New York: Simon and Schuster, 1970.

Millman, J. An unpublished adaptation of Michael Scriven's "Product evaluation checklist" distributed at the 1979 American Educational Research Association presession on meta evaluation.

Murphy, J. T., & Cohen, D. K. Accountability in education—the Michigan experience. *The Public Interest*, 1974, *36*, 53-81.

Provus, M. M. *Discrepancy evaluation*. Berkeley: McCutchan, 1971.

Reinhard, D. L. Methodology development for input evaluations using advocate and design teams. Unpublished doctoral dissertation, Ohio State University, 1972.

Sanders, J. R., & Nafziger, D. H. *A basis for determining the adequacy of evaluation designs*. (Occasional Paper No. 6). Kalamazoo: The Evaluation Center, College of Education, Western Michigan University, 1977.

Schnee, R. Ethical standards for evaluators: The problem. *CEDR Quarterly*, 1977, *10*, 3.

Scriven, M. An introduction to meta-evaluation. *Educational Product Report*, 1969, *2*, 36–38.

Scriven, M. Evaluation perspectives and procedures. In W. J. Popham (ed.), *Evaluation in education: Current applications*. Berkeley: McCutchan, 1974. Pp. 3–93.

Scriven, M. Evaluation bias and its control. In G. V. Glass (ed.), *Evaluation studies review annual* (Vol. 1). Beverly Hills: Sage, 1976. Pp. 119–139.

Scriven, M., Glass, G. V., Hively, W., & Stake, R. E. An evaluation system for regional labs and R & D centers. (Project No. 1-0857, Grant No. OEG-0-71-4558). A report presented to the Division of Research and Development Resources of the National Center for Educational Research and Development, U.S. Office of Education, 1971.

Seligman, R. College guidance program. *Measurement and Evaluation in Guidance*, 1973, *6*, 127–129.

Shepard, L. A. *A checklist for evaluating large-scale assessment programs* (Occasional Paper No. 9). Kalamazoo: The Evaluation Center, College of Education, Western Michigan University, 1977.

Sroufe, G. E. Evaluation and politics. In J. D. Scribner (ed.), *Seventy-sixth yearbook of the National Society for the Study of Education: Part II, The politics of education*. Chicago: University of Chicago Press, 1977. Pp. 287–318.

Stake, R. E. Presentation made at The Evaluation Center, College of Education, Western Michigan University, 1976.

Stufflebeam, D. L. *Meta evaluation* (Occasional Paper No. 3). Kalamazoo: The Evaluation Center, College of Education, Western Michigan University, 1974.

Stufflebeam, D. L. Evaluating the context, input, process & product of education. Paper presented to the International Congress on the Evaluation of Physical Education, Jyvaskyla, Finland, 1976.

Stufflebeam, D. L. Meta evaluation: An overview. *Evaluation and the Health Professions*, 1978, *1*, 17–43.

Stufflebeam, D. L., Brickell, H. M., Guba, E. G., & Michael, W. B. Design for evaluating R & D institutions and programs (Project No. 1-0857, Grant No. OEG-0-71-4558). A report presented to the Division of Research and Development Resources of the National Center for Educational Research and Development, U.S. Office of Education, 1971. (a)

Stufflebeam, D. L., Foley, W. J., Gephart, W. J., Guba, E. G., Hammond, R. L., Merriman, H. O., & Provus, M. M. *Educational evaluation and decision making*. Itasca, Ill.: F. E. Peacock, 1971. (b)

Wolf, R. L. The application of select legal concepts to educational evaluation. Unpublished doctoral dissertation, University of Illinois, 1974.

BIOGRAPHICAL NOTES

RONALD A. BERK is Associate Professor of Education and Director of the annual Johns Hopkins University National Symposium on Educational Research (NSER). He received his Ph.D. degree from the University of Maryland in 1973. Prior to assuming a teaching position at Johns Hopkins, he taught elementary school in the District of Columbia from 1968 to 1972 and served as an evaluator in the Montgomery County (Md.) School System from 1973 to 1976. Dr. Berk has developed over 60 tests and scales and has published more than 30 articles in psychometrics, evaluation, and computer applications. He edited a state-of-the-art book on criterion-referenced measurement that was based on the first NSER held in 1978. He has also been a reviewer for several journals and publishing companies.

LLOYD BOND is Assistant Professor of Psychology and Research Associate at the Learning Research and Development Center at the University of Pittsburgh. He received his Ph.D. degree from The Johns Hopkins University in 1976. Dr. Bond has served as a consultant to the American Association for the Advancement of Science, Educational Testing Service, College Board, National Urban League, and Minority Caucus of Drug and Alcohol Workers of Pennsylvania. He was a Spencer Fellow of the National Academy of Education in 1980. He has published several articles and book reviews on minimum competency testing, aptitude-treatment interaction (ATI), test bias, and the measurement of change. His research interests also include statistical theory and multidimensional scaling.

ANTHONY S. BRYK is Associate Professor at the Harvard Graduate School of Education and Senior Research Associate at the Huron Institute in Cambridge, Massachusetts. He received his Ed.D. degree from Harvard University in 1977. Previously, Dr. Bryk was Supervisor of Research and Program Evaluation for the Brookline (MA) Public Schools Early Education Project from 1973 to 1976. At the Huron Institute, he has served in a variety of research capacities on such projects as the National Project Follow Through Evaluation (1973–1974), the development of evaluation models for Title I programs (1977–present), and the impact of Federal Special Education legislation on children and families (1978–present). Dr. Bryk's journal articles, book chapters, and monographs have focused on the analysis of quasi-experimental design data and quantitative methods for studying individual growth. He is currently a member of the National Academy of Sciences' panel on Measuring Outcomes for Early Childhood Demonstration Projects.

NANCY S. COLE is Professor of Education and Director of the Program in Educational Research Methodology at the University of Pittsburgh. She is also the current vice president of Division D of the American Educational Research Association and serves on the Board of Directors of the National Council on Measurement in Education. She received her Ph.D. degree from the University of North Carolina at Chapel Hill in 1968. Prior to assuming a position at Pittsburgh, Dr. Cole was Director of the Test Development Department of the American College Testing Program in Iowa from 1972 to 1973 and subsequently was Assistant Vice President for Educational and Social Research from 1973 to 1975. She has authored numerous journal articles and book chapters and several monographs on measurement issues related to vocational interest measurement and test bias. Dr. Cole has also been an advisory editor of the *Journal of Educational Measurement* (1972–1976) and *Research in Higher Education* (1973–1975), and a consulting editor for the *American Educational Research Journal* (1975–1977).

WILLIAM W. COOLEY is Professor of Education and Director of the Evaluation Research Unit of the Learning Research and Development Center at the University of Pittsburgh. He received his Ed.D. degree from Harvard University in 1958. Previously, he taught high school science in Wisconsin from 1952 to 1954 and in Hawaii from 1955 to 1956. Dr. Cooley has been Research Associate at Harvard University (1963–1964), Director of Project TALENT at the University of Pittsburgh and American Institutes for Research (1964–1967), and Fellow at the Center for Advanced Study in the Behavioral Sciences (1972–1973). He has published more than 50 articles, book chapters, and book reviews, and seven books and monographs including two popular textbooks with Professor Paul R. Lohnes on introductory and multivariate statistics and, most recently, the volume *Evaluation Research in Education* (1976) with Professor Lohnes.

LOIS-ELLIN DATTA is Associate Director of the National Institute of Education, U.S. Department of Education. She received her Ph.D. degree from Bryn Mawr College in 1961. Dr. Datta is the immediate past president of the Evaluation Research Society. Prior to her current position with NIE, she conducted research on gifted adolescents in the Laboratory of Psychology at the National Institute of Mental Health from 1963 to 1968 and served as National Director of the Project Head Start evaluation and Chief of the Early Childhood Research and Evaluation Branch of the Office of Child Development from 1968 to 1972. Dr. Datta has authored numerous book chapters and articles on evaluation policy and practices in the areas of vocational education and Head Start and, most recently, coedited the book *Improving Evaluations* (1980). She is a member of the editorial boards of *Journal of Educational Psychology* (1976–present), *Evaluation and Change* (1980–present), and *Evaluation Review* (1978–present), and serves as a reviewer on evaluation for *Educational Researcher* and Sage Publications.

RICHARD J. LIGHT is Professor at the Harvard Graduate School of Education and John F. Kennedy School of Government. He received his Ph.D. degree from Harvard University in 1969. Previously, he taught at the University of Pennsylvania from 1962 to 1964. Dr. Light has consulted on several regional, national, and international evaluation projects for the Eastern Educational Television Network, National Center for Child Abuse Prevention, National Day Care Experiment, and the World Bank. The last-named involved the evaluation of health and literacy programs in developing countries from 1975 to 1978. Dr. Light is currently chairman of the National Academy of Sciences' panel on Measuring Outcomes of Demonstration Programs, chairman of the Harvard Evaluation Seminar, and a member of the panel on Evaluation Methodology of the Social Science Research Council (1977–present). He has also published extensively in the areas of evaluation design, qualitative data analysis techniques, and policy and legal issues related to research and evaluation, and has served on the editorial boards of the *Journal of Educational Statistics* (1975–1977), *Evaluation Quarterly* (1976–1979), and *Evaluation Studies Review Annual* (1976–present).

ROBERT L. LINN is Professor of Educational Psychology and Psychology at the University of Illinois, Urbana-Champaign. He is also the current president of the National Council on Measurement in Education. He received his Ph.D. degree from the University of Illinois in 1965. Prior to assuming a teaching position at the University of Illinois, Dr. Linn was a member of the research staff at Educational Testing Service from 1965 to 1973, starting as Associate Research Psychologist and ending as Senior Research Psychologist and Director of the Developmental Research Division. He has been a Visiting Professor at the Graduate School of Education and Visiting Scholar at the Center for the Study of Evaluation at UCLA (1976–1977). Dr. Linn has published over 80 articles and has been editor and advisory editor of the *Journal of Educational Measurement* (1969–present), advisory editor of the *Journal of Educational Psychology* (1976–1978) and *Educational and Psychological Measurement* (1976–present), and associate editor of the *Journal of Educational Statistics* (1976–present). He also received Outstanding Teacher of the Year awards at the University of Illinois in 1976 and 1979.

BOR-JIIN MAO is Statistician and Senior Systems Analyst at the Learning Research and Development Center and Department of Epidemiology at the University of Pittsburgh. She received her Ph.D. degree from Carnegie-Mellon University in 1978. Previously, she was awarded a scholarship from the Republic of China for Distinguished Achievement in Science. Her areas of interest include multivariate and structural data analyses, sampling procedures, statistical computer software packages, and mathematical and statistical modeling.

ANTHONY J. NITKO is Professor of Education in the Program in Educational Research Methodology at the University of Pittsburgh. He received his Ph.D. degree from the University of Iowa in 1968. Since then, Professor Nitko has served as the director of a variety of research projects at the Learning Research and Development Center, University of Pittsburgh, including Test Development for the Individually Prescribed Instruction Project (1968–1970), Measurement and Evaluation Project (1970–1972), and Measurement Project (1972–1974). He has published numerous articles, book chapters, and two textbooks in educational measurement and has been a reviewer for several research, measurement, and statistics journals.

DANIEL L. STUFFLEBEAM is Professor of Education and Director of the Evaluation Center at Western Michigan University. He received his Ph.D. degree from Purdue University in 1964. Previously, Dr. Stufflebeam taught at the elementary and secondary school levels from 1958 to 1960. He was also Professor of Education and Director of the Evaluation Center at Ohio State University from 1963 to 1973. His research on evaluation theory and practices has appeared in numerous journals, book chapters, monographs, and books. He was coauthor of the 1971 volume *Educational Evaluation and Decision Making*. Dr. Stufflebeam has also directed the development of more than 100 standardized achievement tests, supervised evaluation projects throughout the nation, and served as chairman of the Phi Delta Kappa National Study Committee on Educational Evaluation (1967–1970) and National Joint Committee on Guidelines and Standards on Educational Evaluation (1976–1980).

RICHARD M. WOLF is Professor of Psychology and Education at Teachers College, Columbia University. He received his Ph.D. degree from the University of Chicago in 1964. Prior to his teaching position at Columbia, Dr. Wolf was a junior high school teacher in New York from 1958 to 1961 and Research Associate at the University of Chicago from 1963 to 1965. He has taught at the University of Chicago, University of Southern California, and the International Institute for Educational Planning in Paris. Dr. Wolf was a Fulbright Lecturer in New Zealand in 1975 and is currently the U.S. Representative to the International Educational Achievement Association. He has authored more than 40 articles, book chapters, and reviews, and several books and monographs in measurement, evaluation, and computer applications, including *Evaluation in Education* (1979). Dr. Wolf also served as the editor of the 1968 *International Review of Education* and as a reviewer for numerous research journals.